STOP CLUTTER FROM STEALING YOUR LIFE

REVISED EDITION

Discover Why You Clutter &
How You Can Stop

Mike Nelson

New Page Books
A Division of Career Press, Inc.
Franklin Lakes, NJ

Copyright © 2008 by Mike Nelson

All rights reserved under the Pan-American and International Copyright Conventions. This book may not be reproduced, in whole or in part, in any form or by any means electronic or mechanical, including photocopying, recording, or by any information storage and retrieval system now known or hereafter invented, without written permission from the publisher, The Career Press.

STOP CLUTTER FROM STEALING YOUR LIFE, REVISED EDITION
EDITED BY KARA REYNOLDS
TYPESET BY MICHAEL FITZGIBBON
Cover design by The Designworks Group
Printed in the U.S.A. by Book-mart Press

To order this title, please call toll-free 1-800-CAREER-1 (NJ and Canada: 201-848-0310) to order using VISA or MasterCard, or for further information on books from Career Press.

The Career Press, Inc., 3 Tice Road, PO Box 687,
Franklin Lakes, NJ 07417

www.careerpress.com
www.newpagebooks.com

Library of Congress Cataloging-in-Publication Data

Nelson, Mexico Mike, 1950–

    Stop clutter from stealing your life : discover why you clutter & how you can stop / Mike Nelson. — Rev. ed.

    p. cm.

    Includes index.

    ISBN 978-1-60163-008-7

    1. House cleaning. 2. Orderliness. I. Title.

TX324.N45 2008
648'.5--dc22

2007052337

"Mike Nelson has done it again. Whether you're 'practical' or 'emotional' in your approach to solving your organization problems, this book will be of great help."

—Judith Kolberg, founder,
National Study Group on Chronic Disorganization

"As a psychiatrist, I can report that I have 'prescribed' this book and the Clutterless approach to patients with remarkable results. I find that he is grounded in real-world experiences of Clutterers, and offers counsel that appreciates and validates where they are. We don't need to keep beating ourselves—we need practical skills toward results!"

—Kathleen Wong, MD, psychiatrist

"I have enjoyed your candor and perspective as I've read through several of the chapters in your book. I believe it could be a very helpful resource to those who struggle with clutter in their lives (including those suffering with OCD). I am always looking for material that shows people how to make application. Knowing what the problem is, well, that's helpful; knowing what to do about it, that's life-changing."

—Cheryl Williams, licensed professional counselor

"Wow! Talk about hitting the nail on the head! I want to make this mandatory reading for both my employees and my clients! If my clients could recognize why they clutter, and only followed one-tenth of the decluttering [ideas in this book], my job would be much easier. Great reading and advice for anyone, regardless of occupation."

—Maria Fryberger, CEO, president, Residential Cleaning

Dedication

This book is dedicated to Fluffy, the Declutter Dog, who is waiting for me at Rainbow Bridge, and who taught me that pets are more important than stuff; to my sister Pam, who taught me that family is more important than stuff; and to the many clutterers who supported me through my darkest days, teaching me that people are more important than stuff.

Contents

Introduction	**9**
Chapter 1: Are You a Clutterer?	15
Chapter 2: Types of Clutterers	23
Chapter 3: My Story	39
Chapter 4: 40 Ways to Leave Your Clutter	53
Chapter 5: Common Clutterer Traits—Practical and Emotional Solutions	65
Chapter 6: OPC—Other People's Clutter	87
Chapter 7: Paper Clutter and Filing	101
Chapter 8: Clutterers' Stories	117
Chapter 9: The Medical View—Depression, Anxiety, ADD, Hoarding, and OCD	135
Chapter 10: Unpack Your Stuff With TCI	149
Chapter 11: Alternatives to TV-Style Forced Decluttering	155
Chapter 12: Living With Cluttering Kids and Spouses	161
Chapter 13: The Organizers' View	179
Chapter 14: The Spiritual View	189
Chapter 15: Prosperity Is an Inside Job	197
Chapter 16: Offices—Home and Otherwise	205
Chapter 17: Hearses Don't Have Trailer Hitches	219
Chapter 18: Maintenance Steps	223
Chapter 19: Backsliding	229
Chapter 20: Support Groups	235

Appendix I: Decluttering Diary	241
Appendix II: Affirmations and Promises	245
Bibliography and Resources	247
Index	251
About the Author	255

Introduction

This book is about more than just decluttering. It's about balance. A cluttered household is an unbalanced household. It's about not re-cluttering. It's about not having to buy more and more stuff to fill a hole in our souls. It's about learning what's really important in our lives and not using stuff to hide from life. People and pets are important; stuff is not. When we learn to change our cluttering behavior, we learn to balance our need for *things* with our need for *love*.

All the advice on decluttering and organization in the world (including mine) is useless, unless we stop the *stuff* from coming in. There are many good books on how to organize. There are many good books on hoarding, compulsive shopping, ADD (attention deficit disorder), anxiety, and depression—learning to live clutter-less incorporates some knowledge of each of those disciplines.

This book is for those of us who want to overcome our cluttering habits and are willing to do the work necessary to change our lives. Cluttering isn't just about not knowing how to organize. If it were, we'd all be living Zen-like, minimalist lives. Heck, most of us don't even *want* to live in a minimalist environment. We like our stuff. There's nothing wrong with having stuff; stuff doesn't clutter—people clutter. If you stick with me through the journey of this book, you'll come to a place of peace, a sense of acceptance of yourself. Our stuff is part of us, but it need not define us.

This second edition comes after eight years of refining my understanding of cluttering, and after working with hundreds of clutterers. Most of the original truths and insights about cluttering from the first edition remain true, but a few were outdated, and many new insights have been added. In those eight years, I've personally been through a major life-changing event, which was a crucible that clarified my thinking about cluttering and life. May you be lucky enough to learn from my experience and not have to repeat the process. This edition is a better, stronger book; I am a better, stronger person. When you're finished with this book, you will also be better and stronger. Perhaps you will be the Bionic Declutterer.

In rewriting this book, a lot has changed. There is less emphasis on OCD (obsessive-compulsive disorder), which is a basis for hoarding, because, frankly, most people with clutter problems are not hoarders. I've worked with hoarders, and I know the difference between a hoarder's house and that of a clutterer. Less than 1 percent of the general population qualify as hoarders. Some of us have some hoarding-like or OCD-like tendencies, some of us have some ADD-like traits, and many of us are likely to be depressed or anxious. Gee, doesn't that make you feel better? Worrying about your cluttering can make you depressed, and thinking about doing something to declutter can make you anxious, so it's like being a rat in a maze. That's why we have to learn to change our behavior, and not just learn some new decluttering tips.

Most of us clutterers don't have any different psychological issues than other people walking down the street—just more of them. Sure, we're more likely to be depressed, anxious, or have other maladies than the rest of the world, but we're unlikely to have full-blown OCD. I hate to say that, because hoarders and people with OCD make for great television. Many of us may have more ADD traits than the average population, but few of us have full-blown ADD. What we have is cluttering tendencies, and what we can do about it helps us overcome whatever else may be going on in our lives.

Cluttering can be a serious impediment to living a full life, for sure, but discovering the reasons we clutter could take years on a psychiatrist's couch, and most of us don't have that kind of time. Frankly, we don't need to "get to the root of our issues" in order to begin living a decluttered life right now. Neither can we, as one Internet site claims, declutter our house in two days, max. We *can* make immediate progress, but it takes time to change any self-defeating behavior and replace it with a positive behavior.

Cluttering is a behavior; clutter is a symptom. To change a behavior, you've got to treat the causes, not the symptoms, using practical and psychological tools. Until now, you've concentrated on the stuff, better organizing techniques, and finding the right organizing tools to make the messes go away. Those things are valuable, but they're like mowing the weeds in your lawn: Mow them, and the lawn will look good for a few weeks; uproot the weeds, and they'll stay gone. We're gong to stop mowing and start uprooting.

Not only can we take control of our clutter, using the techniques in this book, but we can also learn to maintain control over our clutter. It's just stuff. We are people, and people are more important and more powerful than stuff. Many of the solutions here have practical, emotional/psychological components, but you can just use the practical aspect if that's all you need. If you want to do more inner work on yourself, you'll appreciate the emotional aspects.

Ideally, once you start having some success on the physical issue of your cluttering, you'll start to delve a little deeper, at your own pace, and put the big picture together. Your whole life and outlook on it will change for the better. But don't just sit around and wait for the miracle—get out there and do some work.

You know how to organize; we all do. The reasons you and I clutter are far more complicated than not knowing that there's "a place for everything and everything in its place." Our cluttering habits aren't as simple as the fact that we don't *like* to organize. Who does? We *don't* organize, for more complicated reasons.

That's where this book differs from the many others that clutter the organizing section bookshelves. We do have to learn (or relearn) organizing techniques—and apply them—but we also have to overcome our own blocks to decluttering.

Decluttering is a two-part process:
1. Practical—"Okay, now, do I need to keep this?"
2. Emotional—"Why on earth am I holding onto this? What does it represent in my subconscious?"

Remember, not only is there a prize pony in that pile of clutter, but as you declutter, you will find (or rediscover) your true self.

After eight years, three books on cluttering, and founding a support group for clutterers, I got tired of hearing, "I need those books. I need to go to those meetings." These books and those meetings aren't for people who need them. They are for people who *want* them. Frankly, most people don't really want to do the work necessary to change their lives and live uncluttered. They'd rather complain. Keep doing the same things over and over, and it is highly unlikely that you will get different results.

Most people think of themselves as clutterers in some form or another. Some organizers have said they believe that half the population consists of clutterers. I don't know if I'd put the number that high, but there certainly are a lot of people who have some sort of problem with too much stuff. Otherwise self-storage units wouldn't be such a booming business, and the ranks of professional organizers would not have doubled or nearly tripled since this book was first published in 2001. People who are actually very neat often have closets and storage spaces filled to the brim with stuff they never use. Though it is neatly packaged, it is still clutter.

———◆———

I hope to touch you with humor, love, and compassion. I learned how to change my life and free myself from living a cluttered life. I want to share that freedom with you.

By presenting the opinions of psychiatric professionals, professional organizers, and clutterers similar to you and me who've made progress, in addition to the practical knowledge gained by working with clutterers, I wish to give you understanding that goes far beyond my personal experiences. I was guided to write this by my own pain and the earnest desire to help others similar to myself get to the other side—the joy of living clutter-less.

In this book, you will find ways to handle the feelings that cluttering produces. I've incorporated anecdotal stories about the effect of cluttering on the families of clutterers, as well as professional opinions from psychiatrists and psychologists who deal with the cluttering, hoarding, depression, anxiety, and self-esteem issues that we clutterers seem to have in almost as much abundance as our stuff.

The practical and economic aspects of cluttering (and decluttering) are all covered, so you can see how your life can be positively changed by finding a path out of your own personal maze, whether through therapy, support groups, medication, meditation, or a combination of any of the above.

Living a clutter-less life is more than cleaning up. It involves changing the way we think about possessions, love, and self-worth. It means developing a way of life that celebrates what we have and honors our inner self. Feeling good about ourselves, believing in the abundance of the Universe and a less self-centered way of life are both the results of, and the means to, living without clutter. A joyful, rich life is the payoff.

This is a book about freeing ourselves. We've been trapped in a prison of clutter of our own making. We aren't bad or weak people any more than someone with diabetes is bad or weak. We probably own at least three books about organizing. Like Band-Aids, they have helped superficially and temporarily.

You didn't get where you are in one week. You won't become uncluttered one week after reading this book. But you will get started on a permanent change, so that, *if you are willing to do the work*, you can life a clutter-less life. If you are a clutterer, you need more than a way to organize your clutter. You want a life plan that will lead you into the sunlight of the spirit, where you can live a life without shame, self-doubt, and fear. The first three printings of *Stop Clutter From Stealing Your Life* gave this gift to many thousands of clutterers. May this revised edition bring you more insight and more tools so that you can join us in our journey to clutter-lessness.

Join me on this path to self-understanding. May we meet on the road to joy and peace.

The greatest gift I can give you, the shortest synopsis of this book, is that our new mantra is: "Stuff is not as important in our lives as we make it. People are important. Family is important. Pets are important. Life is all about relationships, not things." You can lose every single item you own, and if you have at least one of those things, you will be richer than the person living in a mansion full of stuff. I had to learn this the hard way. Trust me, and let me be your guide on this incredible journey of discovery.

1 | Are You a Clutterer?

One's own self or material goods, which has more worth? Loss (of self) or possession (of goods), which is the greater evil? He who loves most, spends most. He who hoards much, loses much.

—Lao Tse

If *overwhelmed* and *shame* are synonymous with *clutter* in your mind, welcome to the club. For people such as ourselves, the solutions to our cluttering are more complex than just learning how to organize. We need to learn the *clutter two-step*, which is not a dance, but a paradigm shift. For us, solutions must work on two levels—the practical and the emotional/psychological—because cluttering affects each of us in different ways. Not everyone needs both levels. Take what applies to you and leave the rest. The practical advice helps us get rid of clutter on a physical level. The suggestions on addressing the emotional aspects help us understand why we clutter and how to change our behavior, so we stop re-cluttering. Many of us are so full of negativity that we're like one-sided magnets, repelling any positive changes in our lives.

Clutter is the symptom. Recognizing and changing the reasons for our cluttering are the solutions. There's no *one* reason or *one* type of clutterer. As psychiatrists say, we are across the spectrum of behavior.

One aspect of Dr. C. Robert Cloninger's thought-provoking book on coherent living (*Feeling Good: The Science of Well-Being*), the

Temperament Character Inventory (TCI) scale, shows that some of us have high "persistence" levels, and some of us have low "persistence" levels. Practically, that means that in order to change, some of us should make our beds every day to strengthen our persistence muscles, and others of us should *not* make our beds every day, to learn spontaneity. See why it's so hard for us to stop cluttering? (To learn more about this test and Dr. Cloninger, see *https://psychobiology.wustl.edu/coherence.html*.)

Learning to live clutter-less isn't just about how to declutter; it's about how to *not* re-clutter. The obvious part of that is that once we get something out of our lives, we don't bring more back in. The less obvious part, which is why this approach differs from others, is that it's more about how to change from within and improve both our inner and outer lives. It's about getting a whole new outlook on what's important in life. In books of this genre, there's often too much emphasis on "getting rid of," or "winning the battle against" clutter. Because clutter is such a big part of our lives, most of us are already filled with negative emotions from it. Why make changing your life a negative experience? Negativity is fine on magnets and electrical connections, but only as half the picture. In order to have electrical light in our houses, we need both the negative *and* the positive electrical charges channeled into a light bulb. We do not celebrate the electrical current, but the end result—the light that illuminates our lives.

So it is with changing from lives filled with clutter to lives filled with joy. *Filled* may be too strong a word...let's just shoot for more good days than bad and call that a win. For most of us, it will be a huge change.

We, who've learned to live clutter-less, don't get all worked up about what *not* to do. We give thanks for our abundance, and give that abundance away. We, as reformed clutterers, pass on those things that do not serve us anymore to others who can benefit from them. We help others by giving; we help our planet by recycling; we help our spirits by lightening our emotional loads.

Guilt is no longer part of us. We are innocent. All the negative emotions in the world, all the negative comments others have thrown at us, all the negative self-talk we've unloaded on ourselves, have not gotten rid of one ounce of clutter. An ounce of positive thinking is worth two pounds of negative self-talk.

You *can* declutter. You *can* live clutter-less. You can also define what that means to you. You know, after eight years of working with people just like you and me, one thing I've learned is that we are only going to be successful when we, and we alone, determine what *our* uncluttered life looks like.

Some of us are neat at home, but messy at work. Regardless of how we express it, we're using clutter to make a statement to the world. Others of us can be neat on the outside, yet be cluttered within—emotionally, or time-cluttered.

We are always going to have some clutter in our lives. We will always have a desire to clutter to some degree. We're similar to the overweight person whose success is attaining a healthy, sustainable weight—not fitting into a size-two dress or 26-inch pants at age 55. I have not met one reformed or improving clutterer yet whose house should be spotlighted in *House Beautiful*, *Martha Stewart*, or *Southern Homes and Gardens*. Yet so often others tell us that's what our houses should look like when we've "conquered" clutter.

This isn't a war. It's not an occupation. It's a revolution, yes, but not a revolution of blood and gore. It's a quiet revolution of the spirit. Be revolutionary. Be a gentle warrior, a peaceful warrior. But remember—you are not your enemy. I used to believe that, as Pogo said in the old comic strip by the same name, "We have met the enemy and he is us." You know what? I was wrong. The enemy is negativity. Clutter is the past. Peace and prosperity are the future. Let me gently guide you to your future, one with less clutter, and with lots of positive energy. Together we can create the future.

Are You a Clutterer?

Some Questions Only You Can Answer

1. Do you feel overwhelmed when thinking about your clutter?
2. Have you tried to "clean up" or "organize" yourself repeatedly, with no lasting results?
3. Are you ashamed to have anyone come to your home?
4. Do you feel more confused in your home than at work?
5. Do you find yourself buying more of everything than you need because "you never know when you will run out"?
6. Do you have multiple copies of books, software, clothing, or other items because you couldn't find what you already owned when you needed it?

7. Has your spouse or partner expressed dismay about the way you live?
8. Do you feel like, "What's the use, it will just get messed up again," when you begin to declutter?
9. Do you hold on to broken items because "they might come in handy someday," or "I'm going to fix them someday"?
10. Do you hold on to relationships that do not serve you because "This is the best I can do"?
11. Do you feel that there will never be enough for you? Do you believe that you do not deserve any better than what you have?
12. Do you want to change these things?

Not all of us can answer yes to every single question (except the last, hopefully), but if you're reading this book, you'll probably answer at least three or four yeses. The only one that is really important is the last one. Questions 1 through 11 are the past. Number 12 is the future.

The brief part of my own cluttering story that follows might help you, and certainly will show you that I know of what I speak because I have been where you are.

Xtreme Decluttering

Freedom's just another word for nothing left to lose.

—Kris Kristofferson

As Fluffy, my cocker spaniel, and I watched yellow-red flames turn all our worldly possessions into black soot when our home burned down, my overwhelming emotion was a sense of relief. I was freed from the bondage of *stuff*. There's something to be said for being homeless—it makes moving a lot easier.

I can't speak for Fluffy's thoughts, but he seemed just as accepting. Although I don't recommend this form of "xtreme decluttering," I can share the lessons with you so you won't have to experience it firsthand. I don't want to give you the impression that I was left with absolutely no possessions: I had a bathrobe and a copy of one of my books salvaged from my burned car. See, a clutterer always has something.

And no, I didn't have renter's insurance. So I truly did have to start over from scratch.

Yes, my computer burned up, and I lost a lot of information that truly was irreplaceable, though much of it was backed up on a portable hard drive. When I became aware of the fire, I figured I had enough time to save my dog or my computer. Stuff is not as important as life.

If one of the things holding you back from your own decluttering has been the fear of throwing away something important, trust me—no thing is that important. People are important. Pets are important. Stuff is just ashes waiting to happen.

If one of the fears holding you in bondage to your papers is that they are all valuable, trust me—they can be replaced. My wallet burned up, so I was identity-less, but within a few weeks I was able to convince officialdom (even in post-9/11 America) that I was who I purported to be.

If you dread decluttering that collection of photographs, trust me, you'll remember what you need to. I remember all the important photographs. There was a picture of my mother that I can see perfectly as I write this. There were pictures of me as an innocent young boy that are etched in my memory. Oddly enough, pictures of ex-wives seem to have escaped into the ether. Go figure.

We clutterers are held hostage by "ifs." We've surrendered our lives to our possessions. They own us; we don't own them. We can change that, but we have to change our thinking in order to change our lives. I've done it, and so have thousands of others. One key is willingness to change. Another key is persistence. You didn't get where you are today in one day, and you won't change a lifetime of cluttering in one month. But you *can* change. It will take work and commitment (no, I don't mean we should be committed to an institution), but you can do it, if you truly want a better way of life.

Fear is what's keeping us back. Fear is our captor. Fear keeps us stuck. Fear is false. We have given it more power than it deserves. When we face our fears, they turn into wisps of smoke and waft away into the clear skies of our new clutter-less life.

I've worked with others who've lost everything in fires, floods, and hurricanes. Just losing your stuff won't keep you from cluttering later. Most clutterers I know who experienced these traumatic life events were just as cluttered a few years after their brush with disaster. That's because they didn't change the philosophy behind why they felt a need to fill their lives with stuff in the first place. The same goes for those who were magically "decluttered" on TV. Great TV; bad advice.

It's similar to someone who's been forced to quit smoking, drinking, or doing anything else because of a serious illness. Until that change in the psyche occurs, until the person wants to voluntarily live without whatever he gave up; until the clutterer begins to think of himself as a non-clutterer, he'll revert to the old habits as soon as he can.

That's why decluttering is about a combination of:
1. The practical (the how-tos).
2. The emotional (the why-dos).

I first became aware that I had a major cluttering problem in 1999, in Los Angeles. I can't blame my cluttering on the City of Angels; I brought it with me from Texas.

Get out, and take your clutter with you. Maybe you can come back when you get your life under control. With those sobering words, my former fiancée forced me to realize that cluttering is more than an annoying personality quirk. For some of us, it is a serious problem. But, as I was to discover, there is hope. Cluttering can be controlled. No matter how many books on organizing I bought, no matter how many systems I seriously applied, no matter how many professional organizers I brought into my life, the clutter controlled me, until I found the way out.

Remember the George Carlin skit about "stuff"? We need our stuff. Heck, George could have been writing the clutterer's pledge. It was funny when he did it. Everyone identifies with it. But normal people didn't leave the nightclub after Carlin's routine and have to dodge Big Mac boxes, unfolded maps, overcoats, old clothes, magazines, and newspapers in order to get into their cars. They didn't go home to places that were so full of stuff that there was only one path through their living rooms. Clutterers live that skit every day, and the humor wanes.

I had to admit that I was different from other people. I had to fight an irrational compulsion to create chaos wherever I went, before I could begin to get my life in order for any length of time. Before my fire, I had already made great strides toward living clutter-less for six years. I'd eliminated more than a ton of clutter, learned to keep more clutter from coming back into my life, and, although not perfect, was not ashamed to have people come over to my house. Post-fire, it is *even better*, because I have less attachment to *things* as markers of success. That's not to say I don't have relapses of cluttering—I do. Sometimes, I just make a mess. But today, the messes are smaller, and I clean them up fairly quickly. I use them as markers to my emotional well-being. If I'm cluttering, then something is going on in my emotional life that I need to look at.

I don't know about your cluttering. It could be as simple as that you don't know how to organize. (The Dr. Phil diagnosis.) If that's your problem, you don't have a problem. But if you're like me, it's more likely that you clutter because of what's going on inside. Either way, we're going to find solutions. Either way, you're going to have to do some work. Either way, it has nothing to do with your being a bad person.

2 | Types of Clutterers

It's like clutterers are trying to fill the holes in their souls with stuff.
—Dr. Kathleen Wong, psychiatrist

I've Been Where You Are

How long since you've used your dining room table for dining? Is your closet so full of old clothes you don't wear anymore that the new ones you keep buying are getting crushed (yes, I know that a lot of them still have the tags on them from a year ago or more. I told you I've been there). Do we really need those prescriptions that expired when Reagan was president? How many of us have junk cars in our yards that we are going to restore or that might come in handy for parts?

Degrees of Cluttering

For most people, a desk littered with papers, or a closet or garage stuffed with forgotten items, is a temporary aggravation. Heck, how many "normal" people actually put two cars in their two-car garage? For clutterers such as ourselves, those things have become so much a part of our frozen-soul environment that they're perma-clutter.

Those areas are only the tip of the iceberg, and are an outward manifestation of our inner lives. Inside, many of us are afraid of losing love, so we hang on to every object that comes into our lives. We feel that if we accumulate enough things, love will magically appear. What's truly sad is that clutter usually cuts us off from others. Many of us say we want love and people in our lives, but we're lying to ourselves. Subconsciously, we use clutter as a physical barrier to letting others get close to us. The stuff in our lives isn't the problem—the stuff in our heads is. The solution is a combination of using our heads, emotions, and spirits.

Everyone is different. Although there are broad categories of clutter issues (paper, mail, keepsakes, clothes, memory items, and so on), each type of clutterer approaches the same physical manifestation of cluttering in her own way, based on her own personality. Everyone clutters for different reasons (usually a combination of reasons), and will do their best decluttering in a different way. That's why cookie-cutter decluttering advice works for some, but not for others.

You Are Lucky if This Describes You

The degree of our disorganization will determine how much effort we need to put into changing our behavior.

Mildly Disorganized

If you are fortunate enough to be one of these people, then a little tweaking, such as using your dominant learning skill, or improving decision-making or visualization, is all you need. You are the kind of person who generally maintains a neat desk (with a few scattered papers to add flavor), knows where 90 percent of your files are, and would rather not have a messy desk.

You probably only need to spend about 5 percent of your time on organizing to improve your work life. Your home is probably not in need of any work at all. So why did you buy this book? Even that little bit of cluttering is a big deal to you, and you may be afraid that it is just the tip of the iceberg. If you read a bit more, you'll find out if there is really something behind it, or if you can stop worrying.

You're not going to need the emotional/psychological approach to solving your cluttering problem. The practical information will take care of you, but as long as you're here, read a little of the emotional reasons for cluttering, why don't you. You never know, there may be more going on than you think.

Home- or Office-Only Clutterer

This is another type of clutterer who can be "fixed" without much effort. You seem to live two lives. You're relatively neat at home, and cluttered at the office—or vice-versa. This shows that you have the ability to get and stay organized, but there is a deeper psychological reason why you clutter in one area or the other.

You'll probably have to initially devote 20 percent of your time to understanding what's going on and why it is expressed in disorganization. You've got some ingrained habits that can be changed when you know what's behind them. Once you're back on track, staying there will only require periodic checks.

Solutions

Practical. Learning a bit about a radically different way of filing (in a later chapter) or how to deal with your mail, or whatever your clutter issue at home is, will open a door in your mind and propel you into a clutter-free life—if this is all that is going on.

Emotional. There's probably not a lot going on that you're not aware of, so let's not waste time looking for deeper meanings. Even Freud said, "Sometimes a cigar is just a cigar."

Your Grown Children's Clutter

Sometimes your house or garage is cluttered through no fault of your own. Your grown kids have gone off and left their stuff at your house. You may be a clutterer too, but it's hard to tell with all of their stuff in the way. Only you can decide what's fair and what's unreasonable. If they've gone off to college, maybe it makes sense for them to leave their stuff behind until they get on their feet. But do you want all of their junk blocking your own life for the next four to eight years?

If they've graduated and have lives of their own, the answer is easy: No.

Practical. Have a talk with the owners of the stuff. Tell them that the next time they come to visit (preferably this century), they've got to decide what they want to do with their stuff. They can either take it home (their home!), or rent a storage unit. But your home is no longer in the storage business.

Emotional. This is actually one of the tougher issues to deal with. You love your kids. You'd do anything for them. You don't want to alienate them. And you may actually not want to get rid of all their stuff, because it reminds you of them. Getting rid of it may force you to admit that they're no longer your babies and are really gone.

Clutter Just Happened to Me

If you're a situational clutterer, you started cluttering because of some situation in your life. You lost a spouse (through a breakup, death, or Alzheimer's), family member, job, or had a major illness or some other brush with death. Fortunately, this can be the form of cluttering most likely to be solved. Using the tools in this book, coupled with some good therapy, you can stop cluttering for good. Once you figure out why you're using cluttering as a way to avoid dealing with what's really bothering you, you'll deal with what needs to be dealt with and move on.

You can keep pretty good track of where things are, but when faced with deadlines or extra pressure, you react by losing papers and feeling overwhelmed. Cheer up! The problem isn't that you are chronically disorganized; it is that you have chosen this method to react to doing something you don't want to do, or are afraid of failing at. We can fix this by changing the way you relate to tasks, and lowering your misplaced perfectionism.

About 20 percent of disorganized people were neat until a traumatic event changed their lives. They became messy after the death of a loved one, or the loss of a job or relationship. Although this is thorny emotional ground, changing the cluttering behavior is easy because we know the obvious psychological roots. Yours aren't buried deep in your psychic garden. With a little psychological digging, you can release your uncluttered self and return to your previously uncluttered life.

A word of caution: don't start until you are ready. Your cluttering may be protecting you from dealing with emotions you can't deal with right now. Once you get started, it won't take you much time at all to get back to normal.

Solutions

Practical. For you, there are several practical ways to get started. Once you start, you'll find you can move forward quickly.

Take one item that seems to be hard to get rid of, but that you feel you should. Put it in a plastic sack in the garage. Leave it be until you're ready to get rid of it. Write about it in your Decluttering Diary. Concentrate on what it means to you. Why is it so blasted important? Yes, I know we're dealing with just one thing here, but what I've found is that one thing may be the gatekeeper that's keeping a whole lot more things from escaping your house.

If the clutter isn't your stuff, but belonged to the family member who's deceased or gone to an assisted living home, and you aren't sure what to do with it, do as I did when I got rid of most of my mother's and father's clutter: I asked them for permission to throw things away. Father was dead and Mother was in another state with Alzheimer's, but I clearly visualized them when I asked them. They did not say no, so I continued with getting rid of their stuff (details are in Chapter 3).

If the stuff isn't yours, and you're fearful that you're discarding valuable items, ask one of your spouse's friends with the same interests to help you decide what's valuable and what's not. There was a good book, published in 2000, called *How to Tell What Things Are Really Worth*, by Tommy Vig, Chick Sponder, and Michael Scriven, but it's out of print. If you can find a used copy, it's a good way to help determine the worth of things. However, all is not lost. You can use the Internet to get a general idea of the value of nearly everything. Specialized collectibles often have their own Websites (coins, stamps, dolls, and so on), and everything is on eBay. Another source for the values people put on their collections of stuff is *www.itaggit.com*.

Be aware that there are scumbags who will try to take advantage of you if you have a garage sale or put a lot of stuff up in a classified ad. I personally know a man who makes several thousand dollars a year because he goes to garage sales or follows up on ads for old cameras. He mainly takes advantage of widows and the elderly. Hey, I'm a capitalist, and believe everyone should make a buck for his time, but to tell someone an old camera is worth maybe $25 when you know it's worth $2,500 is unethical.

There are, of course, estate sales companies, but they usually only want to get involved with higher-end collections. Check out the company's reputation before signing anything.

Emotional. You're probably anthropomorphizing your possessions. Things don't represent people. You've lost people, so you're afraid to lose possessions. Easy does it, but as you do it (get rid of one item at a time), you'll process your feelings and come to the realization that after all, it's just stuff.

You're stuck in the past, afraid to move into the present, and the future is scary. You don't trust the Universe to treat you fairly. Everything happens for a reason, and holding on to all the stuff in the world is not going to change the unfolding of your life—only slow it down. If someone you love has moved on, from this world to the next, isn't hanging on to his possessions a way of trying to keep him in this plane of existence? To paraphrase a hackneyed expression from the 1960s, "If you love someone, let them (and their possessions) go."

Nobody's Gonna Tell Me What to Do

If you are a rebellious clutterer, you weren't a clutterer all your life. In fact, when you were a child, your mother forced you to be neat. You know, it doesn't take a PhD to figure this one out. Getting over this may be as simple as accepting that your mother is not running your life anymore, and you don't need to be messy to prove it. In fact, I have worked with many clutterers for whom just accepting this realization and doing something positive with it turned the tide on their cluttering.

Solutions

Practical. The practical won't work until you do a little emotional work. You've got to face whatever demons you're rebelling against before you can show them who's boss.

This type of cluttering is usually easier to stop in the first place. Once you've done the emotional work, just be aware the next time you start to throw your jacket down instead of hanging it up, pitch the mail on the kitchen table instead of the basket you've already set aside, and so on. You see, it's not that we don't have systems to prevent our cluttering. It's that we don't use them. We don't use them because we don't want to. We're like babies throwing a tantrum, refusing to do what's good for us.

As you catch yourself cluttering, stop, and shout (or if you don't live alone and don't want others to think you are crazy, say to yourself), "You're not the boss of me." Silly? Yes. Effective? Yes. Hang up that jacket, and put the mail where it belongs.

After you've done that a few times, you're ready to clear up the mess that your rebellion created previously. Go to an area that bothers you. Vow that you will "show them," and declutter one small area of your house, but reserve the right to clutter the heck out of the rest of it. You're going to show them that you can keep that area clear for one week by declaring it sacred. (This is a concept we'll get into in detail later. It's the cornerstone for building a clutter-free life.)

Emotional. By turning the rebellion on its head, you are owning it and breaking "their" hold on your life. By taking responsibility for your own actions, you empower yourself to build your own life.

If your rebellion stems from other factors of your life you can't control (bosses, traffic, ex-spouses, estranged teenagers, and so on), ask yourself why on earth you are giving them any more control over you.

This type of cluttering is about control. You've given away your emotional control to others and are using your clutter to express your own independence. The problem is that the clutter ends up taking control of your life, so the faster you go, the behinder you get.

Terrorists in Our Heads

Fear-driven clutterers have a Depression mentality: There will never be enough. Never throw anything away. It will come in handy someday. I can fix that, or use it for parts...yeah, when pigs fly.

Solutions

Practical. Take just one broken lamp, toaster, cup, or tool, and throw that sucker away. Don't agonize about which one, or where to donate it. Nobody wants it. Just pitch it. By trashing just one, you won't be too traumatized.

Emotional. Watch your emotions and enter them in your Decluttering Diary. At first, you're going to be terrified that you're making a mistake. Then you'll probably feel as though you're a wasteful person. (Gee, do I hear a self-esteem issue raising its head?) Go back to the space you cleared and look at it. How does it make you feel? (No, you don't need to fill it up again with something else that's broken.) Chart your feelings for a couple of weeks. You'll find that the world did not end, your self-esteem didn't crumble, and you actually feel better. Now find something else to throw away, and repeat. Eventually, you will like the end result (the feeling of being in control) more than the initial fear.

Tomorrow Never Comes

If you are a procrastinating clutterer, your problem really isn't having too much stuff, it's too much putting-off. You tell yourself you could declutter in a weekend if you could just get around to it. Have you ever considered that you get around to other things, that maybe there's a reason you're putting off decluttering?

Solutions

Practical. Come on soldier, drop and give me 15. Take one (just one) decluttering task that you've been putting off for, oh, a couple of years (just kidding, it doesn't matter which one). In fact, there is really no order of difficulty, only that which we make. Some things may be more difficult than others, but few are that much harder to justify our putting them off. Pick a card, any card. Tell yourself that you are going to devote 15 minutes to working on the one task. Then do it. Even a procrastinator can do something for 15 minutes.

Emotional. We put things off so we cannot fail. If we never start, we can't do things imperfectly. If we never start, we never finish, so we can always be working to get things right. Oh, come on! Your world's not going to end if you don't declutter perfectly. In fact, there is no perfect solution. By setting a manageable timeframe instead of a completion goal, you can't help but do it perfectly. Even if you just stare at the project for 15 minutes, you did that for the allotted time. When those 15 are over, go another 15, and so on.

If Only I Wasn't So Busy

For time-clutterers, stuff isn't your problem (you tell yourself). In fact, stuff's only a minor part of your problem. You don't budget your time well enough to take care of everything. Something has to give, and it's usually "getting organized." Unless you are radically different from most people, you have the same 24 hours in a day that the rest of us do. So maybe time isn't the trouble. Budgeting your time is.

Practical. Because you value time so much, just keep a record of how much time you waste looking for keys, important papers, and so on, because of your clutter. Do this for a week. Once you've done that, you can use the practical method for the procrastinator.

Emotional. You're sabotaging yourself by making things harder for yourself. Similar to the procrastinator, you're preparing an excuse for any failure. When we fill our every minute with activity, we prevent ourselves from having quiet time for meditation/visualization or just plain relaxation. At least one of those is necessary for us to recharge our batteries and approach life with a positive attitude. When you realize that doing what is important is more important than doing what is urgent, you will schedule time for meditation/visualization, or relaxation.

Knowledge Is *Not* Power

Information junkies have to know everything. You derive part of your self-worth from or define yourself by the fact that you are the one people turn to when they want to know about something that was in the newspaper three weeks ago. I must be careful in making generalizations here: I used to use the phrase, "You are not the information desk at the library" in my seminars, until someone raised his hand and said, "As a matter of fact, I am."

Practical. This is going to be surprisingly hard, but the next time someone asks you about a three-week-old newspaper article, say, "I don't know." You'll probably stutter, but you'll get it out. You're going to have to deal with this before you can start getting rid of old newspapers and magazines. Once you've made "I don't know" part of your vocabulary, and you see that people don't think any less of you, then you're ready to start getting rid of the accumulated knowledge of the world in your living room. Since this overlaps with other types of cluttering, we'll address it in detail in a later chapter, but the short version is getting rid of the oldest first.

Emotional. Everyone wants to be wanted. There's nothing wrong with that. When we manufacture a reason for people to approach us, maybe we are hiding behind the façade. Our friends will like us for who we are, not for what we know. People who are using us only like us for what we can do for them. Dropping them from our lives is good self-esteem decluttering.

CHAOS Junkie (Change Hurts And Organizing Stinks)

Every aspect of your life overwhelms you. Congratulations! You are a real clutterer. You spend more time *looking* for things than *doing* things. Your office and home are cluttered. You will get better, but it will require some real work on your part. You'll have to understand why you clutter, and decide you want to change the behavior. If you really want to change, you can. Don't change because your boss or spouse is on your back. Change because you want a better life.

The reasons you're disorganized are deep-seated and have to be faced before you can make any permanent progress. Don't worry, I'm not suggesting Freudian analysis. I won't ask you to relate your clutter to your relationship with your mother. While we are on the subject of mothers—no, cluttering is not genetic. It may be learned behavior, but even that doesn't hold up statistically. About half of clutterers came from cluttering families (or obsessively neat families—the flip side of the same coin).

You can make positive changes *immediately* and work on the rest in time. The practical visualization and memory tools here will help you today; behavioral modification will take some time. Cluttering is a habit. Not cluttering is also a habit. It's hard to change alone. Consider attending a support group such as Clutterless (*www.clutterless.org*) or Clutterers Anonymous, and/or psychological counseling. **Changing your outside without changing your inside is only temporary.** Disorganization has stolen your life. You may have to spend 30 percent of your time fighting what comes naturally to you—cluttering. Oh my gosh, you may say, that's a lot of time. That 30-percent investment will result in a 200-percent improvement in the way you work and feel about yourself. Do you get that good of a return from your mutual fund?

An Uncontrollable Clutterer

Some of us will never get organized. All the books, all the best professional organizers, all the best intentions in the world, will not make it happen. The stress of trying to fit into someone else's mold is just too much. Before you jump up and shout "Hooray! I can stop trying!" upset your cluttered desk, and scare the cat, think about this for a minute. If you honestly try and don't really want to change, accept it. Accept the consequences as well. You will always under-earn.

You will never know the joy of living to even half your potential. You will probably always be alone, because you use clutter to keep people out of your life. But maybe that's not important to you. Maybe you have made such a relationship with your demons that you don't need any other kind. Who's to judge?

Hoarding

Hoarding is far more often brought up in the media than "mere" cluttering. Part of that is because *hoarding* is a medical term, and, in the media viewpoint, sexier than someone who's "just" messy.

Today we are inundated with so-called reality shows in which clutterers' and hoarders' houses are magically converted to Simple Living temples. I believe that such shows do more harm than good, but for now, I'd like to clarify the term *hoarding* because the media often misuses it.

Advanced clutterers or hoarders don't get cirrhosis of the liver, age prematurely, or end up in seedy thrift stores with shaking hands, begging for "just a little shot of clutter to get the day started." Or at least very few of us do. If you apply the principles set down in these pages, you'll be able to pass an entire street full of thrift shops and not even be tempted to run in for "just a peek."

Cluttering affects a majority of the population in one way or another. Hoarding does not. Calling someone who clutters a hoarder is like comparing a cold with the flu (respectively). The outward symptoms are somewhat similar, but the flu (hoarding) can kill you. A cold (cluttering) won't. There are degrees to cluttering. You don't have to go to the extremes of some of the people you will meet in later chapters to get a lot out of this book. Even if you are just a disorganized person, you will find great insight and help overcome your slight problem before it becomes a major disability. Almost everyone I talked to when writing this book said, "Oh, I have a problem with that!" So read on before you make any judgments about how serious your cluttering is. You will be able to benefit from the experience, strength, and hope of those who went too far. Maybe you will be able to arrest what is at this point a mere annoyance with the information found here. I sincerely hope so.

Dr. Gail Steketee, one of the nation's leading experts on hoarding, put it into perspective for me. "For those of us who aren't suffering from psychiatric conditions, we are all suffering from flaws. We will always struggle with those things [such as weight]. We will always have to watch what we eat. We still have to be alert."

I was a guest on a radio show with Dr. Randy Frost, another hoarding expert, and we complemented each other well. Hoarding and cluttering behavior may appear similar on the outside, but differ in degree and in severity. Clutterers can fix themselves. Hoarders can't. One of the many things we clutterers should be grateful for is that we are clutterers and not hoarders.

Depression and Anxiety

We're way more likely to have depression or anxiety, or both, than OCD or ADD. Chronic disorganization has psychological roots. Based on 879 responses to a survey on *www.clutterless.org*, 49 percent experienced depression, and 34 percent sought psychiatric counseling. Of those who told their psychiatrist/psychologist about their cluttering, 29 percent felt it helped them to not clutter long-term.

At one of my seminars, a woman shouted, "I dispute your statistics!" As politely as I could, I asked her why. "I think 49 percent are depressed and 51 percent won't admit it." The audience burst into knowing laughter.

So what's that mean? I'm afraid it doesn't let you off the hook. You can't just say, "Oh, I'm depressed, and that's why I clutter." It could be the other way around. Either way, experience has shown that those who work on their clutter issues find their depression and anxiety lessening. It's a chicken and egg thing, and facing your clutter is the start of making a great self-improvement omelet.

Terms

The terms *cluttering, disorganization, chronically disorganized,* and *clutterers* are interchangeable. I don't use *packrat* or other euphemisms. Cluttering is a compulsive behavior. Cluttering is serious, but learning not to take ourselves so seriously is part of getting over it. Lighten up and defuse clutter's hold on you. This isn't a tome. You'll laugh out loud as you identify with other clutterers.

Cluttering is an emotional blockage in our lives that hampers our job performance, steals time from our families, and fosters feelings of inadequacy in people who are far from inadequate. Cluttering is seldom life-threatening, but it does cause accidents at work and at home.

At my very first seminar, I said, "Cluttering, unlike other self-destructive behaviors, isn't life-threatening." A woman raised her left arm, which was in a cast, and said, "Yes it is. I fell down my stairs because of the clutter on them. That's why I'm here."

I use the term *clutterer*, for the most part. Although many people prefer the term *packrat*, I don't like it. I, and many clutterers, find it demeaning. A packrat is a charming rodent; cluttering is serious. Calling oneself a packrat is rather like somebody with a broken arm saying she has a boo-boo. Still, it may be more comfortable for you to say you're a packrat. Maybe you don't have a serious problem, and don't want to be identified with those of us who do. Only you know the truth.

For those of us with a serious cluttering problem, I believe that accepting what we are—clutterers—is more liberating than using gentler terms such as *packrats* or *collectors*. However, we all have to make decisions that we can live with. What is important is that we admit that we have a problem and are willing to take the steps necessary to do something about it.

Some people will object to the word *recovery*. There's a prejudice against it because it denotes an alcoholic or drug addict in many people's minds. We "recover" from all sorts of things: colds, broken legs, financial setbacks, relationships gone sour, and so on. If the word bothers you, substitute *get better*, or something else that makes sense to you. Don't let a little semantics keep you from recovering—oops, I mean getting better. See how easy that was?

Different Methods of Approach

Many different approaches are suggested in this book. Heck, all it takes is some out-of-the-box thinking and new organizing methods to overcome your cluttering problems. Some of us need the two-pronged synthesis of the practical and emotional ways to deal with cluttering.

What I propose has worked, for many clutterers. Similar to any book about clutter and its elimination, there are practical how-to tips here. But you'll notice that I spend more time on the emotional aspects. That's what separates this from mainstream organizing books. As a clutterer myself, I know that we can organize as well as the next person if we want to, or have to. But we cannot *stay* organized unless we change some of our core beliefs about what *things* mean to us and what *stuff* represents. In doing so, we have to tackle some of our ways of looking at *things*, and how we define ourselves.

In short, we must take steps toward living an aware life, a self-actualized life. If you're up for the challenge, you can gain the life you've been missing. But it's all up to you. For many, just doing the exercises in this book is all you'll need. You just needed a little self-awareness to make the changes necessary to live clutter-less.

Although clutterers tend to be introverts and loners, a few of us will be willing to join a support group such as Clutterless or a 12-step group such as Clutterers Anonymous, and find that helps us in many aspects of our life. Some of us may realize that a little therapy could do wonders. Whatever works for you is what you should do.

One thing I've become more convinced of since the first edition is that taking some action for the depression and anxiety that so many of us have is a big step to overcoming our cluttering. Decluttering is a big step to breaking out of depression. A cocktail of all or some of the above may work best for others. Take a look at each path, and start down the road that your heart chooses. If one approach doesn't seem to work for you, try another. Whatever you do, don't give up.

Recognizing the Problem

Some of us have turned our clutter into security blankets. We sleep on beds littered with books, clothes, papers, and boxes so we don't feel so alone when we go to sleep at night. It starts with one book that we read before retiring. Then it is joined by another. It invites its friends. Before long, the books from the library are having a party on our bed, and we are just in the way.

We pile papers and books on our dining room tables until we and our families (if we still have them) have to eat from TV trays or have learned to balance our plates while eating. We don't invite anyone to our houses, out of shame. No one ever rides in our cars, because there is only room for the driver.

In extreme cases, some of us have sold cars rather than deal with the clutter in them. We have moved to larger houses, thinking that the problem is just that we don't have enough room. To some extent, that is valid, but mostly it is hogwash. We rent storage sheds, in ever-increasing sizes, to relieve the pressure. If enough people take the advice in this book, the storage shed industry will go on the skids—so sell your stock now.

Most of us are neat in appearance, and appear normal to the outside world. Oh, maybe our desks are a little messy, but everyone laughs that off. Unlike alcoholics or drug addicts, our clutter seldom gets us fired for not showing up for work. But many of us have been fired for losing important documents, missing deadlines, missing important appointments, or screwing up our boss's travel reservations, sending her to Cancún instead of Chicago.

Stopping the Merry-Go-Round

Can we stop this black tornado of paper and useless items that swirls around us, blocking us from the sunlight of the spirit? Absolutely! It will not be easy, because no one wants to admit that he or she is not in control of every aspect of his or her life. I'll alternate between the male and female pronouns in this book because, although most admitted clutterers are female, that could just be because women are more likely to admit that they have a problem and do something about it. Guys clutter too. I'm not the only poster boy for clutterers. Women have the deck stacked against them because our society (yep, even after the 1960s revolution) expects women to be neater than men.

A sober alcoholic or drug addict doesn't take alcohol or drugs into his body or house. A recovering overeater doesn't ingest more food than he needs. A recovering clutterer doesn't let clutter take back her life once she has won a few battles with it. It is a war. Clutter comes into our lives every day. We get mail that we don't need. We get bills that have to live somewhere until they are paid. Things wear out and break and get replaced by new ones. Clothes shrink (well, maybe we grow), lose buttons, fade, or go out of style. The newspaper comes every day, if we still take it. Eventually we learn to view these events as calls to arms. The world throws clutter at us. We learn to throw it back. Before long, you will be hitting clutter out of your life like a big-league ballplayer.

Bad News for Sports Car Enthusiasts

This will be bitter medicine for sports car aficionados, but even a 1965 Alfa-Romeo Spyder *is* a junk car when it hasn't run in 15 years.

However, we insist on calling them "project cars," which is a euphemism for unfulfilled dreams. Don't get suckered into this. I've been struggling with the temptation to get another project car the last couple of years. Maybe it has to do with yet another midlife crisis. One thing that's saved me is the realization that I never was a mechanic, so what makes me think I can start now, in my 50s? The other is that crawling around on the floor and twisting and turning to try to put tools where they weren't meant to go (in the engine compartment, that is) is realistically impossible given my current physical condition: old guy.

I speak from experience. I owned that 1965 Alfa. It didn't run the day I bought it, and it didn't run five years later when I sold it for $100. The stories in this book are from people just like me and you. I've had stuff littering my life, stopping me from becoming the person I wanted to be. Yes, all this stuff really affects our personalities. It makes us shy, fearful, and angry, feeds our low self-esteem, and makes us feel "less than." So get rid of the clutter and take back control of your life!

3 | My Story

> *One doesn't discover new lands without consenting to lose sight of the shore for a very long time.*
> —André Gide

First, the good news: I (and many others similar to me) have gotten my cluttering under control. Although our battles will never make a Tom Clancy novel, they feel just as exciting to us.

In the years between publishing the first edition of this book and my losing all my worldly possessions in a fire, I had made a lot of personal progress against clutter. I think it's important to know that, even for me, Mr. Clutterless, Grand Poo-Bah of the Clutterless Groups, Revered Author, clutter is still an ongoing struggle. I've always stated this in my books, but this may be the first of them you've read. Yep, friend, we will always struggle with cluttering, but the engagements will be mere skirmishes instead of pitched battles.

After I moved to Galveston (the end of the saga in the previous edition), I moved three more times, once to a single room (lesson: there's such a thing as too much downsizing), but with a garage for storage. My last one-bedroom apartment was presentable, most of the time. When I moved to Austin, I was able to rent the second-smallest Ryder truck and fill it with mostly furniture.

But there were still the several thousand slides I'd taken and meant to organize and catalog in order to sell. Actually, except for maybe four or five banker's boxes of papers, there wasn't much else that was clutter. I had stuff, but all of it had a purpose. (Okay, I seldom went fishing, but the nets and rods and reels *did* get used a couple of times a year.) I can't swear to this, but I think I only had one old non-working computer I was going to fix and use for a backup device. Now that's progress.

No One of Us Is Unique—Lessons From Losing It All

If you read the introduction, you know that all my possessions were destroyed in a fire. I am not unique. Fire, flood, hurricanes, tornadoes, and other natural disasters destroy the homes of thousands of people every year in the United States.

What *was* unique was the effect that losing all my stuff had on me. I honestly do not think I would have reacted the way I did, with acceptance and relief, had I not spent the previous years helping others and myself overcome our cluttering habits. I've known and worked with too many people who lost everything, and within a few years were just as cluttered as before, and others who were not clutterers until the disaster, but became that way in reaction to their losses.

The positive news I can give you from my own experience is that, although occasionally I will remember and even briefly miss something that was destroyed, there has not been one thing that I have *needed* to continue living.

Yes, my computer (and the external tape backup—which seemed like a good idea) was destroyed. So I did lose data that I will never get back. I did lose addresses that I had accumulated throughout 20 years. I did lose tax records. Yes, on the surface, it would seem that there were losses that could not be replaced. There were, in fact. But not one of them has kept me from going on. Not one of them was invaluable.

I sincerely hope that you don't go through a natural disaster such as that, but know that some small percentage of those of you reading will face this in your future. When that happens, I hope you can take hope from my own experience, and that it will make going on a little bit easier. From a practical standpoint, even if you are a renter, get insurance. I wish I had read that a couple of years ago.

The other lesson from the fire was that our lives go on, and they go on the way they're supposed to. I moved around for a few months after the fire, leaving Austin and eventually landing in San Antonio. I felt free to live anywhere. When I had all my stuff, moving was a royal pain. When all you own can fit in the trunk of a mid-sized car, you can go where you want to go.

I made a trip to Mexico and rediscovered my love for that country and began writing about it again. While I was in Austin, I was comfortable and stagnant. AF (After the Fire), I had to hustle again. As clutterers, we tend to get into our comfort zones and stay there, never growing emotionally or spiritually.

Starting Over—Again?

I ended up coming back to the Rio Grande Valley of Texas—Mission, to be specific. Fluffy and I rented a 300-square-foot trailer in a Winter Texan trailer park. I have to admit that I was a little depressed at first, because I could survey my realm in a couple of rapid eye movements. But it taught me that, just as I preach, our self-esteem does not come from people, places, or things. Being 56 and starting over took a lot of inner resources.

What's this got to do with clutter? Plenty. Living in such a small space, I had to plan before I brought any item into my house. There were no impetuous purchases at the thrift stores. It also taught me to honor and cherish those items I owned.

Today, I live in a nice house in a middle-class neighborhood, with a nice office that is neat and clean 75 percent of the time, with a woman who loves me, a dog who adores me, a cat who tolerates me, and several birds I tolerate. I am where I am supposed to be. Fluffy, the Declutter Dog, left this vale, and has moved on to Rainbow Bridge to wait for me. Misty, the new member of our family, doesn't know clutter, and I'd like to keep it that way. It made me sad to keep the Fluffball's bed, dishes, and other paraphernalia around, so I donated them to homeless animals. If you're keeping something that reminds you of someone, give it new life by giving it away.

Losing Teaches Us the Meaning of Loving

Losing Fluffy hurt one hell of a lot more than losing all my stuff. That's the way it should be. I almost never think about the stuff I no longer have; I think about Fluffy frequently. That doesn't mean I don't love Misty. It means that the Fluffball's memory will always have a spot in my heart. There are two lessons here for the rest of us. One is that we don't need to keep stuff around to remind us of those we love. The other is that we will lose people and animals in our lives, and we will grieve, but we should not let that be an excuse for us to re-hoard or re-clutter and shut ourselves off from others again. Unfortunately, I have seen that happen—someone dies and the surviving spouse clutters to fill the hole left by that person.

Occasionally, I get frustrated with the lack of success of Clutterless groups. I get tons of calls and e-mails, but nobody wants to start meetings. One week I had had it with those groups. I had decided to throw in the towel and disband the meeting in McAllen, where I now live. Before the meeting started, and before I could make my announcement, a lady said, "I just wanted to thank you for being led to write your book. I am so happy that you decided to move down to McAllen and start this meeting. It has saved my life. Thank you."

As if that wasn't enough to make me feel like a heel for considering quitting, two other people echoed the sentiment.

I, like you, will be put in the right place at the right time. Follow your heart. Forget your clutter.

One Ton and Counting

When I began writing the first edition of this book, I had recycled more than 1,075 pounds of paper (not including newspapers) and given away 230 pounds of books, 63 pounds of clothes, three old computers, and hundreds of floppy disks. I had thrown out a pottery pink flamingo with a broken leg (and gave its mate to a CNN reporter who interviewed me for a story on cluttering), 10 cans of old paint, two tents without poles, and a partridge in a pear tree (just kidding about the bird). And all of that is just since I started keeping track. As a side benefit, I dropped 6 pounds, probably from carting all that stuff to the recycler. By the time I left Los Angeles, I had discarded more than a ton (2,100 pounds) of clutter.

Today my desk is clear, I can walk around any room of my house in the dark without fear of tripping, I can find a book when I need it, and I haven't spent any time looking for my keys or wallet in years. That's one Clutterless habit I have down pat. It took acceptance, determination, work, and the support of fellow clutterers to get this far. I am just a guy who has a problem and sought help. Thank God there are organizations of people in the same boat. I mention them so that you too can avail yourself of their support if you choose.

I am not going to preach at you and say, "You'd better get into a support group, or else." You may not be a group person. You could just need to apply the concepts in this book to your life to get back on track. It's similar to quitting smoking or any other habit. You *can* do it alone, but it's usually easier to do it with the support of others. If you want to know more about support groups, Chapter 20 is all about them.

Different Approaches

I disagree with typical organizing books in a number of areas. That isn't to say they are wrong; I can only speak from my heart and the words of those I interviewed. I don't believe in the statement, "If you haven't used it in a year (or three years, or some other arbitrary number), throw it out." If you are a clutterer, you probably couldn't *find* it for three years. No one can make that decision for you, and that is one thing that makes decluttering so hard.

One of our dilemmas is that our possessions give us feelings. *That* is what we have to deal with. Some stuff, like old love letters, family mementos, and pictures, have value. What I had to do was to evaluate each of those items. At first it was hard, so I just threw them all into a box marked "memories." Later, when I had dealt with the bigger and easier stuff, I went back and sorted through the memories. In my case, about 70 percent could be discarded. Since the fire, I have not started another memory box. But from a practical perspective, I'd like to point something out. If you've got a few containers (plastic, not cargo-ship-size) of memory items, so what? Spend your time decluttering other, less emotionally laden items.

Brief Family History

I don't think I was born a clutterer, though it did run in my family. (Some research suggests there is a genetic disposition to hoarding, which is not to say there is for cluttering.) While decluttering my home, I had to go through many boxes of my mother's stuff. She had saved a few important papers, but mostly, she saved junk. I found folder after folder of contests she entered from 1956 to 1973. I also found every letter I had written to her during my vagabond youth. They were instructive, and gave me a feeling of continuity. Okay, those letters are some of the things I wish I had not lost in the fire. But you know what? Even things as important and personal as they were do not haunt me the way I thought they would. So if your fear of making a mistake is keeping you from discarding anything, trust me—trust yourself.

When I was a child, I was neat. I ironed my clothes, washed dishes, and made my bed. We were poor, so I didn't have a lot of stuff to clutter up my room. I grew up on a farm, which is the devil's playground for a clutterer. The shed in back was bigger than the house, and I loved it. I probably thought, "When I grow up, I'm going to become a clutterer!" Old 78 rpm records, newspapers older than I, broken farm equipment, and assorted junk filled most of it. My father believed that everything would come in handy someday, so he kept everything. My mother ragged on him from time to time, but she had her own way of cluttering.

She filed everything. When the filing cabinets were full, she transferred the bulging folders to cardboard boxes and stored them in the garage for safekeeping. The rats ate chunks out of most of them. A good rule of thumb is that when the rats are eating better than you, it's time to start decluttering.

My first piece of clutter came with wheels. I got a sports car (a silver Datsun Fairlady 1500, which never became a classic, or at least not a valuable one. There are a few "project cars" on the Internet, but few are running, and they are not expensive. This is just one more warning to middle-aged guys and gals not to hang on to a car just because it's old). That gave me a rationalization for keeping old spark plugs, distributor caps, and tires (you never know when you will need a spare). I justified the tires because the odd-sized tires were difficult to find in 1967. The Datsun eventually broke and spent more time behind a tow truck than on the road, but I couldn't part with it.

After high school, I spent two years hitchhiking around the country, and now see that my cluttering was beginning to take on unreal proportions. Unlike most hitchhikers, I carried a duffel bag because it held more stuff than a backpack. I had a sleeping bag and several changes of clothes. But why did I carry a three-pound statue of a Greek goddess? Because it was given to me by a girlfriend. I couldn't have her, so I kept a thing to give me love. Funny, that statue didn't keep me warm at night.

Wives Don't Appreciate Junk Cars or Phonebook Collections (Go Figure!)

When my first ex-wife (I mention the ex-wives because cluttering often got in the way of my relationships) and I moved to New Orleans, we didn't have much stuff, but we towed my broken-down sports car. All our possessions fit in the one room we rented. As we became more affluent, we rented a house.

I acquired a 1965 Alfa-Romeo Spyder (one of the last with an oil temperature gauge). Clutterers are like parrots: We're fascinated by geegaws. It was my dream car. It didn't run, but it gave me a project. I had grown up! I had a wife, a garage, and two sports cars. I had become the clutterer I had only dreamed about being as a boy. Before long, the garage was home to a broken refrigerator for beer, the Alfa, and a lot of broken tools. But it was my garage. The broken-down Datsun lived in the yard.

In college, I needed a lot of books for research. I wanted to be a writer, so I had five dictionaries. Elaine (name changed to protect me from a lawsuit) bought me a new IBM Selectric typewriter. I couldn't throw the old manual one away, so I kept it for a spare—in case the electricity ever went out. But really, how likely was it that I would type by candlelight? Clutterers have all sorts of illogical excuses for keeping their junk.

Notice that there were a lot of "I" statements there. "We" didn't have a sofa, or extra chairs for guests, or a dining room table. Similar to most clutterers, I was self-absorbed.

I loved garage sales. Every weekend I came home with some new piece of junk. Before long we had to move to a larger house. I blamed it on the furniture my wife bought. She began to complain about my junk encroaching on her space. I think it was the collection of phonebooks from every major city in the United States, Mexico, Canada, and France that finally did her in. Our arguments often ended with, "Take your junk and get out."

It was 30 years until I really heard that statement. After all, I was an artist. I was allowed to be eccentric.

Bachelorhood = More Clutter

The marriage ended, but I can't blame it all on my cluttering. My active alcoholism and irresponsibility had a lot to do with it. Very few wives would have understood why I wanted to quit college and become a jungle explorer (which I did eventually become, paddling a dugout canoe up the Amazon). After getting heat stroke in the middle of the river and being saved from certain death by a kindly native, I decided that my career as a jungle explorer should be short-lived if I wanted to be long-lifed.

I left South America and moved back to the Big Easy. I moved into a small, furnished apartment, crammed wall to ceiling with books and junk. I was happy. My possessions gave me a feeling of security and love. My bed was a minefield; there was barely enough room for me. Several girlfriends came over and tried to help me "get organized." Fortunately for them, there was no way for two people to get into the bed at the same time. They usually gave up on the project, and me, after a couple of weeks. For solace, I went to more garage sales and carted home more junk.

A Billboard?

The most bizarre thing I accumulated was a billboard. In a bourbon-induced haze, three friends and I stole it in some small Louisiana town. I took it with me to Memphis and back to New Orleans a year later. You should have seen the looks on the movers' faces.

It was a look that I saw more and more frequently as I grew older. Without saying a word, people conveyed amazement and disgust at the way I lived. I had no shame, and invited people to my house. Once, my apartment was burglarized. When the cops saw my living room, they said, "Man, they really did a number on this place." In fact, the burglars hadn't touched a thing in my living room. That was the way it normally looked.

I had always had a golden touch and was able to make a lot of money at executive positions. At work, I was a neat freak. My desk was always cleared when I went home. I made to-do lists. I was the model of efficiency. My cluttering downfall came when I went into business for myself as a stock trader in the 1980s. The Internet was in its infancy, so I had a ticker tape, which consumed rolls of yellow paper, best suited for throwing out the window during parades. New Orleans had a lot of parades, but I kept that ticker tape. My closet began to fill. I had to save the *Wall Street Journal*, *Barron's*, and the *New York Times*, for "research."

When I went bust and moved, I left behind an entire room full of old papers and ticker tapes. I was sure that someone else would appreciate the valuable library. All I took with me fit into the back of a pickup truck. I then lived clutter-free in a one-room house in Puerto Escondido, Oaxaca, Mexico. I owned nothing but a duffel bag and a few books. When I left a year later, I left behind a clutter mess. Poor people in Mexico hang on to everything that crosses their paths. There was a difference, though: They used those things. I just collected them. I returned to the United States with only a half-full duffel bag and lived in a furnished room in Seattle. My fortunes increased again, and so did my stuff. I moved to sunny Southern California. By the time I left San Diego, I had to rent a storage space for my stuff. One clue that I was out of control again should have been when I had to hire a moving company to transport my junk from California to my mother's home in Texas. She, the ultimate clutterer, said, "How did you ever collect so much junk?"

Married to a Neat Freak

Then I married a compulsive neat freak. That is common with clutterers. We often marry people with whom our clutter will cause conflicts. We do so in the hopes that their neatness, which we equate with goodness, will rub off on us. It doesn't. They just get frustrated and angry. Many clutterers have unhappy spouses and think the problem with their lives is their spouse. "If only he or she would stop nagging, life would be perfect."

Lost Job Due to Cluttering

I garnered a dream job writing guidebooks to Mexico, which I then lost, to a large degree because of my cluttering. Because I was a recognized eccentric and artist, I cluttered my office with papers and books and statuary. The six-foot wooden doorjambs from Michoacán, Mexico, were probably the most bizarre. How I got away with it, heaven only knows. A reporter for a news magazine interviewed me and couldn't take a picture of me behind my desk because everything was piled too high. He took the shot outside. When new management came in, they started their decluttering with me.

Moving Didn't Help

Thinking a change of address would help, I tried to sell my house to move back to Los Angeles. It took six months to sell. People came in, and although I had done what I thought was an exemplary job of stuffing things into my garage, they were appalled. Books (a common clutter problem—we just can't part with the written word) overflowed the shelves, papers were jammed everywhere, and it was always an adventure when prospective buyers opened a closet door. One lady was actually covered in an avalanche of papers and audiotapes that fell on her head when a sagging shelf collapsed.

To move, I rented a small U-Haul trailer. Clutterers often have a poor sense of space utilization. After three subsequent trips to U-Haul, each time getting a bigger trailer, I had to get a Ryder truck. I got the biggest truck available. It wasn't big enough. When the guys started loading it, they gave me that now-familiar look. I left half a garage and a pickup truck behind, as I had two cars again. This time my Alfa ran, though.

The move cost me $2,000. Had I decluttered before I left, it would have cost me about $400. My clutter was now causing me financial losses.

The end was near. I rented a two-bedroom apartment and had to pay $300 a month extra for the second bedroom just to store all my things. I stopped inviting people to my home. My truck was just as bad.

The Dawning

When I met the woman in Los Angeles who became my fiancée, I was able to keep her away from my apartment for three months. I'm surprised she didn't think I was married. Whenever we went anywhere, we went in her car, as my truck was too cluttered. I moved to her place. When she finally saw my apartment, she, too, gave me "The Look." But she was a kind person and thought she could help me. She tried to do it herself. When it was obvious that either the relationship or my clutter had to go, she hired a professional organizer. The organizer estimated that it would cost at least $1,000 just to get a good start at cleaning up the wreckage.

Gradually, my stuff overflowed into my beloved's neat house. At first I had space in her closet. Then I got my own closet. Then we bought a portable closet for the garage. By the end, I had taken over her extra bedroom. Finally, she too gave up on me.

The Beginning of the End

What sane man would choose stacks of useless items instead of a woman who loved him?

My business suffered. I missed deadlines because I couldn't find papers. It took too much research to find my research notes. Even with the Internet, I couldn't find files I needed because of the clutter in my computer. My income spiraled downward. I was alone and broke. It all seemed hopeless.

That's when I found a self-help group. When I first heard of it, I refused to go. I thought it was a silly California over-the-top self-help group for the terminally needy. After a few more weeks of vacillation, I went. That's when I found out that I was not the only person with this problem. Others had stories that made mine seem insignificant. Some just had minor disorganization difficulties. Most were somewhere in between. Most importantly, some had actually made progress in their battle with cluttering. They had been in the same hole of depression and negativity as I was, and had climbed back out to live happy, orderly lives. One of the most important life-changing concepts that I grasped quickly was that when I changed from thinking and living in negativity, I could change the physical clutter in my life. Never before had I read or heard that clutter and my belief systems were intertwined.

Once I realized that my clutter was an outward expression of my inner conflicts or emotions, I was able to do something about the problem and not just treat the symptoms by organizing my mess. Even doing just a little bit of decluttering at a time helped me start to get out of my depression, overcome my anxiety, and get back on track. I was not able to change a lifetime of habits or overcome serious depression all by myself all at once. But, bit by bit, little by little, everything got better. My mental fog gradually lifted and my business improved.

Suze Orman, financial advisor and author, addresses clutter in her books *The Courage To Be Rich* and *Nine Steps to Financial Freedom*. She says that having too much stuff keeps wealth from flowing into our lives. If you are religious or spiritual, you'll see that most religions or spiritual movements see clutter as something that gets between a person and his God. By crowding our lives with things, we edge out our spiritual awareness. If we believe that people are inherently good and are expressions of God, we have to make room in our lives for the good to flow in. Our lives get better when we get rid of negative thoughts and things and replace them with positive ones. Joel Osteen, in *Becoming a Better You*, says that living a positive life is part of the path to material and spiritual abundance.

Spirituality is about losing yourself in something greater than yourself. I was given a story about a lecturer who talked to a group about his experience with spirituality after visiting a great spiritual leader and learning to pray for hours at a time. The properly awed group oohed and ahhed about his achievement. After the lecture, a little old lady wearing an old-fashioned suit and a pillbox hat went up to him and said, "I know what you mean. I crochet." Because so many clutterers sew or make quilts or just collect fabric, maybe we are all closer to our God and just don't know it.

You cannot hold on to your mistakes. Catherine Ponder, a spiritual prosperity writer, says clutter holds us back from our ultimate good. Our outside is a reflection of our state of mind. Abundance doesn't mean having more stuff, a bigger house, and more money in the bank. Those things are fine, but if they are the focus of your life, you're missing the point, in my opinion. Abundance is appreciating the good you have and being able to share it. Abundance is having a life that's full of joy, energy, and compassion. Stuff's fine, but inner stuff is divine.

We're living in a society that puts too much emphasis on *things*. We need to find a balance. We generally aren't happy being minimalists, but we seem to create our own set of problems trying to be maximalists. In moderation, all things.

The more I delved into cluttering from other aspects than merely how to organize it, the more I began to realize that cluttering has emotional and spiritual roots. I finally got it. Thus began my road to living clutter-less. Even now, after eight years and counting, what I wrote in 2000 is true. Living clutter-less is a new way of life, not a one-time event. It is a neverending journey that has hills and valleys and curves. There are times when clutter creeps back into my life. When it does, so does depression, negative thinking, and confusion. Fortunately, I now have the tools to take charge—if I want to. It is always tempting to just let things pile up, to return to the old ways. Each bout of recidivism lasts a shorter time.

4 | 40 Ways to Leave Your Clutter

Q: *What decluttering tips/advice haven't worked for you?*

A: *Anything that uses words like* have to, should, ought to, need to, why don't you, you should have, what are you doing. *Any observation that starts out with* you *stops me from listening. It puts me on the defensive and makes me want to protect and defend the way I do things.*

—Response to online survey question

Clutter is the Past. Order is the Present. Peace and prosperity are the Future.
—Clutterless Affirmations

Some organizing books are like angel-food cake: easy to digest, but half an hour later, you want some substance. Others (some say similar to mine) are like seven-course dinners—lots of substance, but maybe a little hard to absorb in one sitting.

So here's an appetizer. The meat and potatoes are spread throughout the chapters, but this is the essence of this book, distilled into a few pages. If all you want to do is declutter your living room and not think about why it got cluttered in the first place, you could probably get by with these tips, though some are a bit cerebral. Trust me, if you want the real meal deal, these tidbits should entice you to read the rest of the story.

Decluttering in a Nutshell (Not That You're a Squirrel)

1. Be kind to yourself. You didn't get this way overnight, and you won't be decluttered in a day, week, or month. But you will get better, a little bit every day.
2. Start small. Make small, reachable goals for yourself. It's important at first to feel successful. You know what failure feels like. Try the other side for a change.
3. You will probably never be completely decluttered. This is a positive statement. You are who you are, and we clutterers like to have more possessions around us than many people. Stuff doesn't clutter. People clutter.
4. Your goal is to have a home where *you* feel comfortable. Don't let someone else's idea of beauty be forced on you. It's *your* house.
5. Clutter is an excess of abundance. Celebrate your abundance, and share it.
6. Shoot the next person who tells you, "If you haven't seen it in six months, you don't need it." If you haven't seen it, how do you know you didn't need it? By their reasoning, the lost tomb of Ramses the Great had no value.
7. Visualize what you want. When you make things real on the mental level, it's easier to make them real on the physical level.
8. Keep a Decluttering Diary (see Appendix I). By keeping track of where you've been, you can map out where you want to go.
9. Decluttering is also about your emotional, mental, and spiritual life. A cluttered mind is a dangerous place to be. So is a cluttered soul.
10. Take digital pictures. Keeping track of where you've been is the best way to keep from getting discouraged after you start.
11. Think locally, not globally. Try decluttering in 15-minute increments. If you find you work better in

longer sessions, do that. The 15-minute concept is 15 minutes at a stretch. You *can* keep going.

12. Goodness gracious, you'll be overwhelmed sometimes. You'll start looking at the Big Picture. Mellow out. Lighten up.

13. Keep thinking small when it comes to projects. A square foot is a lot to declutter in a session at first.

14. Make cluttering an area you've decluttered a crime in your house. Some people have bought police tape (or any colorful wide plastic tape) and put it around each area they declutter.

15. Make spaces sacred after you've decluttered them. One sacred space at a time will grow to be a whole house. Think of them as pieces to a jigsaw puzzle.

16. A sacred space is one where you promise yourself you will not clutter. You give yourself permission to clutter somewhere else (which takes the pressure off and makes it more likely that you'll keep at your decluttering efforts).

17. If you love books, let them fly free. Well, donate them to a library book sale, hospital, church, or somewhere else they'll be appreciated. If you really miss them, you can go to the library book sale and buy them back. The hope is that you'll procrastinate and not get there in time.

18. Having a garage sale may be too much work and stress for you. Take some good stuff to a resale shop. You'd be surprised at what others want. Once something's out of your house, it's easier to not bring back in. If it doesn't sell, donate it.

19. If the clutter belonged to someone else, there's no easy way to get rid of it. Fortunately, there is a chapter of not-too-painful ways to deal with the issue (Chapter 6).

20. Once it's out the door, it's gone. You no longer control stuff that's gone.

21. Shopping is not a sport. The less you buy, the less you have to declutter. If you don't learn to stop shopping, you might as well just shoot yourself in the foot.

22. Get a clutter buddy. Another clutterer or a nonjudgmental friend who will help you declutter.
23. Mail is everyone's Waterloo. Turn it into your Elba. Honestly, if you dedicate 15 minutes a day to the mail, you can eliminate a lot of anxiety about clutter.
24. You're allowed to have more than one shredder. Have one by the door (for mail), by your TV chair, in your office, wherever you might want to deal with papers or mail. Saving things up to shred is just another excuse for cluttering.
25. Sooner or later, you're going to have to deal with your emotions about clutter. Otherwise, these tips will be like smoke up a chimney. Nice, but fleeting.
26. If your clutter isn't overwhelming, invite a friend over for dinner. There's nothing that motivates someone more than company.
27. If your clutter *is* overwhelming, invite an imaginary friend over. Set a date and time and shoot for at least a decluttered sofa, but give yourself enough time.
28. It's a good idea to give your excess stuff away, but don't overthink it. Whoever gets it *is* "just the right person." Putting stuff in the alley is as good as carting it to Goodwill.
29. If recycling is keeping you from actually decluttering, rethink that. Have you turned your home into the landfill you're trying to prevent? Sometimes our best intentions are just excuses to not get rid of things.
30. How important is it? Ask yourself that about everything you spend half an hour trying to decide what to do with.
31. What's the worst that can happen? If you throw something away unintentionally, will it kill you?
32. Almost everything can be replaced, including important documents. Don't stress about stuff that's not really important.
33. People and pets are important. All the things we own shouldn't own us.

34. Reward yourself. Give yourself a treat for decluttering.
35. Decluttering is boring. So?
36. We agonize over decisions. That's the absolute worst thing we do to sabotage ourselves.
37. I promise you that you'll either find unexpected money or receive unexpected money when you declutter. So, it's a bribe. It's worked for me. When I need money, I declutter.
38. Tell yourself, "I'm worth it." You are. You deserve to live in a clutter-less environment.
39. Never, ever, ever, ever give up. I have enough faith in you for both of us.
40. Say the Clutterless Affirmations (see Appendix II) until they come true in your life.

15 Minutes to Change Your Life?

The phrase, "You can do anything for 15 minutes," has been used so often, it's hackneyed. So why am I using it? Because it is an important part of the solution to our cluttering problem. The number of minutes is immaterial. Make your personal mantra "I can do anything for X minutes."

Naysayers abound. There are always people who laugh and say, "That will never work for me. At 15 minutes a day, I'll be 150 before I get my living room decluttered."

The idea is not that you will *only* work 15 fifteen minutes a day. It's that you are only committing to decluttering for 15 minutes. If, after you've done that, you feel like going on, do it—but only in 15-minute increments. I am not going to promise you that this will be an easy process. Nor will I promise that it will be quick. You've taken years to accumulate all your stuff. You aren't going to physically get rid of it in a few weeks. More importantly, you aren't going to change your cluttering habits and psychological behaviors that quickly either.

You'll progress at your own speed, in your own time. Reread that sentence, please. You *own* your time. You are in charge; not your clutter, not me, not someone else telling you what to do.

You can do this.

You can do it alone if that's the route you choose, though it will be harder.

You can do it with another person, which will make it easier.

You can do it with a group, which will be the easiest of all. What's important is that *you* are in charge and *you* make those decisions. Be true to yourself, not to someone else's vision of how you should live. Too tidy is too stressful. I spent a night at a Zen master's house and felt as though my soul was flying apart.

There's nothing wrong with having stuff around you. We clutterers have an acceptable need to have more things around us to feel comfortable than some other people. So what? Everyone deserves to be happy. Once we get rid of what is truly clutter, we should be able to enjoy those possessions we cherish. We feel uncomfortable in a Zen-like minimalist environment.

The Physical Stuff

We cannot start with our emotions. We have to start with physical clutter. Once we start decluttering our stuff, we then begin to deal with the attendant emotions. This chapter is just a warm-up. We've gotta start somewhere.

The big picture, your final destination on the decluttering express, will just overwhelm you. Start small. Pick one small area to declutter. This could be a square foot of a desk, table, floor, bed, or sofa. It does not matter one little bit where you start, except that it is an area that makes the most sense to you.

I started with the area around my desk. The desk itself was too big a project to tackle all at once. Getting the papers off the floor, and the sunflower seeds (some of which were starting to sprout) out of the carpet, made me feel victorious. In four 15-minute increments, I had a small area that made me feel good. I congratulated myself and stood back, surveying my realm. I was the king of all I surveyed. How long since you've felt that way?

If paper is your biggest issue (which many people say), then declutter one inch, one lousy inch, of paper as your goal. By starting with something small and doable, you get immediate gratification and a feeling of success. Start with projects that you feel you will accomplish. You won't always succeed, because what seems small physically may be extra-large emotionally. That's why you'll keep a Decluttering Diary. Pick a method of working that works for you. Do it whichever way fits your personality. You know how to fail at decluttering; you've done that enough times. This time, let's succeed.

Sacred Spaces

This is the "secret" that will enable you to succeed in not recluttering. Decluttering is only one-third the challenge. Next you declare an area that you've decluttered as sacred. It can be as small as a square foot at first, eventually as large as a chair or desk, and finally a whole room. *Sacred* means that you promise yourself that you will not clutter in that one area. You can clutter anywhere else you want (and you will), but not there. The idea is that each sacred space interlocks like a jigsaw puzzle until you have several of them making a complete room.

Other Points to Keep in Mind

- You'll find that visualizing what you want will make it easier to get what you deserve. You may not be able to do this at first, but trust me, you will be amazed at how it helps once you do it.
- You'll learn to keep a Decluttering Diary to chart your emotional progress. This diary will chronicle not only *what* you did to declutter, but also *how you felt* when you did it. There are only so many emotions. Sooner or later you'll find which ones predominate, and what you can do to defang the beasts.
- Recycling may just be an excuse for not decluttering. Sometimes the good is the enemy of the greater. If much of your clutter consist of bags and boxes of stuff you're going to get around to recycling, maybe it's time to realize that the landfill you wanted to save is now your house.
- Giving things to "just the right person" is an excuse. When you get something out of your house, you give up control

of it. If you believe in the Grand Scheme of Things, whatever you get rid of *does* go to the right person. If we just put something out on the curb or in the alley behind our house, and someone picks it up, that is the right person.

- You'll probably find lost money. Most every clutterer I know, including me, has found money or valuables stuffed away that we'd forgotten about.
- The reason we've gotten this way is that we have assigned emotions to our things. If we did it, we can undo it. It won't be easy, and we may need the help of a therapist, but we can untangle ourselves from our stuff.
- The bad news: We will experience shame, guilt, fear, anxiety, depression, sadness, a sense of loss, hurt, and probably more, as we declutter.
- The good news: As we face these emotions, we can put them in their proper places. As we face our fears related to getting rid of things, we can overcome them. We can overcome our depression. We can live richer, fuller lives.

The Right Way

Declutter yourself and face each emotion as you go through things. This is how I faced some of the emotions I ran into. Don't feel that you have to get rid of all mementos. Sure, it is best to be tough, but don't be ruthless. I held on to a lot of old letters, for instance. Great sadness came up when I reread some of them. Similar to the scene in *Indiana Jones and the Raiders of the Lost Ark*, when the Ark is finally discovered, ghosts of the past swirled around me. Lost loves, professions of undying devotion, opportunities gone forever—all floated through the room like sad wraiths.

The toughest emotions that will come up grab us when we tackle boxes containing memories of relatives and friends who are no longer in this world. I was working away like a madman, having recycled more than 70 pounds of useless papers, when I hit the boxes of my mother's stuff. I uncovered every letter I had ever written her, pictures of me taking my first communion, me as a little boy, snapshots of her and my father having fun, and so on. She was such a vibrant, fun-loving woman, and now she has Alzheimer's. It was like looking through a keyhole at another life and time.

I couldn't just toss those items. I had to see them and experience the emotions. I went into a trance, becoming the innocent little boy I had once been. I remembered my mother with fondness, and rejoiced in the softness and warmth with which she handled everything in my young life. I felt sorry for all the times I had lied to her or disappointed her.

I overcame my resentment of my father. I saw for the first time that he was a human being, with fears and joys similar to mine. Letters from his Army days made me realize that some things never change, and that we are all cut from the same cloth. Mementos of his failed businesses and the despair he experienced during financial setbacks made me see that we weren't so different.

These were all things I would have missed if I had hired someone to clean up for me. Sure, spending time on those items slowed my progress at decluttering, but they pushed me forward emotionally. I lost track of time, but when it was time to resurface to the real world, I was able to discard about 30 percent of the items and keep the ones that made the most sense to me. More importantly, I was able to file them where I could find them again. It was one of the most emotional experiences of my life, and one of the most rewarding.

The Wrong Way

Or, we can just hire someone to come into our homes and "neaten them up" for us, a la TV decluttering. If we do this, we don't face our emotions, and we re-clutter. The choice is always ours.

"I get anxious when I try to throw X away." The item itself is not important. There is no order in difficulties of items, only difficulties inside us. *We* are not our clutter. We have power over our stuff. We have given our stuff our power, but we can take it back. This is where the Decluttering Diary will come in handy.

It doesn't matter a whit what we're agonizing about getting rid of. The bottom line is that we have a hard time with:
- Making a decision.
- Making a value judgment.
- Making a commitment.

Hey, it's okay. That doesn't mean we're bad, stupid, lazy, or crazy. It just means that we're reading the right book.

I'm going to use the word *discard* instead of *throw away*, *recycle*, or *donate*. We're smart enough to know which of those applies to what items. But don't get hung up on the terminology.

Okay, let's first put things into their hierarchy of values a la Abraham Maslow. Dr. Abraham Maslow developed a widely used set of criteria to explain different stages of growth of individuals. For now, let's just apply the most basic of human needs, that of psychological needs, for whatever we're trying to do. Ask yourself: "If I discard the wrong thing, right now, will it kill me?" I'm serious. We need to start putting things into perspective. What's important here, from a practical perspective, is that we try to put a little logic into what shouldn't be an emotional decision. For us, all decluttering is emotional. If it weren't, we wouldn't have such a problem.

Make a decision—imagine the very worst thing that could happen if you discarded the wrong thing. So far, so good. We know that throwing "X" away isn't going to kill us. (Actually, there are some severe hoarders who might really have such grave fears. If that describes you, psychiatric assistance is probably called for.) Make a value judgment—in the grand scheme of your life, imagine how important this item is. "Will getting rid of 'X' affect my security or stability?" Nah, probably not. (Part of that second need deals with the need for order, structure, and freedom from fear, but for now, let's stick to the basics.)

Now we get to the third need, in simple terms, of belongingness and love. Here's where we get stuck. Obviously, this doesn't apply to some items. I've known a lot of clutterers and a few hoarders, but so far, not one who has been under the delusion that her collection of plastic sacks or cardboard boxes loved her.

On our thinking level, we *know* that "X" does not love us (it's inanimate, for gosh sakes), bring us love, or represent someone else's love. On our emotional level, we think it might. Non-clutterers (and those who are only mildly disorganized) will scoff. The rest of us will nod knowingly. Although that dress or suit that hasn't fit since Reagan was president may not "love" us, it could represent a time when we felt better about ourselves, a special occasion that we wore it for that brought us happiness, or it could remind us of a special person. That's a lot of emotional baggage for a piece of cloth. That's terribly illogical. But that's what we do.

This was just a taste. The full-course meal is the rest of the book. Stick around; all you have to lose is your clutter.

5 | Common Clutterer Traits—Practical and Emotional Solutions

As I clear my physical clutter, I clear my mental and emotional clutter. My life is clutter-free on all levels.
—Clutterless Affirmations

Why Clutterers Clutter

Why do we clutter? Remember, I am addressing cluttering, not hoarding. Although some of the same irrational and magical thinking we use may apply to hoarders to some degree, not all hoarders can change the behavior without professional help. Hold on, excuse-makers—before you use that as an excuse, the mere fact that you bought this book and want to do something to change your behavior indicates that you probably aren't a hoarder.

Most of us have a combination of personality traits that contribute to our cluttering. A lot of us have some psychological issues that add to the mix, such as depression or anxiety, and a few of us actually have ADD, though it's more likely we have ADD-like tendencies. Most everyone has some kind of "issue" to deal with. They're very real to the person who has them. Some of us deal with them, and others of us ignore them. Either way, clutter is often a physical manifestation of our inner turmoil.

When we work on the physical issue (the clutter), the emotional issues come into line. When we work on the emotional challenges we face, our decluttering gets better. Approach this from either side you want. Just do it, and you will be rewarded.

No matter what your reasons for your personal cluttering, eliminate the following excuses: "I am an artist. Artists are messy." "I am a genius (Einstein was a clutterer). We are allowed." "I am a Latvian (or any nationality). It's part of my culture."

There's no difference between someone who calls himself a clutterer and someone who calls himself a packrat. Both are self-diagnosed terms. A hoarder is someone who has a medically recognized personality disorder. A collector is someone who keeps memorabilia or sets of items that are related to each other. Collectors can be hoarders or clutterers, but not all hoarders or clutterers are collectors (though they may rationalize their disorder by calling it a collection). When I collected phonebooks and bottle caps, I was cluttering. When I collected stamps and coins, I was collecting.

Many clutterers rationalize their accumulation of stuff by calling it a collection. If a specific type of stuff (the complete Zane Grey novels) is in one area (the Zane Grey wing of your mansion), and you can find it, then it's a collection. If it gives you pleasure, then it's a collection worth keeping. If it doesn't, why let it rent space from you?

Just because you've got some clutter and are having a hard time getting rid of it doesn't mean you need therapy. It doesn't even mean that you *need* a support group. Maybe you just need the insight from this book to help you to start a decluttering program that works for you.

We've all got "issues" of some sort. So what? That doesn't mean everyone belongs on a therapist's couch. Even when the root cause of our cluttering is our underlying depression or low self-esteem, we could overcome the cluttering as a manifestation of those issues and never address the core problem. We could be uncluttered and as neurotic as we wanted to be. Or we could resolve the core issues and live much happier lives. In the long run, it's up to us what we do. Do you want to just clean up your living room, or also clean up your life?

Most of us can develop the self-awareness necessary to both declutter and live more fulfilling lives without therapy; others cannot. For some, a combination of a support group and therapy works best. Willingness to change is necessary in either case. Any therapist worth her salt will tell you that a person who doesn't want to change will have limited results from therapy. Ya gotta wanna. Read this chapter. See what applies to you. Put some of the practical steps into action. If that's all you need, you're done. Congratulations. If you apply some of the practical steps and the results don't last, then you might want to revisit the emotional components. You'll probably do a lot better if you try a support group or get a clutter buddy.

Support groups aren't for everyone. People who have never been to one generally have misconceptions about them. If there's not a clutter support group near you and you don't want to start one, I'd be willing to bet there's a support group for something in your town that would apply to you.

Think of a support group as a bunch of friends who share a similar interest, and get together to talk about that interest. That's it. No hocus-pocus, no chanting, no being tackled by insistent huggers. It's really a lot more low-key than you'd think, though some people do get pretty emotional when it's the first time they could talk about their problem. But in a few weeks, they're usually laughing with everyone else at our illogical behavior when it comes to cluttering.

If that still doesn't sell you, find a group of people interested in anything you're interested in: boating, chess, model airplanes, UFOs, philosophy, books, and so on. Because clutterers are likely to be isolationists, they could use some friends. Once you make friends, you might find someone to confide in, or a clutter buddy.

So What Are You Afraid Of?

Fear is at the root of most clutter issues. We don't discard things, because we are afraid. These are the Big Picture fears. In the paragraphs that follow are ways to deal with the specific fears.

Our fears include, but are not limited to:
1. Fear of making a mistake.
2. Fear of failure.
3. Fear of admitting failure.
4. Fear of commitment.
5. Fear of someone in our past (parent, sibling, bully); ghosts.
6. Fear of not having enough.
7. Fear of not being good enough (to deserve better things); low self-esteem.

8. Fear of not knowing everything.
9. Fear that we'll need it someday.
10. Fear that we will be judged as wasteful if we throw something out that once cost good money.
11. Fear of flying. Oops, that one just sneaked in.

You can pick your own fear to add to the list. You've probably never thought about fear having anything to do with why you can't get neat and stay neat.

Save these fears for times when you need them. Fear is a good thing. It makes us stop, look, and listen, if used positively. If we use it negatively, it just makes us stop, freezing in the headlights of what we're afraid of until it runs over us.

Solutions

Practical. First of all, identify your fears. Name them. As long as they're unnamed, they're too big to tackle. Give them a name and you know what you're dealing with. Look at the fears logically (he said optimistically). Fears come in all sizes, shapes, and colors. Cluttering fears are pretty small, in the grand scheme of things.

Remember the fear you had (well, some of you) about a monster in your closet or under your bed? Now you have a monster of your own making there. It's all your abundance of stuff. But you're big enough to know it's not going to gobble you up, right? Right?

Enter the fear, the item, how you felt when trying to deal with it, and how you felt if you actually did something about it, in your Decluttering Diary (Appendix I). It's not going to take terribly long before you see that most of your decluttering challenges are lumped together in a small universe of fears all of your own making. You made them, which means you can unmake them.

Emotional. Throwing out a busted lamp, coffee maker, pile of newspapers, shoes, and old clothes that don't fit, is not going to shorten our lives, sabotage our careers or marriages (unless our partner happens to love that lamp), or affect our lives in any big way.

If you have paper paranoia, welcome to the club. Papers are so much more complicated than most other types of clutter because they apply to our home *and* business lives. If someone could come up with a pill or a magic spell that would eliminate shoe and paper clutter from our lives, she'd retire a rich person. But the bottom line about the fear of discarding important papers is:

- Almost everything exists in another format, such as digital.
- Almost everything paper can be replaced.
- Ninety percent of the papers we keep are never referred to again.

For anything else, get rid of just one lamp, book, dress, shoe (okay, that wouldn't make much sense, so one *pair* of shoes), or inch of papers. See how you feel. Write it down in your Decluttering Diary. Did your world end?

Following is a list—and amplication—of some of the fears and emotions that come up when we try to declutter, and, if we let them, sabotage our efforts.

1. Making a Mistake

You will. So what? *How Important Is It?* is our new mantra. We spend $10 of time agonizing over 10 cents of importance. Start small. If you are paralyzed by a fear of making a mistake, then don't declutter papers at first. Declutter something that, if you got rid of it tomorrow and needed it the day after tomorrow, your world would not end.

Solution

Practical. Okay, what have you got around the house that makes absolutely no sense to keep? Pick any one item that is broken and easily replaced if you needed to. How about the umbrella with the end that's unattached to the spokes? That portable phone that "just needs a new battery." The busted picture frame? The book without a cover? You get the idea. Not one of those things will make a big difference in your life if you get rid of it today. Do it. Just one item. Trash it.

Now, after a few days, did you have to go buy a new umbrella or phone, or did you use the ones that were already in your closet? The idea is to desensitize the fear by facing it. Keep a list of this stuff in your Decluttering Diary.

2. Insecurity

This is another variation of one of the fears listed previously, and is a core cause of cluttering. We keep useless stuff because we are afraid that there won't be any more for us. We cling to the things we have (including relationships), even if they are broken, because we don't feel we deserve any better. Our rationalizations include: "Saving for a rainy day," "Waste not, want not," "A penny saved is a penny earned," or some other platitude from *Poor Richard's Almanac*. "Poor" Richard was rich Ben Franklin, and those sayings were a product of the Puritan beliefs of the time. Back then, goods were in short supply and people really did "fix it up, use it up, or wear it out." Today we don't have to.

Solution

Practical. Be honest. Are you really going to fix that broken vase? Do you even know where the glue is? If you could find it, could you get the cap off? It's not the vase. It's the fear that we'll never get another one, or that we don't deserve anything better. There are never enough things to fill that hole in our guts.

3. Feeling Unloved

We fill our lives with things to replace the love we don't feel we are getting, or didn't get a long time ago. Even if we have loving spouses (and it takes a lot of love to live with a clutterer), we are afraid we will lose them or are not worthy of them, so we get more things. But things don't love you; only people love you. That teddy bear with the missing eye and stuffing falling out (I got rid of mine after a couple of years of decluttering) doesn't love you. It was an expression of love from the person who gave it to you. But you can carry that love in your heart. Bury the bear. Nobody wants a ratty old bear.

There's an opposite side to this. Sometimes the things (or money) that someone gave us don't resolve our feelings about them—generally, anger. Who hasn't heard of the divorcee who spends as much of the money she got in a settlement as fast as she can? Those who began compulsive shopping or cluttering after the death of a spouse really have to watch this. Marsha's story, which you will read later, is classic. Here's a synopsis:

After Michael died, I showed him how mad I was by going through his blood money from the insurance as fast as I could. No matter how much I spent, it couldn't fill the hole in my heart.

Solution

Practical. Spend some time with real people. Volunteer at a school, nursing home, homeless shelter, library, hospital, animal rescue shelter, or the like. Once you get some real love, you should be able to wean yourself from the "thing-love" you've filled your life with. Get a pet, but only if you're willing to spend the time and energy necessary to take care of it.

4. Feeling as Though We Don't Deserve Better

We feel as though we are not as good, smart, or attractive as other people. So we fill our lives with stuff to make us feel better. Our junk doesn't make us any "more than." If we took an inventory (ugh!) of all our stuff and carried it with us, do you think it would make anyone think any more of us? Imagine going to a party and holding out the list of your junk, saying, "Hi, my name is Sally, and this is who I am." We are not our stuff.

In fact, if we could grasp this one concept, many of us would make a huge leap in understanding and then dealing with our cluttering problem. The spiritual concept of "You are not guilty," should help every one of us overcome this feeling. It may not happen overnight, but if we keep repeating that to ourselves, we will eventually believe it, and more importantly, live it.

Solution

Practical. Instead of an inventory of your possessions, why not make an inventory of your inner stuff? What are your best qualities? Your greatest assets may not be things you have done, but the person you are. To start with, you are the only living being qualified to be you. If you are kind and loving, you should celebrate that. If you have done others good turns in life, that makes you a contributor to the betterment of mankind. We can't all be Mother Teresa, but we can all make a difference in at least one person's life. Mother Teresa herself suffered grave doubts about her inner goodness and worthiness, yet she rose above them to keep on keeping on. My friend, if you and I could do half as well at doing the best we can with what we have (emotionally), we would be truly blessed.

We all have great qualities, if we think about it. If nothing springs to mind immediately, you can say, "When I am really happy, I like to _____." You may like to go to museums, and that makes you good at appreciating art. You may like to fish, and that brings to mind your successes in fishing. You may get pleasure from gardening. That could be one of your best qualities. The list goes on and on, and so do your good qualities.

We weren't always this way. We may be so down on ourselves that we have to go back to childhood to find a time we excelled at something. Maybe we played the saxophone well as a kid. It doesn't matter if we were first chair or seventh chair, we played it better than those who never tried. When I did this exercise, I started playing the saxophone again.

5. Fear of Someone in Our Past (Parent, Sibling, Bully); Ghosts

Fortunately, we won't have to get a priest or the Ghostbusters to exorcize these ghosts. We can take care of them on our own. Many of us were told we were no good, would never amount to anything, or as a Woody Guthrie song says, "too old, too fat, too thin, too this, or too that." Chances are, we were told this when we were children. We aren't children anymore. Let's let those people go and stop giving them power over us. We are adults. We all have an inner child, and we can all tell our inner child that playtime is over. Our inner child has replaced our old outward bully. It's trying to run our lives on a false assumption—that we aren't good enough. We are.

Here is a brief tale from Lila, a clutterer.

You know, I didn't make any progress at all in my decluttering until I finally realized that it all came from how I grew up. I'm not one of those who want to blame everything on my mother, but this is so obvious that even I can see it—now. When I was a little girl and a teenager, my sister handled my things and threw them out to make room for hers. Mother always sided with her because she was older. In fact, Mother sided with her about everything. I never felt supported.

Now, I am an adult, and when my mother or sister comes to visit, they insist on staying with me, and still go through my things and throw them out. If I mention it, they just laugh and call me a clutterbug. They say they are only trying to help me, like the people they see on those awful TV shows. It hurts that they don't respect me or my feelings.

Since going to these meetings, I finally realized that I was holding on to stuff to get back at them. I was afraid they were going to come in and take everything from me. I was able to tell them how I felt, both then and now. After I did that, I started to declutter, and have kept it up. When my family comes to visit, they can stay at a motel, or, if they want to stay with me, they have to promise not to touch my stuff. So far, it's worked. The biggest payoff has been that I am just plain happier.

Often there are people in our lives today who give us similar negative talk. They may not realize the power their words have on us. Until we get the courage to ask them to stop, we can learn to discount their negative statements. We are not alone. Advice columns are filled with people with this same problem. If this comes from a spouse, maybe our cluttering is contributing to the negativity. Quite possibly, we are giving ourselves this same negative talk.

Most of us have the habit of belittling ourselves. I have a self-deprecating sense of humor, which some people say is the same thing. It probably stems from some childhood experience such as I was told not to brag. I am an adult now. I could get over that if I wanted to. But I don't see it as a problem, and it has become something of a trademark of my writing style, so I keep it. The point is that you will have to decide what level of self-praise you're comfortable with, and work up from there. If something is true, and you state it, that is not bragging. If it is not true yet, it is an affirmation. Affirmations can change our attitudes and make things real. Now obviously, just saying, "I live in a clutter-free environment, mentally, physically, emotionally," isn't going to make your house any less cluttered. What it will do is set your mind into believing that you can do those things, and that will allow you to actually do them.

Solution

Practical. When we catch ourselves in negative self-talk, we can learn to say, "Wait, that's not true. I am really good at _____." We may not believe it at first, but if we say it often enough, we will. As time goes on, we will remember more and more things we do well.

6. Needing to Save for a "Rainy Day"

We were taught the rainy day concept by our parents. What if there is a shortage, or another depression? What if we lose our jobs? What if the sky falls? Those "what ifs" are keeping us from enjoying a full life right now. Sometimes, the "what ifs" happen. But instead of ruining our lives, they can enhance them. If you want to save for a rainy day, do just that.

When my rainy day came in the form of the fire, I started over again with literally nothing. So has every other person who's been flooded, burned out, or wiped out by any natural disaster. Those of us who've recovered our sense of self and serenity have moved on, with a greater respect for things in their proper hierarchy of importance.

Solution

Practical. Every time you *don't* buy something, put that amount of money in the bank. Every time you have a garage sale or sell some of your clutter, put that money in the bank. Believe me, if the Red Cross says that cash is more important than things when the going gets tough, they know what they're talking about.

Our parents did the best they could in raising us. They experienced the Depression, or, if you are younger, a couple of recessions. Fear and scarcity ruled their lives. But you are not your parents. We live in a world that is substantially different from theirs. There is great abundance in the world. More importantly, there is great abundance in you. I believe that when you believe in lack, you experience lack. When you believe in abundance, your life will be filled with as much love and prosperity as you can handle. It's really your choice.

Suze Orman addresses this same issue. She is as practical as they come, so even if you don't believe in the abundance principle, listen to her. Suze says *save*, don't squirrel. Besides, squirrels save nuts. And you aren't saving nuts, are you? (Are you?) Suze points out practical ways to save money and to put it to work for you. She writes that money flows, and that if we block the flow of it, it will cease flowing to us.

My favorite practical spiritual author, Katherine Ponder, writes in *The Dynamic Laws of Prosperity* of the "Vacuum law of prosperity." She says, "The vacuum law of prosperity is one of the most powerful, though it takes bold faith to put it into operation. If you want great good, greater prosperity in your life, start forming a vacuum to receive it. In other words, **get rid of what you don't want, to make room for what you do want.**"

This has been demonstrated over and over again in my life, sometimes in immediate ways. I found $1,100 the first time I decluttered. The second time yielded $730. The third netted me $260. How much more good would that cash have done me if I used it to pay off high-interest bills? Or done something fun such as going on a vacation? Recently, I took my penny jar to a coin machine to cash it in. Yes, I got a windfall of $87.23, but I had to pay 10 percent for the privilege. Pretty sorry money management, don't you think?

That's just great, you may say, for the first few times, but sooner or later, you're going to find all the cash you've misplaced. True. But my experience and that of many more clutterers I've talked to, is that the amount of abundance in the world is not finite; neither are the manifestations. I, and others, have experienced money flowing into our lives in unexpected checks, gifts, and the sales of items we've "found" when we decluttered. I still find an occasional check or cash because I am still not perfect in my dealing with the mail, but I find fewer checks now than I used to.

7. Compulsive Shopping

Shopping isn't a competitive sport. I don't think all of us clutterers qualify as compulsive shoppers, but we are likely to be among those most likely to get a get-well card from local merchants if we go to the hospital.

Few of us are physicists, but we seem to have the concept of multiverses down pat: There are several parallel universes that make up our reality. Each is filled with stuff we bought. Because we only live in one universe at a time, that stuff doesn't exist all the time. For that reason, we have to buy more—one for each universe we inhabit. All this sounds perfectly logical to me.

Like Pavlov's dogs, we begin panting and salivating when we see a two-for-one sale ad in the newspaper. Clutterers routinely buy two, three, or a dozen of everything. Three-for-two sales are our downfall. We turn them into six-for-four sales. Lord knows I'm not about to argue against saving money. When clutterers talk about getting any item, they are most animated when they start with, "And I really got a good deal on this...." But before you pay "just a little bit more," for a second or third of something, we might want to think about it. Two boxes of ballpoint pens are seldom a good deal, because the ink dries out before we use the second one. Think about the space the second thing is going to take up in our house. Someday, we get to the point that clear space is worth more than whatever might take it up. Now, I do have space for a Faberge egg, and if they were to go on sale at two-for-one or three-for-two, I might be able to make more room.

As we declutter, we're likely to find enough file folders, labels, pens, staplers, and so on to start a stationery store. Those things had value, but they cost me more than they were worth in storage and confusion. What good are spares if we can't find them when we need them?

Those of us who grew up financially poor have a real problem with this. We didn't have many possessions growing up, and want to make up for it now. As children, we never had enough to throw away. Now we are adults on the outside, but still scared little kids inside. We can gently grow up and claim our adulthood. See the comments on dealing with our ghosts for more of this.

We could lose our jobs tomorrow. I think, in today's world, this is not an unreasonable fear. Before I started working for myself I'd been laid off, quit, or gotten fired several times. My 12 pairs of scissors, three old computers, seven staplers, and boxes of God-knows-what didn't cushion the blow. They didn't make me feel rich. When I came to believe in abundance, I realized that better jobs and situations always came along.

If you use a lot of something, then of course, buy the economy size—if you have room—and if you realistically expect to use the item up. Think through the limited utility of purchasing the economy-size version of something that has a "Best If Used By" date of next week.

We currently buy steaks and meat wholesale and stuff them into our average-sized freezer. It creates an inconvenience for a few weeks, but the reward is that we eat better for months than if we bought small quantities at the supermarket. Weigh the advantages versus the disadvantages to decide if something's a bargain or not.

When I had a publishing business, I used Styrofoam peanuts to ship books, so I bought some. Maybe it was a case of abundance-thinking gone awry, but I bought an industrial-sized sack. It was so big that I couldn't put it in my Alfa-Romeo convertible (this one ran), so I returned to the store in my truck. That was in 1996. I moved several times since then, and still had enough peanuts to feed a circus's worth of Styrofoam elephants. That sack of Styrofoam took up space in my rental truck when I moved to Los Angeles. In 2000, when I moved from there to Galveston, my friend who came to help me said, "I hate these things. We're getting bubble wrap." So I tossed them. Years later, I have not been tempted to get another bag of Styrofoam peanuts, and have shipped a lot of books. Did I really save money buying the extra-large, economy, industrial size?

Solution

Practical. Just for fun, buy just one of something that's three-for-two. Then, watch and see if it doesn't go on sale one more time the next time you need it. By paying attention to these things, not only will you have less stuff taking up your space, but you will also be less likely to be taken in by advertising.

Stay out of thrift stores. I know, this is going to hurt, but there are just too many "bargains" there to pass up. Avoid garage sales like the plague, unless you're buying a garage. If you must go to garage sales, sleep in. At least then most of the good stuff will be gone. Use eBay only for selling. Or, if you must visit it, make a deal with yourself that you can only buy something if you sell two items there. When you list something on eBay, do not put a reserve price. Let it go.

I wonder if people with ADD are more vulnerable to Screamin' Deals! Limited Time Offer! Only 3 Left On The Shelf! Spend $50 for Free Shipping! Buy Now And Get Free Gift!

8. Feeling Overwhelmed

Well, duh! Of course we get overwhelmed. There's a good reason for it—our clutter is overwhelming if we look at the whole mess. It didn't get this way overnight. What do we expect, that a genie will come in and make it all go away in eight hours? Think about how long it took to accumulate all that stuff. Then be thankful that it won't take as long to get rid of it, though it may seem that way.

As Teddy Roosevelt said, "Do what you can, with what you have, where you are." The important thing is that we start. Many have found it best to start with something manageable that will show the results of our efforts quickly.

Solutions

Practical. Focus on just one little area of clutter. Pick something you can manage. Pick a square foot of a table, an inch of papers, half a foot of your closet clothes rack. Take a picture so you'll be able to see your progress. Work for just 15 minutes at a time. Do whatever it takes to see the little picture instead of the big picture. Clear a spot of floor or a square of desk space and then stand back and admire it. Seeing wood or carpet is often a clutterer's first phase of getting better.

Emotional. The specific emotional components will vary according to the items being decluttered, but the general fear is of being a failure, or simply not being able to trust your decisions. We can't deny our emotions, but we can tell them to take a short hike for just 15 minutes.

9. Feeling Guilty

I've come to believe that guilt is one of the most common, and most overlooked, stumbling blocks to getting over our cluttering. Clutterers wear their guilt like a shroud. They revel in it like a dog rolling in something dead. All we're missing is a hair shirt and a cat o' nine tails. "Guilty, guilty," we lament, while whipping ourselves. Stop it! Take to heart one of the lessons in The Foundation for Inner Peace's *A Course In Miracles*: "You are innocent." Even if that book is not right up your alley, take this one simple idea to heart. You are innocent. Believe me, when you stop feeling guilty, you will start getting over your cluttering.

Solutions

Practical. This is one of those cases in which we have to read the emotional components first. No matter how bad the giver's taste may have been, he brought you a gift. He may have put a lot of thought into it, or he may have grabbed it at the airport before he left. Either way, you'll never know, and it doesn't matter today. Mentally thank him for it and toss it, or give it to a charity. Some other poor clutterer or beer stein–collector may be pining away for it. Or, you could accidentally drop it (preferably on a concrete floor), then truthfully say, "Oh, that gift? I dropped it and it broke, so I had to throw it away. But that's okay, I will always remember it." You're certainly not telling any tales there.

Emotional. We're in a real bind here. We feel guilty because we have all this junk, and we feel guilty if we throw it away. If it's something that Aunt Tillie gave us, we feel we're being disloyal to her memory if we get rid of it. Never mind that the hula dancer with the clock in her belly is hideous. She brought it all the way from Honolulu. Never mind that the beer stein in the shape of Santa Claus is ugly and awkward to drink out of; Uncle George went to a lot of trouble to bring it back from Germany.

So what?

They may not notice that you don't have it anymore.

They may have forgotten all about it.

If it means so much to them, do they have one on *their* mantle?

One of the emotional components of cluttering is control. If the giver expects you to have their gift always displayed prominently in your house, they're exercising control over you, remotely. This comes under the purview of the fear of ghosts. The whole point of this book is to help us take back control of our lives. In any decluttering situation, that is always the higher good.

We may be holding on to the items people have given us because we don't want to lose the person, but we can't stop the natural cycle of life and death. Things are not people. Sooner or later, we need to let them both go, so that they can fulfill their destinies.

10. Feeling Like a Failure

One reason some clutterers have not made serious inroads to decluttering is our plain and simple low self-esteem. Regardless of our cluttering situation, many of us felt that we were somehow inferior human beings.

Once we decide to do something and take a serious look at our physical clutter and the attendant emotional blockages, we will probably be overwhelmed and feel not only inferior, but as though we are complete failures. We'll get some small projects done. At first we'll feel great and successful. After awhile, especially if we have negative friends or spouses, we'll start feeling down again. No wonder we never did this before.

Don't worry. This is a sign of getting better. Feelings of failure when confronting our clutter are common. It's like starting to exercise. You're going to be sore at first, until your muscles get into the habit of being used.

Solutions

Practical. We start with something we know we can do, until our decluttering muscles are built up enough to enter the decluttering triathlon. A walk around the block is a start. Decluttering one small area is a start. Remember those pictures you took when you started? Now's the time to get them out. It's easy to feel like a failure when we start looking at that blasted Big Picture again. Many of us have so much clutter that we can't see the forest for the tress (if there were any trees in our living rooms).

Reread your Decluttering Diary. See how you felt when you started. See how you feel now. I'll bet that overall you feel better about yourself and your stuff. But you can't know that without knowing where you came from. Small segments of decluttering at a time will leave you feeling that you have succeeded, rather than failed, in your mission. If you end on a positive note, with something you have set out to do, and accomplished, you will feel successful.

We're going to have setbacks. We didn't become perfect when we started to clean up our mess. If we don't have a support group such as Clutterless (*www.clutterless.org*), where we will find other clutterers who have been where we are, or a therapist, we find a friend who will listen to us nonjudgmentally. The important thing is that we don't let these feelings of failure take root and grow, and that we don't isolate.

After I'd cleared my bedroom to the point that anyone would be proud to sleep there, and cleaned my office until it sparkled, I still got blindsided by failure feelings. When I went into my second bedroom and saw the piles and piles of junk, I felt that I hadn't done anything at all. I went into a tailspin, and the next thing I knew, my desk was cluttered and piles of clothes and books started sprouting on my bed. There's an old joke (the only kind I seem to know) about a bird that flies backwards so that it can see where it's been. Maybe it's time for us to start flying backwards for a while.

Emotional. Feelings are what they are. Feeling bad, down, or overwhelmed about life situations doesn't make us failures. Not using those feelings as goads to grow is what keeps us in a state of negativity. Wallowing in those feelings, using cluttering, compulsive shopping, or anything else to numb them, are common escapes we use to avoid taking appropriate actions. We're going to continue to feel as though we are failures as long as we keep acting as failures.

11. Feeling Confused

Mental clutter is common. When we first start to face our problem, chances are we are walking around in a mental fog. Lynda Warren, a San Bernardino psychologist, describes clutterers as "people who have an enormous problem making decisions, and can't stay focused."

We forget things. We may be worried that Alzheimer's is sneaking up on us even though we are relatively young. But cheer up! None of my research indicated a correlation between Alzheimer's and cluttering.

When I was in the throes of my cluttering, it was difficult to keep an assistant for my home offices. The more cluttered my office, the less time they stayed. Each said he felt as though he was descending into a black hole when he came to work. If they felt this way being here only a few hours a day, imagine what it did to me.

Solutions

Practical. Write down your decluttering goals and your progress in your Decluttering Diary. Committing things to paper forces us to look at them clearly. Clarity clears confusion. Using a Decluttering Diary to keep track of our progress (or lack thereof) will keep us from going around in circles, which is our natural tendency.

Emotional. It's another chicken and egg thing: Which do we get rid of first, the cluttered mind or the cluttered life? Although the physical clutter is probably the first thing we can change, let's not forget about our minds. Even clutterers who had never tried visualization and meditation told me that they help. They visualized a clutter-less home long before they had one, but reported that actually doing something after visualizing was easier and more effective. Visualize exactly how your beautiful, neat living room will look when you're done. Then imagine the looks of surprise and pleasure on the faces of those you invite over to celebrate your success.

Visualizing and meditating on peace and order will give your confusion a rest, and the direction to tackle the disorder will flow. If you are unfamiliar with visualization or meditation techniques, there are many books on the subjects.

Of course, don't just imagine what your home will look like. You still have to do the work, but it will become surprisingly easier after you have envisioned it.

12. Time Clutter

Ah, the time trap. If we are vague about everything else in our lives, why should time be any different? We often have a poor sense of time and miss deadlines—not because we can't do the work, but because we forgot the deadline date. We wake up one day and there is a due date for some project unforgivingly staring at us from our calendar.

We don't keep track of time, and don't prioritize. We get distracted by other projects and don't allow enough time for them.

Solutions

Practical. So, what to do? Well, the old standby, a to-do list, helps. For clutterers, however, that has drawbacks. We have to put deadlines on it, yet still make it flexible enough to allow for the added projects that we know we will tackle. That is part of our nature, and instead of rigorously adhering to the conventional wisdom of what works for other people, we should adapt their programs to our personalities.

A common problem with to-do lists is that we lose them and then start new ones. I've found that keeping mine on my computer works best. If you want a simple one that you can also send to your phone, try *www.tadalist.com*. It is free, and it's a very, very simple check-off to-do list. For a comparison of to-do lists and simple project managers, go to *www.techcrunch.com/2006/05/08/do-more-online-to-do-lists-compared*. I rather like "Remember the Milk," which is sophisticated enough, but not overwhelming: *www.rememberthemilk.com*.

If we take it a step further and get a simple project-manager program, we will really triumph. A project-manager program lets us create a list of the projects we want to complete, with a checklist of the steps necessary to get there. Don't get bogged down in making sure you write down each step that could possibly occur. Just add a few blank lines for the ones you cannot envision yet. Then allow yourself 50 percent more time than you think it will take.

This process has worked for me in designing book projects. At first I would feel elated that I had "finally gotten organized." Later, I would feel overwhelmed that I could never do all the tasks. Then came the feeling of being straightjacketed by the timeline. I got around this problem and still kept a reasonable schedule by putting in several little steps that I knew I could complete in less than the allotted time. When I checked those off, I was able to feel better about the whole thing, and get the project done.

Emotional Components: Feelings of being overwhelmed, and rebellion, are the main emotional barricades we set up to succeeding. Fear of success is pretty common among us: If we succeed and do what we're supposed to, then people (or bosses) will ask us to do more, and then we will fail big time. Come on, let's tell that naysaying part of our personality to chill out. You know, most of the stuff we agonize over isn't worth it. We aren't nuclear scientists (as sure as I say that, I'll get an e-mail from one).

13. Over-Committing to Others

Talk about an oxymoron—an over-committed clutterer. How can we, who can't commit to doing anything about our clutter or showing up on time, be asked by others to do things for them?

We often get ourselves over-committed from a feeling of lack of love. When people ask us to do things for them, we feel they won't love us if we don't. More people love us than we know, and they don't base their love on what we do for them. There are also some who take advantage of us. They shove their work on us and ask us to help them do things because they are using us. We must learn to say no. The trick is to learn to say it softly but firmly. People respect us more once they realize we value ourselves and our time.

Another time-stealer is people who ask us to run their lives for them. Frankly, because we have so much difficulty managing our own, we wonder what shape they must be in to depend on us. We have to learn to be kind to them and wean them away. This takes time, but it can be done. We could honestly tell them that we don't have time right now because we have to organize our sock drawer—they've seen our sock drawer, and may believe it. After that, there is the underwear drawer, the pajama drawer, and the closet. The last one is good for at least three excuses. If you have a garage, you can milk that one for six months. Everyone can identify with an untidy garage. Unless your friend is a real dunderhead, he will get the message.

Solution

Practical. The next time someone asks you to do something for her, say you will, *if* she will do X for you—preferably help you declutter. The chances are, she will beg off and not bother you again. But if she does, by golly, you've had some help decluttering.

14. Thinking Our Children Will Appreciate It

Ha! When was the last time your children appreciated anything? Okay, some of us may have wonderful kids, but even they are not going to be thrilled to clean out a house of garbage when we die. Believe me, because I have had to do this. The feelings that welled up in me as I sweated in the 100-degree South Texas heat were many, but appreciation was pretty far down the list.

Yes, there are some things that should be saved. Photo albums can preserve moments of our past, but double prints are probably overdoing it. Jewelry is nice to hand down to your children; pins from every state you visited are superfluous. The ratty old moose you shot on a trip to Canada should probably be buried and given a chance to get to the happy non-hunting grounds in the sky. Clippings from the school newspaper may by enjoyed, but the whole paper, complete with lunch menus, will not.

I would leave things such as this for the last attack on clutter. This is a personal area, and one minefield you will have to traverse all alone.

Do it only after you have some success under your belt. Then you will have a better eye for what to keep and what to discard.

Just imagine your children going through the stuff. You do want them to remember you with love, don't you?

Solution

Practical. There's a whole chapter about this (Chapter 17).

6 | OPC—Other People's Clutter

The hardest thing I ever did was put Jesse into an assisted living facility. The second hardest was to come back home and start to get rid of his clutter. It was like having the pain of not having him there, but having his ghost in the collection of stuff.

—Sandy, not a clutterer

As if the world didn't have enough acronyms, I'd like to add another. This won't make the top-10 charts as did ADD, OCD, or even IBM, but it seems that, if we can give something a name, then we can take the first step to doing something about it—disassociation of the condition from the person. When it's no longer "Mother's clutter," but "OPC," it's not as personal.

Dealing with your relatives' clutter after they have gone from this earth, or gone to a nursing home, will be one of the hardest things you'll ever do. Not dealing with it is impossible. Welcome to adulthood.

Linda Durham, a professional organizer and owner of Organizing Matters (*www.organizingmatters.com*) in Houston, Texas, offered these thoughts:

> *Grief and "stuff" complicate lives because it is the last moments, the last things touched, the last things said, and the last gifts given that become so precious. The lipstick message on the mirror, the sound of a voice on the answering*

machine, the silly note stuck on the car seat, that become treasures overnight. Holding on to the stuff helps hold on to the memories. Letting go of the stuff opens us up to letting go of the person.

Sorting through things and making decisions with deadlines looming make the process of going through things and letting go unbearable. The passage of time doesn't lessen the pain or make it easier. Procrastination, feeling powerless and overwhelmed, compounds the pain of loss, making sorting even harder.

While it's tempting to keep everything, it's usually not wise. When you keep everything, you can't love anything. You can shuffle it, compress it, contain it, and organize it, but there's only so much that you can see, touch, and enjoy in your daily life. It's better to have one item that is dearly treasured than hundreds of items that are meaningless.

It's not just clutter in the traditional sense that we're working on here. When people go, either by leaving this world or by moving to assisted-living situations, they leave behind lots of stuff—valuable stuff. Unfortunately, those of us left behind are not equipped to determine what's valuable and what's not. Although there are services that, for a pretty penny, will assess estates, not all of us have enough to be called an estate. Our children may be well-meaning, but haven't a clue to what to do. We can't get John Edwards or some other person who speaks to the dead to ask them what we're supposed to do. In short, we're in a bind.

The Bright Side (Yeah! There Is One)

Okay, now that I have thoroughly discouraged you, let's look on the bright side.

While our loved ones are still around, it's possible to do some preventive maintenance and ease your burden later. Actually, if you can work together, not only will you keep yourself from having a frustrating problem later, but you'll also be doing them a favor. Your parents and relatives are probably paralyzed by indecision. That frustrates them. They are afraid of leaving a mess for their heirs, but are unable to decide what to do about it, so the problem gets ignored. It's like the elephant in the living room (although few people have real live elephants, they frequently have enough stuff to camouflage one) that everyone walks around, pretending not to notice.

The results of taking care of the issue before it becomes a problem can actually be rewarding—in some cases. I put that caveat in because it all depends on the type of clutterer your relative is. If he's just a little disorganized, this could be a breeze. If he's severely cluttered, but not a hoarder, it could still work out. If he's a hoarder, I'm afraid there's not a lot of hope for change. You'll have to work with psychiatrists or psychologists who specialize in hoarders, and follow their lead.

In most cases, this issue comes up when only one parent is living or still at home. When they are both around, few people think about this eventuality. But I'll operate on the principle that we faced this when they are both around. You aren't doing this for selfish reasons (Oh my God, what am *I* going to do with all this stuff?!), but with love, because you don't want your parents to have to deal with all that stuff. When we all go to our heavenly reward, we all leave our worldly stuff behind for someone else to deal with. When one parent dies or goes into a nursing home, the other has to sort through the years of accumulated things. By your taking the clutter by the horns, you're helping them too.

The key and main element that can make this effort a success on all levels is to frame it as a way to help your parents while you still can. It's not about deciding who gets what; it's about easing their minds about the future. Things are the past; legacies are the future.

Although somebody is going to be stuck with brother, sister, aunt, uncle, and cousin clutter eventually, I'm going to use the example of parents, because this is the most common. We all have parents. Not everyone is as lucky as my sister to have a clutterer brother.

Why This Isn't Just About the Final Curtain Call

My own dear mother has Alzheimer's, and I work with spouses of Alzheimer's patients. While they are not gone, they are far, far away. There are other debilitating diseases that strike families. The surviving or present spouse has to deal with her own emotions, the sense of loss and helplessness, and myriad other debilitating emotions when her partner is institutionalized. Add to that the guilt of discarding the possessions of her absent spouse, and it's a sure recipe for depression.

The following is a composite of several people I've worked with whose spouses have moved to assisted living facilities because of

Alzheimer's or some other condition. Marty is struggling to take care of her husband's accumulation of a lifetime of work George left behind as a real estate developer. She has no idea what is valuable and what is not. There are survey maps and soil samples going back 20 years. Does she need to keep them? There are financial records for the last 25 years. He owned other companies, some of which had patents. How long does she need to keep these things for liability purposes? Some of his computer files are password-protected. Does she need to get into them, or would they reveal things she would rather not know?

Occasionally, when she visits him, he will remember some item he left behind and ask her about it. Because of this, she is terrified of getting rid of anything without his permission—something that is unlikely to happen now.

Added to this are the remnants of his personal interests: photography, coin collecting, fishing, hunting, antique cars, old books, and so on. It isn't fair to her to have to make decisions about all these things that are out of her paradigm. It isn't fair to put this added burden on her to wade through years of accumulated memories, when every time she does, she remembers George as the vibrant man who had such varied interests. It just isn't fair.

This could have been avoided. That's what's not fair. Let's do what we can to bring some fairness to the situation. That's why I'm here.

The Good News

If your relative is a mild to moderate clutterer, she will welcome your attention and help in making decisions, which is the root of her problem. The two of you (this is not limited to just you; you could involve your brothers and sisters as well) could actually spend some time bonding and reliving past pleasant memories. People, young or old, like to talk about themselves, and to share those things that are valuable to them. Going through mementos could bring up a wealth of life experiences that you may never have known about. I've seen parents reveal things about themselves in these decluttering sessions about their lives and feelings that gave the children a new understanding of them as people, not just as parents.

The key to making this work is to be as patient and nonjudgmental as you can. It's going to be a long process. You'll make some progress in a weekend, but a week would be better. It all depends on how motivated your parent is to change things.

Practical Preparation

1. Prepare yourself mentally. The process of clearing out your mother or father's (or even brother's or sister's) home comes from a realization that they aren't going to be around forever. Yep, Mr. Death is lurking behind all this. It's similar to making a will—something that people put off because they don't want to face their own mortality. Have you made one yourself? Now you see the dilemma.
2. Make an honest self-assessment of your suitability to this task. Maybe you aren't the right person for the job. Some of us are simply more naturally judgmental or critical than others. If this is you, undertaking (there's Mr. Death again) this task is going to be hell for both you and your parent. If you're the one who's aware of the potential problem and is willing to face it, you'll probably find that the rest of the family is just as aware, but were afraid to talk about it.
3. Talk to your parents. This is not going to be easy, but it's got to be done. Let them know that, because of your love for them, you want to make it easier for them to ease their minds about leaving a burden for their children. You'll be surprised at how this phrase can open up the floodgates of emotion and dialogue. Believe me, this has been on their minds.
4. Talk with the other family members. If possible, do this in person, rather than over the phone. With our geographically fragmented society, this may be difficult, but timing it for a time when everyone's there, such as Christmas or Thanksgiving, would be great. If that sounds like an odd time to talk about a serious issue, think of this as a meeting to give thanks for the life your parents gave you, and a gift-giving occasion for them.
5. This family meeting may be the most fun, depending on how dysfunctional your family is. Because "dysfunctional"

describes most families to one degree or another, it's just a question of severity. Nobody wants to deal with the actual issues or do the work, but everyone will have ideas about what should be done. If you found yourself described in step two, try to enlist one of the less judgmental of your siblings to help. You can offer moral support to him, but it's probably best if he is the one to do the actual work with your parent. Give him this checklist and this book.

6. Be prepared for some resistance from your siblings. They haven't taken step one, and may just want to put this issue off. Should you run into this kind of resistance, try selling the idea on how much easier it's going to make things for them. After all, you're doing the heavy lifting here.

7. Everyone's aware of the big things—the antiques, the jewelry, the cars, the personal mementos—but no one is cognizant of the Big Picture. Hiding all the good stuff is a ton of junk, or at least papers and knick-knacks that are of no value to anyone except your parent. Maybe 30 percent of stuff in a parent's house is of interest to family members. But you gotta deal with that other 70 percent.

8. Based on #7, ask everybody what pieces of the big stuff they each want. Point out, before you get into a tug-of-war about the good stuff, that the final decision is up to your parent. (Now you see why it was important to talk to your parents first. The more avaricious of your family may approach your parents to ask for certain things.)

9. When you're together with your parents, have someone act as secretary to keep track of who gets what. Put adhesive labels on the backs or undersides of items with each child's name on it. That'll take care of the big things.

10. Now the little things: photographs. Parents probably have thousands of photographs, from both the dark ages of print film and today. Digital photography hasn't eliminated the urge to print memories. Pull the boxes and albums of photos out, put 'em on the dining room table (after clearing the turkey), and let everyone choose the ones they want. You'll find that maybe 10 percent of the pictures have value, and the rest can be discarded, either now or when the time comes.

11. Personal interest items: fishing, hunting equipment, tools, woodworking equipment, old books, and so on come into play here. If no one wants them, and they have value, make an agreement that they will be sold and the money split among the heirs or donated to charity. If somebody is an avid eBayer, put her in charge of this stuff. If not, find out who can honestly appraise it.

12. Clothes. These are one of the real minefields of decluttering your parents' (or your spouse's) stuff. Many are going to be so full of memories that it'll be like a stroll through the Elysian Fields to deal with them. This is especially hard for spouses. Make it easy on everyone: Donate them. Local theater groups or even college or university theater groups always need period pieces.

Why Your Relatives Hold On to Things

Sofia seems to have it all. She is a professional, likes her interesting career and is only three house payments away from being debt-free. Yet the impending ghosts of OPC (other people's clutter) looms heavy, an ominous cloud on her horizon. Her mother is a full-fledged hoarder.

You probably have the same cloud above you, but, in most cases, are more fortunate. Your relative is more likely to be a clutterer than a hoarder. That alone should give you some hope. Clutterers can change, and there are strategies in this book to help you and them. Hoarders (less than 1 percent of the population) are very difficult to help, even with OCD medication and psychiatric care.

I've dealt with my own mother's clutter, and know how emotionally devastating it can be. I've worked with hundreds of clutterers and their families to address the real issues of letting go of possessions on a psychological/emotional level. Stuff is never the issue. The reasons people hold on to things are a combination of fear, anxiety, and depression, or a manifestation of the symptoms of attention deficit disorder. Treating the *stuff* as the problem is like cutting the tops off crabgrass in your yard: Unless you get to the roots, it will come back.

One thing I can guarantee you is that, if you are not a clutterer yourself, you won't understand the reasons for your relatives' clutter. Getting a steam shovel and a dump truck is not the answer. The approach used by popular "get organized" TV shows is useless—there are no quick fixes. I'm giving you some great tools to help your cluttering relative and yourself, but you are going to have to do some work. There are no easy solutions.

What You Can Do About It Now, for Yourself

For your own sanity, you'll need to disassociate the clutter from the clutterer. You can help, but not until you gain this perspective. You may also have to accept that your clutterer doesn't want to change. If that's the case, stop wasting your energy on trying to change them, and prepare for the steps you'll have to take when they are gone. Believe me, preparing now can save you months of agony later. It should be no surprise that people die. You already know that your clutterer has a houseful of stuff. Start now to prepare a plan to get the problem of the stuff taken care of when the time comes. Know that there are valuables secreted in all the mess. Then let it go. You've done what you can. Learn to love the clutterers while they are still here, and don't let things come between you and your loved ones.

Sofia is not unique. She is only one of many thousands of you who dread having to deal with your relatives' clutter when they pass from this life. This is a nascent problem, little talked about, and little understood. There is more shame to being a clutterer today than there is to being an alcoholic. It's a (forgive the pun) closet disorder. How many of you have a relative who, though they may not live in squalor as Jane's mother, have houses so full of tchotchkes that it is difficult to even walk around? How many of you look at the future with dread, knowing that you will have to wade through this mess?

The Difference Between Clutterers and Hoarders

There are significant differences between people who clutter and hoarders. The short version is that a hoarder can't tell trash from things of value. A clutterer may have an overwhelming abundance of possessions, but won't mix trash or garbage into it. A clutterer and a hoarder go to a fast-food restaurant. The clutterer takes extra ketchup packages, salt and pepper, and napkins because "they might come in handy later." The hoarder saves the half-eaten sandwich and the box it came in because "I may run out of food."

If you're thinking of getting a TV-style organizing intervention to resolve your relative's cluttering issues, don't. Read Chapter 11, "Alternatives to TV-Style Forced Decluttering," first.

Intervention—A Dangerous Weapon

Jane lives in fear of what she will have to do when her mother passes on. Her mother's house is full to overflowing with trash, randomly mixed in with treasures. I've been to her mother's house and done an intervention-type decluttering session. I don't usually recommend such measures, but in extreme cases, they are the only choice. They usually fail in the long run. Sometimes, at least temporarily, it gives hope to the family member. For the hoarder or clutterer, most of the time, these interventions only make them more anxious about their possessions that are gone. In this case, the mother was appreciative and thankful, but three months later, the house was back to the same state of disorder.

We were lucky. In most cases of intervention, the clutterer becomes far more anxious or depressed, resents the family member who tried to help, and often shuts herself completely off from her family. Decide right now, what's more important to you—having your relative live for a short time in what you consider a neat house, or losing contact with her permanently?

Why I Understand the Problem—From Both Sides

My own mother was a clutterer. As with most clutterers, she stuffed things into boxes, in a vague attempt to organize them. I was lucky enough to inherit both her tendency to clutter and her collection of useless and useful items when she went into a nursing home for her Alzheimer's. As a clutterer myself, I carted her many, many boxes of things across the country every time I moved. The good news is that the techniques I learned in overcoming my own cluttering and in eliminating the decades of my mother's clutter can be applied by anyone to help themselves and the clutterers in their family.

I should have known I was a clutterer when the homeless guys I hired to help me unload my moving truck in Los Angeles opened the back and declared, "My God, what a lot of crap." While this remark hurt me, it was true. When I finally started dealing with my problem, I got rid of more than one ton of useless papers and items. Half of that was my mother's.

Emotions and Things

The reason my mother held on to items that had no intrinsic value, and the reason it was so hard for me to get rid of the same items, is that clutterers attach emotions to things. The reason you can't just help your relative get organized is that it is too frustrating for you to go through piles of papers that (to you) obviously have no value, and it is too painful to them to have you around and not understand why it's so hard for them.

When I learned that I was surrounding myself with things because I had either an emotional attachment to them or an unreasoning fear of not having enough, I began to deal with the core issues. Stuff wasn't the problem. I was. And if the problem was intrinsic instead of extrinsic, then I also had the solution. My other three books on cluttering chronicle how I climbed out of that hole. Here, all you need to know is that it takes baby steps and appreciation by someone else for a clutterer to continue to change. Compliment them on what they have done, and don't criticize them for what they haven't, if you want to win their trust.

Getting Permission to Discard Things

What worked for me, and a technique that's been used by many of the people who've attended my seminars, was to ask for permission from the absent parent to get rid of her possessions. Close your eyes, visualize your parent, and say something similar to: "Mother, you know I love you. I know that these possessions are not you. They are just stuff you had. Some of it must have been important to you. But to me, *you* are important, not these things. They're causing a blockage in my own life, and I know you wouldn't want that. So I'm asking your permission to discard these items and make more room for the true memories of you."

If the heavens don't open up, nor lightning strike you, then it's probably okay to declutter the stuff. Believe me, it will be a lot easier than it was when you first started.

Auctioning the Lot

First of all, if the collection of stuff consists of specific types of items, such as coins, stamps, guns, airplanes, and vintage or exotic cars, get someone who knows the value of those things to give you an idea of what they're worth. They will not sell for as much at an auction as they will to those who know about them.

The biggest fear of having someone auction off your relative's things is that you will get cheated. Maybe, but, as one auctioneer told me, "Nobody's cheated until something sells." In the next breath (which, as you know if you've ever been to an auction, wasn't long), he told me that because things don't have a value unless somebody's willing to pay for them, nobody ever gets cheated.

I asked auctioneers about the importance of having things appraised first. Because some of them are both auctioneers and appraisers, they thought it was a good idea. Finally, one who does both, but has retired, said it was the biggest waste of money there is. An appraiser will charge you a fee, based on the amount of things to be appraised, his time, or any combination of criteria he chooses, walk through your relative's house, and tell you what he thinks things should sell for.

There are two kinds of auctions—reserve and absolute. If you know what something is worth or have had an appraisal, you would have a reserve auction. It's similar to eBay: You set a minimum price, and if those bidding exceed it, they buy the item. If they don't, it comes off the block. The drawback to that is, generally, you will have agreed to pay the auctioneer his percentage of the reserve, regardless.

In an absolute auction, everything goes, regardless of the bid. Will things go for less than they're worth? That depends. If you believe in the free market system, things are only worth what people will pay for them. If, however, you have a couple of Picassos and you live in an area where few people know or care about the difference between Picasso and Dogs Playing Poker or Velvet Elvises (I used to import them from Mexico before I saw the light), then you won't get the right price. But, generally, for most stuff, you get what it's worth on a wholesale basis.

Sure, you could get more if you sold the items retail, but you probably just want to get this over with. I'd go for the absolute auction.

The auctioneer will (generally) be responsible for getting the stuff out of the house, displaying it, and returning what doesn't sell if you go the reserve route. In an absolute auction, as long as someone bids a dollar (or a penny), the item goes.

You can find an auctioneer who's a member of the National Auctioneers Association at *www.auctioneers.org*.

If You Want to Sort Through Things Yourself

You may want to go through all these things at the relative's house, or bring the stuff to your own. Only bring it to your own if it would distress you too much to be at the relative's house, or you're not a clutterer yourself. Although it is usually easier to deal with someone else's clutter and get it out of your house before it takes a long-term lease, there may be so much emotional baggage among the Samsonite here that you should keep it from coming in.

As we go through your loved one's things, always keep in mind that they are just things, not her. It helps most people to have music or the TV on. It also helps to have someone else there with you. Being alone with all those memories is just too much to bear for many of us. This can be a relative or just a friend who will be there. It doesn't even have to be another clutterer or a nonjudgmental friend, because the emotions attached to the items are not yours.

Categories of Stuff

- **Papers.** Save papers for last, because there is always a chance that there is something valuable in them. Plus, sorting through papers is more time-consuming and seems less rewarding than sorting through the big stuff.
- **Clothing.** Clothing may be the easiest group of items to eliminate. If the pieces are old but in good shape, a theater group can use them. Everything else that is not tattered can be given to battered women's shelters, the Salvation Army, and so on. Stuff that's missing buttons, stained, and in poor shape, is trash, and can be thrown away. Remember, you aren't throwing away the person or the memories of

the person. It's only stuff. Chances are, at least once you'll have to remind yourself of that. I did. One emotion that might come up is, "How could Mother/Father have gone around in such tattered clothes?" There's no way to answer that, but the most important thing is to not blame yourself.

- **Photos.** See my other comments about photos, but the bottom line is there will probably be a few you want to keep, and most you will want to toss. If they are really old, the local historical society may want them, but ask them first before you start saving some "just in case."
- **Dishes and kitchen stuff.** Unless the dishes are china, they are essentially worthless. Donate them, but don't agonize over them. I've seen too many people collect gravy boats from their relatives. How many gravy boats do you need?
- **Paintings.** We often read about a famous painting that's hidden behind a Dogs Playing Poker piece of "art." If you know an art student or at least someone artistic, ask them to look at whatever paintings there are before you toss them. Velvet paintings are probably not hiding great art, but (now that I no longer sell them—a long story), they are collectibles.
- **Furniture.** Unless this looks like a collection of antiques, just sell it.
- **Computers.** Be sure to either wipe the data from them or smash the hard drives before giving them to someone.

Okay, What If It's Just Junk?

Junk is a loaded word, but sometimes it applies. What if your "inheritance" is piles of old papers, magazines, plastic milk cartons, enough paper and plastic sacks to supply a grocery store for a week, and so on?

How much time do you want to spend on this? The quick method is to hire some manual laborers and an industrial trash container and dump it. Then pay to have it hauled to the dump. Or, if the stuff is recyclable, have it hauled to the recycle center. If you just don't want to sort through the stuff and feel that there's nothing of value in it, you can call a company such as 1-800-GOT-JUNK, and, for a fee, they will cart it away for you. Check out the Website at *http://1800gotjunk.com/us_en/homepage.aspx*.

7 | Paper Clutter and Filing

Knowing our learning style will help us in all areas of decluttering and staying organized, and nowhere is it more valuable than when organizing our paper clutter. When we learn *how* we learn, we can apply the organizing techniques here and in other books a lot more effectively. Maybe our problem has merely been one of trying to do things that work for auditory people when we're kinesthetic.

Most of us don't really know, though. I'm convinced I'm a visual/logical learner. Girlfriends have often reminded me that I don't remember what color hair theirs has been (I swear it *was* red once), or ever notice what they have worn. I thought that was just being male. Don't even get them started on the "logical" spreadsheet calculations I made to decide which car to buy. ("If you take the square root of the gas mileage and multiply that by the mean average of cubic feet of trunk space....")

The following questions are short and simple. Many of us want to "do well" on tests and anticipate the "correct" answers. "But Mr. Author, you said to anticipate in the first chapter!" Belay that for the test. We often figure out the pattern, and try to make sure we fall into that pattern. Please don't do that here. The first answer that comes to you is correct. There are no trick questions here:

1. When I agree with someone, I might say:
    A. I see what you are saying.
    B. I hear you.
    C. I feel that you are right.

D. I think you are right.

E. I think you've touched on the right point.

2. When I feel under pressure, I might say:

    A. I'm under the gun.

    B. I hear the clock ticking.

    C. I feel overwhelmed.

    D. I know I will get this done.

    E. This thing's got ahold of me.

3. When I look for something, I might say:

    A. I'll see if I can find it.

    B. That sounds familiar.

    C. I feel as though it's in that pile.

    D. I just know it's around here somewhere.

    E. I know I can put my hands on it.

4. When I decide to try to clean up my office, I might think:

    A. I can't clearly see my way.

    B. That pile of clutter is calling to me.

    C. I can't breathe. I'm drowning in clutter.

    D. I can't believe I let it get this bad.

    E. I'm going to get a handle on this mess.

5. When I try to declutter, I might think:

    A. I'll start with the area that looks the worst.

    B. I'm going to try a new technique I heard about.

    C. This pile is calling to me.

    D. I'll start at the left corner of my desk and work to the right.

    E. I'll grab the first thing I see and start there.

6. At home, my worst clutter is:

    A. In my entrance.

    B. In my living room.

    C. In my bedroom.

    D. In my reading area.

    E. In my kitchen or garage.

7. When faced with a new demand on my time, I might think:
   A. I'll see if I can fit this in.
   B. It sounds like a lot of work to me.
   C. This doesn't seem fair.
   D. I have enough responsibilities. I don't know how this will fit in.
   E. I'll try to juggle some other things so I can squeeze it in.
8. When I meet people for the first time, the initial thing that strikes me is:
   A. Their overall appearance.
   B. The sound of their voice.
   C. How sincere they seem to be.
   D. A combination of body language and what they are saying.
   E. The strength of their handshake.
9. When I shop for a new car, I am most attracted to:
   A. How it looks.
   B. The opinions of others I've talked to.
   C. An overall impression of how I'd feel about owning it.
   D. Gas mileage, reliability, and a good deal on financing.
   E. How it handles, how I feel behind the wheel.
10. I feel that I learn best through:
    A. Workshops and group presentations.
    B. Tapes to play in my car or at home.
    C. One-on-one discussions.
    D. Reading.
    E. Just doing it. Hands-on.

Results

You've probably already figured out that there are four broad categories of learning types. This is the basis of NLP (Neuro Linquistic Programming), as put forth by Tony Robbins and others.

The key to learning and remembering is finding the way your brain works and utilizing your dominant styles. No one is a pure type, of course, but you will have a general tendency toward one style, with another coming in second. Use the following methods to help you to remember, to file, and to avoid cluttering. A main reason for disorganization is that we don't trust our memories. By discovering our dominant learning style, we can improve our memories.

(Note: Number 10 fits all styles. Reading is auditory, visual, logical, and kinesthetic to some degree. If you chose "reading," but not many other *D* answers, figure out your predominant learning sense from your other responses.)

*A*s—Visual

If you answered mainly *A*s, you are a visual learner. The question that gave you the most trouble was number 10, because visual people learn both from workshops and reading. So, even if you had a *D* for the last question, you are still visual.

*B*s—Auditory

*B*s are auditory learners. Because reading is an auditory skill for many of us (we mentally say the words as we read), in question 10, both *B* and *D* can be considered auditory answers. You learn best by verbal communication. You are more likely to get the most out of a conference, lecture, or tape. You probably have an extensive music collection. You wish this book was on tape.

*C*s—Emotional

*C*s are emotional learners. There are two types within this broad category: *Inter*personal types are concerned with how things affect others. *Intra*personal types internalize everything. How things affect them inside is the most important. This can be a good thing, if they have a highly intuitive, sixth sense, or a self-defeating behavior, if their self-esteem is so low that it goes up and down like a yo-yo with every decision.

*D*s—Logical

*D*s learn best by understanding "why" something works or needs to be done. They like to have a lot of graphs, flowcharts, and orderly steps to get something done. Few disorganized people are truly logical, but many of us have a mistaken belief that we are. I fit in this category. Most of us should count this as a secondary skill, because we are probably hoping we will be logical when we grow up. Maybe we will.

Logical people are organized and efficient. We often tell ourselves (myself included) that what we are doing is logical. We take logical steps to arrive at an illogical conclusion. If you answered with a lot of *D*s, then check your number-two responses. They are probably more accurate. You are probably an *A* but want to be a *D*. If your talent is to be logical, you can develop that trait. But to get started, you'll have to learn to get organized to know what it feels like. Thus, you should apply the *A* techniques until they become habit, and the *D* traits will start to emerge as your true self. In a sense, visual is more logical than the other categories. We feel that we can trust what we see more than what we hear or feel.

*E*s—Kinesthetic

*E*s are kinesthetic learners. They have to have some kind of physical contact to enhance learning. Great typists are kinesthetic. Graphic artists work in that mode combined with the visual mode. Kinesthetics would rather shop in a store than buy online. They want to see a working model before saying yes to a design.

But I Thought I Was Something Else

If your answers don't seem to be "right," you didn't flunk. Some of us don't really know how we learn, and are more likely to have put down how we *think* we learn. Later, we'll do a visualization exercise that will clarify it for us. If there is a discrepancy between your answers here and the results of the visualization, go with the style that is dominant in your visualization. We are complicated people, and this little test is only a first step on the journey to understanding ourselves.

Paper Clutter Represents More Than You Think

Or so we think now. We can move beyond that. Before we deal with the papers, let's explore some of the insecurities the papers represent, and banish them. They are literally paper tigers. Let's make 'em toothless pussycats.

The problem is our way of looking at the papers. The pile of papers is intimidating because we have imagined it as a minefield that could sink our careers. Traditional advice tells us, "All you have to do is start with the piece of paper at the top of your pile and work your way down. Once you've gotten rid of it, and implemented a system, you won't let it pile up again."

That might work for organized people. We clutterers have to overcome our feelings to do even the simplest tasks. We know logically that "all we have to do" is to set up a filing system and be religious about putting stuff into it. Once a year, or once a month, we know that we should go through it and purge it. Gee, how simple is that?

1. Date all files.
2. Reduce decision-making.

Only about 20 percent of the papers you file are referred to again. Yet, an average of 60 percent of each person's time is now spent processing documents. (From *Data Smog: Surviving the Information Glut*, by David Shenk, derived from *Beyond Paper*, by Patrick Ames.)

Make your filing system work the way your brain does, based on your learning style. There is no one perfect system. The only "have to" is to write the date filed (month/date/year, or simply month/year, as you choose) in the upper right-hand corner of every file. Why? Once you've learned to trust your decisions, you'll actually enjoy purging your filing cabinet. This makes it easier. "Every file older than X date goes," will reduce decision-making. The fewer decisions we have to make, the easier it is to stay decluttered.

Computer-Based Solutions

Myth 1: A Scanner Will Solve All My Filing Problems

I have a paper document from a potential supplier about a new telephone system. I take about three minutes to place it on the scanner, scan it, and then file it on my hard drive. Oops, make that six minutes, because the OCR (optical character recognition) missed a few words. Because hard drives crash, and I'm not very good at backing up, I'd better file this paper just to be safe. That takes another two minutes. Total time elapsed: eight minutes. Likelihood this will be important: 20 percent.

Solution

Before filing or scanning anything, say HIII (How Important Is It?). Is this new information, or merely a follow-up to something else? A typical business letter contains about 30 percent fluff. From the letterhead to the inside address, there's nothing useful.

If the letter or fax is merely an acknowledgment of your last fax or letter, then a quick note in your contact manager will suffice. If it contains new, useful information, can it be summarized and computerized, or do you need the paper as a CYA (Cover Your Ass) document? Finding a system that balances clutter-proofing with your personal style is a trial and error process. If you try to apply a rigid system that makes you feel uncomfortable, it will fail. Finding balance is the goal.

Myth 2: If I Keep Everything in My Computer, I Can Find It

Having everything on your computer or PDA is no guarantee you'll be able to find it easily. Instead of doing a "Find" search for "Appleton" every time you need his documents, learn to file intelligently. **Do not put everything into "My Documents" without creating directories such as WordDocs, Spreadsheets, and such.** A proper filing system saves you from wading through dozens of documents to find the one you want.

Solution

Keep it simple, but not too simple. The problem with taking a Zen minimalist approach to filing (computer or paper) is that we are *not* Zen masters. Our minds are more akin to a fragmented computer file. Have you ever defragged your files? You should, at least once a week. Otherwise, you won't be able to find anything.

Our minds don't file information sequentially, by priority, or alphabetically. We mentally file by association. **Visualization is the key.**

Strive for Dominance

When you have a scene firmly in your mind, what sense seems to be dominant? Your emotions? The colors of the surroundings? The roaring of the crowd? Your boss's or spouse's voice? The feeling of being physically touched by your spouse, boss, or teammates? That dominant emotion is the key to helping you remember. If the dominant feeling conflicts with your answers on the questionnaire, go with your feelings now. Sometimes we are too logical when taking a test. Our feelings don't lie. You are probably a combination of two learning types, and one might fit better with using a filing system. Try both for a while and see which one works. You'll know pretty quickly. Don't forget the power of humor! Whatever you can do to make a project humorous will make it stick with you. You could visualize the telephone project as a skit about someone getting lost in voice-mail hell, or a Lucille Ball–type episode of a harried old-fashioned telephone operator.

Don't Just File It and Forget It

Reviewing what you did after you've done it has proven to dramatically improve retention. Remember those nerds in school who always had the right answers? If you had asked them what they did that was different, they would have said they took good notes and reviewed them before the day was over. The short amount of time you'll spend reviewing where you just filed things will pay big rewards in finding them later.

Memory by Association

Make a mental "hanger" to prod your memory to put the project in its right place. Memory experts (you know, those smart alecks who can recite everyone's name in a crowd of a hundred) tell us that one secret is to associate a person's name with something else. "Mike Nelson" might be too common to remember, but if you visualize a **mic**rophone on a **nail**, you might remember me. The wackier the image, the better you'll remember it. "Janis Wilson" is common, but if you make a play on her name: **Jan** (picture a January calendar) **is wil**ling and **sun**ny (visualize a bright cartoon sun on that January calendar), you won't forget her. Personalize the hanger using your dominant learning type.

Visual: "I See the Light Filing"

A quick visualization will imprint a file's location in your memory faster and better than anything else. You don't have to get cross-legged and chant in order to visualize. Visualization is merely creating a mental image of what you want to remember. You then associate the image with pegs that jog your particular type of memory: sounds, colors, emotions, funny images, whatever helps you to remember. You are creating what psychologists call *attachment*. Attachment means that we make things personal.

Another reason for visualization is that it makes work more fun. The project may be boring, and you may resent it, but at least you can get a giggle from it when you have to work on it. Making dreary work fun will help you organize.

We are more likely to sabotage ourselves and misfile things when we aren't happy. Although we can't all have dream jobs and still feed our families, we can make what we do less of a chore. It will pay off in the long run in being organized.

First, let's double-check the test you took on learning styles. Think of any strongly positive event that has been deeply imbedded in your consciousness. Examples are, the time you were praised by your boss for doing something spectacular, the day your spouse proposed, or the time you won a high school football game. Take some time to relive this without distractions.

Marita Adair is a visual, creative person. Her secret to being able to find anything later is to *see* it. She uses four-legged wire shelves, to put the scanner above her printer, under-shelf wire baskets, plastic see-through crates as book dividers on her shelves, and clear literature containers. "I can organize my clutter better if I can see it. I mark on my daily calendar to put away 12 things. I often accomplish a lot more, particularly if I grab items as I pass by them rather than leaving them out of place day after day."

Visual people should use transparent "Action" files on their desks while working on a project, then transfer them to transparent filing crates as it loses its immediacy. Once it goes into the metal monster filing cabinet, it is like declaring them dead and buried.

Use see-through filing systems whenever possible. Use flowcharts (both visual and logical tools) to map activities. Use charts on the wall to keep track of where you are in your task list. Map the filing system in the file cabinets you use. Keep the map where you can see it. That way you can "see your way through."

Kinesthetic: "Touchy-Feely Filing"

Kinesthetic people can keep a file folder filled with sticky notes with the names of each file, which they can move around as they use them. Make a file folder (a legal size is best for you) that you can access readily. Keep it on your desk instead of the files themselves. Write the names of the real file folders on sticky notes. This frees you to put the files in a real file drawer and not feel as though you have "lost touch" with them. When you need a file, go to your sticky note folder. As the project moves forward, you can move the notes into different stages, like "waiting on a call from Appleton," "submitted bid to Appleton," "pending installation," and such.

Auditory: "I Can Hear You Knocking"

Auditory people can associate a sound with the file. Because reading has a strong auditory component for many of us, go ahead and say it out loud. You are already "saying" it in your mind. This reinforces it. For instance, when you begin this telephone project, say out loud, "Telephone Systems." Then visualize a phone ringing. Embed that sound into your mind. Pull in a little association, and visualize an apple tree with a ringing phone for Appleton. Hear the phone ring again. You could imagine an old-fashioned page-boy walking through the office saying, "Phone message for Mr. Appleton. Phone message for Mr. Appleton." Now you have the entire project and the individual characters in the plot impressed on your auditory senses. If you've talked to any of the people involved, recall the sound of their voices as you create files for them. Whenever someone sounds similar to somebody you already know, or a TV or radio voice, associate the name with the name of the person he sounds like.

Logical Learners

Logical learners won't need the redundant filing system. If they've set the files up in a logical manner, they will feel comfortable that they can find them.

Emotional: "I Feel Filing"

Emotional learners will add their own emotional reactions to the previous mental visualizations to make the project and people important to them. In fact, you should probably drop all pretenses to being logical right now. You could visualize a telephone call in which you got some good news. Hear the voice on the other end, but in a different way than the auditory learners. Hear the emotions in the other person's voice and feel the emotions in yours. Then add in the main players in the project, or the names of the folders in a conversation with the person giving you the news. Hear Appleton excitedly telling you about his proposal.

Some Filing Ideas

How should you file? You decided a letter or fax is important enough to file. You made a folder. Now the decision-making process begins.

Color-Coding

Color-coding works well for most people, especially visual learners. Make the project files all the same color. Unfortunately, there are only so many colors and way too many projects. To choose a color, use visualization. Think about the project with your eyes closed and see what color comes to you.

What does red look like? What does it sound like?

Use emotions, sounds, logic, sights—whatever works for you to determine the "right" color. If you think of the red hotline in the president's office, red wins. If you visualize people yelling at each other, use yellow. If you visualize people talking until they are blue in the face, go for blue. There is no one way to choose a color. Clutterers agonize over the most trivial things. We are likely to waste 20 minutes picking the "right" color for a project file, when two minutes would have been plenty.

Don't use a rainbow when one color will do. Using small, colored dots rather than colored folders is better. Tape them to the folder, because they fall off when you use the files repeatedly. Do not use colored plastic tabs for the hanging folders. They may add an artistic flair, but it is nearly impossible to read the labels. Don't stop with just choosing a cute color: Make a color key map and tape it to the front of the filing cabinet, and write a note named "color code" in your contact manager. This makes it easier for you and everyone else to find files.

More Filing Myths

Myth 3: I Can Find It—If I Make It Too Easy for Others, I Will Lose My Importance

We've all heard stories about companies that begged the retired secretary or office assistant to come back to work because no one could find anything. Some people purposely create complicated, secretive filing systems to increase their own value to their employer.

Sometimes they know their jobs so well that their system isn't created out of fear, but because of their intimate knowledge. Sometimes a cluttered filing system is caused by a cluttered mind. Regardless of the reason, the results are the same: an incomprehensible system to anyone else.

Here is an example given to me by an employee of a nonprofit historical foundation. It could be representative of any organization that puts on festivals or annual entertainment events, but career coaches and professional organizers unanimously agree that nonprofits tend to be the most disorganized types of businesses.

Among other activities, this organization put on an annual event based on Charles Dickens characters. The person in charge of filing knew the Dickens characters, so she filed information by character. Because she wanted to ensure her value and her job, she took it a step further. The filing system worked, but only as long as she did. Due to her superior knowledge, she could justify it.

A logical filing system might have looked this way:

Dickens Festival
    Characters
        Queen Victoria
        Mr. Bumble
        Tiny Tim
        Etc.

Talent
    Performer 1
    Performer 2
Suppliers
    Banners
    Refreshments
    Etc.
Instead, she did this:
Victoria, Queen
Tim, Tiny
Mr., Bumble
Mondo (Name of Talent)
Bill Smith (Company Owner's Name of Banner Supplier)
Gonzalez, Hank (Salesman for Coca-Cola Supplier)
Withers, Ann (name of person who played Queen Victoria)

There was no hierarchy. She obfuscated the information by making the first word one less likely to be someone's first thought. Most of us think of "Queen Victoria" and "Tiny Tim." We tend to ignore Mr., Ms., Mrs., and think of a person's name—for example, "Bumble." A newcomer would be unlikely to know that Mondo was the contact for The Texas Magician's Union. If we didn't know that Bill Smith was the owner of Acme Graphics, the banner supplier, or that Hank (whose first name was actaully Enrique) Gonzalez was the salesman for Coca-Cola, we'd never know where to look.

This all came to a head when she left of her own accord and a new person took over. It took months to unravel the mess.

Solution

This is a difficult situation. If only one person is doing this, she may need reassurance. If more than one person has adopted this, or other paranoia-induced job-protection measures, you have a bigger problem.

Myth 4: Action Files Will Keep Me on Track

These can be useful, but they are more often overused. It's okay to have a portable file container on your desk with things you really, really need to work on today, but the chances for abuse are great. Look at it this way: If you are trying to lose weight, you might take an appetite suppressant for a few days. But if you keep them around and gobble one every time you feel a little hungry, you will become addicted. The same goes for "action" files. You need to change your habits so that these helpers don't become a way of life.

Ongoing projects shouldn't be kept in action files when there's no action occurring. Re-file them when you complete an action. Every day there's a new set of things that cry out for action. If nothing ever moves out of there, you can't take any action, because "in-action" files have taken over your desk.

Solution

Allow yourself three action files. If something comes up during the day that you need to work on, get the file from the filing cabinet. If you need to make a new file, replace something from your so-called action area with the new one, or file it away. Make it a habit to stop an hour before you leave. Finish up the files on your desk. Then file them where they belong. If you need them tomorrow, you will know right where they are.

Make a set of "pending" files you can keep nearby (so they won't feel left out) in a rollaway hanging file basket. When we get them off the desk, into a pending folder, we can give all our attention to the project at hand.

This Is Only the Start

You will find new tools and techniques based on your individual style. Use them. What have you got to lose? Only your clutter. When you discover something that works for you, you feel creative. The suggestions here will open your mind, which has been stuck in thinking there is only one way to do things. There are many paths to the same destination. Some may take the scenic route, and if that's what works for you, meander along. No matter how odd your style may seem to an organized person, if it works for you, *and* you can leave a trail of breadcrumbs for them to follow, you'll get to Grandma's cottage just the same. It will be more fun because your reward will be milk and cookies instead of a Big Bad Wolf of disorganization.

8 | Clutterers' Stories

Life (and all psychological expressions as part of life) moves ever toward overcoming, toward perfection, toward superiority, toward success. You cannot train or condition a living being for defeat.

—Alfred Adler

Nearly everyone has a story about some family member or friend who is a clutterer, but those stories deal with the problem, not the solution. The stories in this chapter, however, are from clutterers themselves and give you a sense of how others have conquered the same problem. Names have been changed, and all are used with permission.

Marsha

On October 1, 1997, my late physician husband, Michael, and I were traveling home from a glorious car trip around Ireland. When we arrived into Gatwick Airport in London to change planes, he fell to the carpeted floor, dying of a massive heart attack. Three hours later I was a widow in a foreign country, all alone. Two days later following all of the arrangements to transport his body, I came home to a household of friends and relatives.

My life had to begin all over again, except this time around, being single meant a 16-year-old son still at home.

Time for grieving was not an option that I felt I could afford to enjoy. My son didn't need to see me crying, so I just buried myself in work to relieve the emotions. Interestingly enough, I was cocreating the Creative Journal Expressive Arts certification program with my business partner, Lucia Capacchione, PhD, ATR, REAT.

I fortunately had a personal assistant to help me deal with the business details of the death. Other than my son, my immediate family lives in California, and I was 1,500 miles from my nearest relative. Friends helped me hold it together; I appeared as if I was doing terrifically. My behaviors spelled a different story. I would go out each day and roam around the stores. I owned four homes, all filled with lovely things. I needed nothing materially.

I was trying to stuff a broken heart with things. Day after day, I would travel out and buy stuff. I would give it away, save it for the holidays, etc., etc. I got so that I would sneak it into the house after my assistant left so that he would not see what I was doing. As if he didn't know—he was the one who received my credit card bills each month. My husband's children tried to sue me during this period, and another one of my two sons was struggling with a drug problem in California. Life was raw and real.

I dated and was looking good. Life was good for this 49-year-old widow. After a breakup with a boyfriend of two years, five years after my husband's death, I finally hit bottom; I crashed and burned. I cried endlessly for six weeks. My heart was broken, and all of the stuff that I had used to fill my abandonment was useless to kill this pain. One day my business partner told me to get on an online dating site and see what I could find. I did, and I immediately found my future husband. Within eight months I was happily married. Coach Dan Nelson and I are going to be celebrating five years of marriage next month. Oh, and the shopping?! Well, I hate to go to the store; he does most of the shopping.

This is a perfect example of what we do unconsciously to ourselves. We are our own worst enemies. As Eleanor Roosevelt said, "No one can do anything to me that I am not already doing to myself."

Vicki

I had seen the advertisements for Clutterless Groups in the newspaper for some time. I always thought about my cousin Nina when I read them, because she has storage rooms, and rooms with so much stuff in them you can't walk into them. I asked her to come from Belton to a seminar during the summer, and she did. We both enjoyed the seminar, and we each bought a book (Stop Clutter From Stealing Your Life *and* Clutter-Proof Your Business), and discussed what we had brought away with us from the information Mike had shared. Mike invited those present to a support group that would be meeting weekly. I decided to go because the location was close to my house, and I thought others in the audience would be attending. Because of my counseling background, I feel comfortable in support groups, and thought it would be interesting. I liked the framework of the meetings—especially the guided imagery and the affirmations at the end. I also enjoyed doing "personal work" that helped me deal with decisions I had to make, whether clutter-related or not.

I worked on issues such as: compulsive shopping because "I deserve it," holding on to things that were no longer useful or I had duplicates of (or triplicates!), getting rid of reading materials and holding on to old articles (when the computer can give me whatever info I need, many times much more current than what's in an old tattered folder). I worked though the issue that having a lot of stuff meant that in some way I was not "poor." That having lots of stuff was defining me as a successful person.

We also laughed as a group when I discussed not being able to throw out jars of half full beauty cream or wrinkle remover. Part of it may have been the cost of the item, or feeling that the next jar of miracle cream was going to be better than the jar I was currently using. What if I was getting all old and shriveled up using Cream A when somewhere out there was Cream B, and it was better?! And then there were the plastic gloves that came with some hair color. When I opened the cabinet, a mountain of plastic gloves fell on me. What was I saving them for? I wasn't going to perform surgery!

The biggest decision that came about since attending the group is the decision to quit the job I was in. I feel that this was due to the *affirmations dealing with getting rid of people or things that no longer serve me, and that I have enough money for my needs. It was a huge decision, but it was like closing a small closet door and opening up a big glass sliding door. Not only do I feel better about myself (my husband has also noticed the difference), but I also have time to devote to cleaning and uncluttering my home. I am finally doing things I've had on my "to do" list for 10-plus years. I have the energy to do them, the time to do them, and I enjoy seeing the results.*

One thing I found myself holding on to were notes from seminars, workshops, classes, or magazine articles. An exercise we were asked to do was to write with our non-dominate hand the answer to the question, "Why is clutter a problem for me?" With my left hand I wrote, "because I can't find what I need, and people will think I'm a dumb Mexican." After waking up at 2 a.m. to ponder that statement, I realized that being seen as a smart, capable Mexican-American woman who is in control was how I defined myself. If I didn't know something and couldn't put my hand on what I needed ASAP, then people might think I'm dumb or lazy (negative stereotypes attributed to Mexicans), and that I might not be taken seriously. I felt I had to work twice as hard and be twice as perfect to prove myself to teachers and the people I worked with. It also has to do with being a perfectionist.

I feel that I clutter in large part because I'm sentimental and can't let go of my box of work from kindergarten and the first grade, notes, a really good project from elementary school, or my high school music books from when I won first place in solo competition. I find the old stuff affirming (it makes me feel happy and makes me smile) that I worked hard, and that it's a part of me, and vice versa. I need to separate who I am from what, like you've said before, could go up in a puff of smoke. Lots of people say, and it's true, that "this stuff is only important to me."

Linda

My experience with cluttering began as an only child raised by parents who grew up during the Great Depression. My grandmother's and mother's motto was "save everything—you never know when you'll get another one."

If my mom had 10 hats, she wore only the two or three oldest and most worn ones, saving the "good ones for Sunday." But it wasn't just any Sunday. That meant "for good," or in my estimation as a young child, never.

When I helped my now 89-year-old mother move from her home of 54 years—the home where I was raised—her closets were filled with hats from the 1950s in pristine condition, mostly unworn—waiting in their boxes for that day special enough to warrant being worn.

Like any daughter raised by a mother and grandmother who lived through the Depression, I couldn't bear to throw out those nostalgic hats. I had looked longingly at them growing up and wondered when the time was going to be special enough for my mom to don one of them, put on a dress equally special, a touch of perfume, and go out into the world.

But at 89 my mom still has her special things that she's saving. She parted with the hats from the '50s, my dad's neckties from the '50s through the '90s, her material room filled to the brim with fabric which would one day be made into good, wearable, everyday clothing for me or for her. Now her macular degeneration prevents sewing. So, it was easier for her to part with that collection when she moved to the senior apartment.

When I went into practice as a clinical psychologist some 25-plus years ago, I took all my education, but I also took all my baggage, and that of my mother and grandmother. My father, who was of the same generation, dealt with "things" differently. He was rather indifferent, and instead spent his spare time not shopping for wonderful things to put on the shelf, but busied himself reading the first "self-help" books—How to Win Friends and Influence People *by Dale Carnegie;* Psychocybernetics *by Maxwell Maltz.*

So, like most people, I am an amalgam of both my parents, with lots of education about the human condition and the treatment of its disorders thrown in on top of that. I didn't pick a specialty, even though some people pressed me on the subject. Instead I enjoyed treating people of all ages, colors, and disorders of living.

Somewhere along the way I met Mike Nelson. I guess by that time I considered myself a recovering clutterer of the mild variety. I attended a workshop he was doing in Oklahoma City where I reside. I liked his approach to cluttering and having support groups for self-identified clutterers. I put my name on his professional page, as someone who treats clutterers.

Ask many clutterers and they will admit to being perfectionistic. It's that black-and-white thinking again: If I can't clean it and make it look perfect, why try at all? So many give up on cleaning and clearing. So I help in correcting the thinking using a cognitive behavioral model. The premise is that if we correct our thinking, we can begin to correct our behavior. But again, it's not magic. It takes time and a great deal of effort.

Therapy requires of us self-honesty. It requires looking at ourselves over and over again and correcting the incorrect perceptions that helped us survive growing up in our families. However, most of the time those models of childhood survival are not adaptive for us as adults.

I like to think of myself as a guide, a teacher just a few steps ahead of my student. When I am asked by a new client who is a self-identified clutterer how I got into the area, I tell them I'm a recovering clutterer myself.

In lieu of therapy, self-help, etc., the alternative can also be to buy a second home for the overflow, and hire a maid who will clear as you bring in more stuff. I personally have adopted a little of all of the above.

Mary

I can't believe I'm writing this. No one knows about my clutter problem, except those at Clutterless meetings. I didn't have a problem with clutter in my life until my divorce. Until then, I was a little messy (I often left the housework for a couple of weeks), but we lived a pretty normal life. I don't know, but after the marriage ended, I felt as if any reason to stay neat was gone too. I was in a depression, and went to a therapist. She helped a lot, and I took medication for a while, which, together with the therapy, helped me over that hurdle. But we didn't talk much about my cluttering. When the depression ended, I stopped seeing my therapist, thinking the cluttering would go away too.

I kept a steady job for which I had to keep detailed records of phone calls. Because everything was done on a computer, this presented no problems, and I used a filing system that made sense to me and to others. I was neat and presentable in my appearance, and my cubicle was always clean and orderly when I left work.

But when I went home, it was like a Ms. Hyde replaced the Dr. Jekyll in my life. Newspapers piled up, on the couch at first, then the coffee table, and finally spilled onto the floor. I loved to read, but just didn't seem to have the time anymore.

My dishes were rinsed and put into the dishwasher at first, but for some reason, I seldom ran it. I just washed what I needed for the evening and put the rest off until later. I began to retreat to bed at night and read tons of mystery novels. I began eating in bed, and somehow the dishes stayed on the floor...

The First Step

I saw a notice for a Clutterers Anonymous meeting in the city where I lived at the time. Although the "anonymous" put me off (after all, I wasn't an alcoholic or drug user), I thought I would give it a try. The meetings helped me a great deal. Just finding a group of people who were like me made me feel a lot more like tackling my cluttering problem. I started decluttering, and things got better. Because I didn't have a 12-step background, some of the concepts were difficult for me to grasp, but some of them did seem to apply, so I took what worked and left the rest, as they say.

Later, I went to OC [obsessive-compulsive] support groups, and, although I respected them and the good they did for others, I felt like I didn't fit in, since I wasn't taking medication or seeing a therapist. I certainly didn't feel like I qualified as a "hoarder."

I moved to a city where there was no CLA [Clutterers Anonymous], and I didn't want to go back to the OC groups. Fortunately, Clutterless self-help meetings had just started, and they really spoke to me. My clutter problem was not as serious as many of the people in CLA, and I didn't have a hoarding problem like those in OC groups, so, like in Goldilocks and the Three Bears, this felt "just right."

"Living in Lack" Hit Home

When the concept of "living in lack" took root, I realized that that was what I was doing. I thought I would never find another love, and wasn't worthy, so why bother? This was the real turning point for me. I tackled my messy house and started to feel good about myself again. My whole personality changed. I shed my depression as I shed my useless possessions. With the help of a buddy, I tackled the boxes of things related to my ex, and we had a big bonfire in the backyard. God, did I feel relieved! The physical act of burning his stuff burned him out of my consciousness.

Clutterless made me realize that my stuff wasn't my problem. I was creating a way of life that was untrue, and I had the power to change it into as good a life as I wanted. This made sense to me. I now have a full life, a clean house, and give dinner parties again. I found that I didn't have to have a man in my life to feel worthwhile any more than I had to have a lot of junk surrounding me. The odd thing is that I now do have a man in my life, but do not feel dependent on him, my stuff, or anyone else for my self-worth. As they say in the meetings, true value comes from within.

Marilyn

Marilyn has been improving for 16 years. She is a bright, cheerful person who talks about the dark days of her cluttering with humor. She grew up in Beverly Hills, but not in a rich family. She was surrounded by "kids who had everything," and she felt phony. Her father was ill, so her mother had to work.

I never knew anyone like me. I felt like I always had a special relationship with God, having been a chaplain. It was so hard on me. If people only knew all these crazy stories I had to make up to keep people who thought I was together from knowing I was not together. It makes it easy now, to just tell people I am a clutterer. But they still only guess what a clutterer might be.

My kids say, "Mom didn't used to be a clutterer." I've got a five-bedroom house. When the kids lived there, I wasn't a clutterer. When they moved out, gradually, I filled their rooms. I'd just open a door to one of their rooms and fling something in instead of putting it away. As long as the main part of the house looked okay,

> *I figured nobody would know. I'll take care of it tomorrow...and tomorrow never came.*
>
> *For me, if it isn't done now, it's so easy for me to say "later" or "tomorrow." There's hardly ever "now" for me. I was so involved in est [Erhard Seminars Training, Werner Erhard's self-growth seminars in the 1970s] when it was big. All the "be here now," "do this now," made me think I would change my life then. At the end, I never did think I got it. I had to take it a second time. I still wasn't sure if I got it, but I had to say I did, because I'd be too embarrassed to say that I was the only who hadn't gotten it.*
>
> *If a repairman had to come to the house, I couldn't sleep the night before. I made up all kinds of crazy stories. It was all lies. I couldn't have people over to the house, I was too embarrassed. We would take our friends out to dinner instead of having them over to the house.*

After the Northridge, California, earthquake of 1994, there was no damage to Marilyn's house, but the disarray caused by the quake was a great excuse that she used for years to justify her clutter. She had a gas oven, but wouldn't let a repairman in the house when it developed problems. A neighbor came to the front door and smelled gas. This led to a visit by the gas company. Marilyn had had a gas leak for two years.

Failure and Loss

Part of Marilyn's story revolves around a business that she no longer operates and the difficulty in letting things from that go.

> *My cluttering was just starting then. I got in est about the time I wanted a restaurant. I wanted that restaurant so badly. It took a year to get it together. It was my dream. I loved it. But after about a year and a half, I realized that 16 hours a day wasn't for me. I had no sense of management. People couldn't believe we closed. We always had business. Some Hollywood stars were my best customers.*
>
> *After that, I was so down. I was depressed for a time. That was my* dream, *and I couldn't make it work. I was surrounded by all the dishes that had been picked out, the antique chairs, etc. It took me so long to get it all together, the recipes, all this stuff, and there wasn't any of that anymore. I just couldn't get rid of them.*

A crisis occurred when Marilyn's family attempted to declutter for her while she was out of town for two weeks:

> My husband and daughter worked nonstop while I was gone. I wasn't grateful, and had a minor nervous breakdown. They had thrown out stuff that had sentimental value, like a little blue hand my son had made as a child, and a luau dress. My daughter thought the dress was tacky, but I liked it. I don't put a lot of value on monetary things. It's the sentimental value that matters. I had boxes and boxes of LA Times food sections. Whole rooms of them. It was crazy, because I made my own recipes. I didn't even miss those.
>
> If I'd been a part of it, I think I'd have let [the neatness] last, because in almost nothing flat, I started messing it up again. I cried a lot for two weeks. I wasn't grateful. Not being sure what a nervous breakdown was, I think I had a mini nervous breakdown.
>
> My husband kept hoping I would be different. I would see the beauty of stuff and not the clutter. My children loved me, but they never did want to come home. I could work nonstop. There was no way to declutter it. I would put out a pot with a pretty flower in it, and just see the beauty, and not the clutter.
>
> My son wouldn't bring my granddaughter over for fear that she would get lost in the clutter. The phrase, "someday it's gonna be different" was a common refrain around the house. We didn't work on this well together. I love my husband, but his way of doing something is different from mine. He is fast, and I am very, very slow. And rebellious. I think he just gave up. He didn't make threats or anything else. He just gave up. He never picked up after me because I didn't want him to. I figure, if I messed it up, I gotta pick it up myself.

Getting Better

This conviction of Marilyn's led to her roundabout route to getting better. She started looking for Packrats Anonymous, and couldn't find it. She called AA and they referred her to Clutterers Anonymous. She recalls of her first meeting:

> I just thought I was a packrat. I didn't know what a "clutterer" was. I'd never belonged to groups. I thought I was going to grab a handful of literature and never go back. When I heard others' stories, I realized that I was a clutterer.

My husband was happy when I got into CLA. I think he thought, "Thank God, there's hope." Now I don't believe he ever throws anything away without thinking "Is this something that's going to upset her?" I think he has so much better an idea of what I am like. I don't know, it's hard to say, but I think he's turned into a little bit of a clutterer too.

With me it's hard to work with a family member [on decluttering]. A fellow clutterer can get me to do something that a family member never in a million years can get me to do. A family member or a close friend, I don't care what they say, they will never in a million years understand a clutterer. We just don't think like other people. I don't think anyone can help me other than myself or another clutterer, or turn it over to God.

Intervention didn't work for me. But maybe other people aren't as stubborn, or maybe controlling, as I was.

Time and the Buddy System

I absolutely believe in the buddy system. Most of my [buddy encouragement] has worked over the phone for me.

I have kind of a thing for numbers. I want everything to total up. Certain numbers: like threes, fives, eights. Three is for God. Five is for Jesus. Eight is a combination of God and Jesus. At a meeting we were talking about how much you can accomplish if you commit to a certain amount of time. An hour to me sounds overwhelming. Or I don't think I have an hour. So we talked about 17 minutes. I thought, good, I like 17 minutes. Seven and one adds up to eight. That equals God and Jesus.

I had a four-poster bed, and each of the bedposts had a lot of clothes on them. In talking to one of the girls, she said that she bet I could really declutter a post in 17 minutes. She was right. I would call her after 17 minutes and we would decide whether to go for another 17 minutes. For me, it's too easy to get sidetracked with longer periods of time. I get overwhelmed easily.

I've got to have that daily list and check things off. If I don't have a list, my memory tells me that I didn't do anything, even if I have. I have a daily list, a roadmap of what I am to do that day. If I don't have that list, I feel like I give myself permission to do nothing.

I liked it that God could be an even bigger part of my life with CLA. I just know that, like alcoholics, they don't just go to meetings and say, "now I'm cured," and never go back. It's forever. And Clutterers Anonymous meetings are forever with me. If I didn't have 'em, I wouldn't have the constant reminders, and I'd be exactly back where I was before.

Slips

I have slips all the time. While my house certainly looks better than it did when my family decluttered it...whenever anything happens that's hard to deal with, like medical bills, car repairs, or whatever, that's when I slip. I categorize clutterers as organized or disorganized clutterers. I rebel against organization. If anything is going on that is hard for me to handle, like junk mail, if I don't handle right away, it fills up any empty container available. I belong to so many organizations like the SPCA, Save the Whales, Save the Ladybugs, and I get so much mail that I feel I have to go through. If I am upset, I can't deal with it right away. If it isn't done now, it is so easy to say "later." Once something gets messed up, it's hard for me to unmess it.

Richard

I came to Clutterless because my boss suggested I needed to get organized. He had attended a few meetings and felt that it could help me. He'd spent a fortune sending me to organizing workshops, and they always seemed to help for a few weeks afterwards, but I found myself slipping into old patterns again.

I'd been a slob since childhood. I was a sloppy kid and grew up to be a sloppy adult. My mother constantly picked up after me when I lived at home. At college, I finally had to get an apartment by myself because I couldn't keep a roommate. I was a computer programmer, so I made plenty of money even then, so the extra expense didn't really bother me. I loved the cleanness and orderliness of programming. I would lose myself in that world and ignore the chaos around me.

Computer Clutter

I had a really good job and plenty of money. I remained a bachelor, probably because I was an introvert. I spent most of my after-work time working on my computers. I had enough money to buy a house, and just picked out some furniture. It didn't matter what the house looked like, because I lived in my computer rooms. I had six computers, several printers, and loads of other stuff like cables, motherboards, etc. Old hard drives were like molehills on my floor. I learned to walk around them. I kept getting bigger and bigger hard drives and faster processors because I would never delete files. After all, there might just be some bit of code in one of the files that I could reuse. I couldn't throw out the old computers because they might come in handy for parts. I knew this was illogical, as old technology and new technology usually don't mix, but I kept them.

Technical journals were strewn all over my home. I could never find the article I needed when I needed it, and didn't actually have time to read half of them. Sure, lots of things are on the Internet, but not always what you need.

Hitting Bottom

At work, I was never neat, but I was a genius, and got away with it. Then, things gradually went to pot. My company lost a huge contract because I was in charge of the development team and I lost track of our deadlines. Some of them complained that I was giving them redundant tasks and instructions that didn't make any sense. I had slipped into a fog. I was perpetually confused and spent most of my day looking for files in the jumble of my hard drive. Or just being distracted.

It all came to a head one day when I was sick and someone had to try to find some important files. They couldn't, and I couldn't explain how to find them on the phone. That's when my boss sent me to Clutterless. It felt good to know I wasn't alone. It felt better to know that I could change the self-destructive behavior. By focusing on what was right about my life, I learned that I could spill that over into the parts that were illogical. By concentrating on my success, I could create more success. By visualizing orderliness, I could bring orderliness into my life. It all made sense.

I haven't been going to meetings for long, but already I've seen improvement. Learning to break things into large subcategories and then into manageable tasks was just like writing a program. How could I have done that in programming and then forgotten to apply it to my life? But they taught me not to beat myself up for what was, and to concentrate on what is. I can make things the way I want. I had just been wanting things to be a mess.

D.T.

I've been in therapy most of my adult life. I take SSRIs [antidepressants]. My cluttering is an on-again, off-again problem. When the meds are working and I am following my therapist's suggestions, my clutter problem is very small. When I slip into depression, my stuff takes over my life. Most of the time, I look like I live a normal life to the outside world. But when things get bad, the piles of stuff take over.

OCD support groups helped me, but I like Clutterless groups too. I like the "we're all in this boat together" attitude and humor at Clutterless, which is different than at my therapist's groups. I like the feeling of support at both from others who won't laugh at me for my crazy thoughts or inability to deal with my stuff. When I am in good shape, I can help others.

I don't know that I will ever be "finished" with therapy. I don't know that I will ever get my clutter under complete control. All I know is that I feel better after the meetings and have made some progress in cleaning out my life. They say this goes beyond just the stuff, and I can see some of that. I feel better when I attack the clutter, and it is a great feeling to go back to the group and tell them of my progress. In fact, that is sometimes the only thing that spurs me on to do something about it.

But I don't always succeed. Sometimes I have to go and tell them that I didn't do a damn thing. They don't judge, but are supportive. This helps, and I don't feel like such a failure. I like going to meetings, and think I may be getting a little better. I know I feel better.

Joe King Carrasco

Joe King Carrasco (name used with permission) is a rock-and-roll musician. We don't think of people who live on the road as having a clutter problem, so his story is interesting to see how many different kinds of people cluttering affects.

Since Joe wrote this story, he has gotten rid of the refrigerators, a lot of shirts, many of the magazines, and has at the very least reduced the size of his storage unit.

Magical Thinking

I don't know if it is a problem, but I have shirts from when I was 14 years old. I'm 54. I feel sometimes that the stuff you touch in your life has some magical properties. I feel that life is so magic. And when you find stuff, there is a magical reason. I've never thrown away any stage clothes. Some clothes seem to bring you good luck. I keep my bus from my road trips. It stopped running in 1992 or 1993. I use it for storage now. Nine bunks, and each has a different item stored in it. It's kinda organized.

I drove my band crazy because I would bring six-month-old newspapers on the bus. When they realized the newspapers they were reading were six months old, they freaked. I collect cactus. Every time the bus stops on the side of the highway, I go dig up a cactus. The band used to get upset, but now they are used to it. They say, "If it's not nailed down, Joe's going to take it." I save every song I've written on cassette. There are 130 tapes now. When I get to a hotel room, I throw stuff all over. People say it looks like a hand grenade went off.

I was heavy on the road in the 1970s and became a Stephen C. Schlesinger fan [author of Bitter Fruit*] and he wrote for* The New York Times. *So anywhere in the world I went I got the* Times. *I saved whole newspapers for 10 years. I have newspapers from my tours of Sweden and France and all over the world. I have every magazine I've ever subscribed to, notably 20 years of* Texas Monthly *and 10 years of* Outside. *Maybe I should donate them? A library?*

When I lived in Austin, I kept the stuff in garbage cans. Two ladies surprised me by cleaning my apartment and threw the stuff away. I freaked out. That's when I thought I had a problem.

27 Refrigerators

I've got over 27 refrigerators in my field [Joe lives in the country], since I was going to build a fence of them. Today my refrigerator is out and I don't have a working one. I have about 1,000 bottles. I bought 2,000 license plates from 1959 to 1961. Paid $150. It was a deal...

I'm really big on recycling. I feel that when I am recycling and when I collect things, I am giving them a second chance. I drop all my trash in a chicken wire fence and stucco over it. I haven't thrown away any trash in 2 years, except food trash. I am trying to make it into adobe walls. I keep Fruitopia bottles to try to sell to my fans—paint 'em and put pebbles in them. Nobody wanted to buy them, so now we give them away.

You can take a stack of magazines and dip them into cement and make a brick out of it. I think everything should be recycled into walls. My new cabin has walls made out of trash. I'm into recycling but I think I have gone overboard. You know when you have 27 refrigerators you are out of touch with reality. You can't explain them to people.

I have a storage unit I rented in 1994 and I still haven't really gotten into it. You could drive a bus into it. So far I've paid $2,500 in rent. Last time I went there was a fox and black widow spiders. It was scary going in there.

Efforts to Get Better

I've taken efforts to clean up. I guess I am getting better, but I sure would love to go to a Clutterless meeting if there was one in Austin. I live in a one-room house. It kinda keeps me under control. The more rooms you have the more stuff you can save. I solved the dishwashing problem by not having many dishes, so I have to wash them to eat. I read the newspapers on the Internet. The Internet has helped a lot. But I will always get Texas Monthly *and* Outside. *Forever.*

All that stuff weighs you down, like anchors. It takes a whole lot of effort to get rid of stuff. In some ways I think I am eccentric. Andy Warhol was eccentric like this too. I feel sorry for whoever has to go through my shit when I die.

9 | The Medical View—Depression, Anxiety, ADD, Hoarding, and OCD

I am now the most miserable man living. If what I feel were equally distributed to the whole human family, there would be not one cheerful face on earth. Whether I shall ever be better, I cannot tell. I awfully forebode I shall not. To remain as I am is impossible. I must die or be better it appears to me.

—Abraham Lincoln

Knowing isn't enough. Once I was counseling an 8-year-old little boy and told him to try hard and have a better week. He smiled and said, "Remember what Yoda said: 'Do, or do not. There is no try.'"

—Virginia Mann, counselor, M.Ed

In the first edition of this book, I spent a lot of ink on hoarding and OCD. When that edition was published, it was breaking ground in the examination of cluttering and psychology. Since then, some of my conclusions and research have been used by university researchers and the understanding of cluttering has expanded. The reason for this book is to help people like me—real clutterers. OCD is unlikely to be our problem. We are way more likely to have experienced the joys of depression and anxiety. These are more likely to be the elephants in our living rooms that are blocking us from getting over our cluttering. There's still a bit about hoarding in this chapter, however, because we can still learn from it.

Clutterers and hoarders both accumulate way too much stuff, and both limit their lives to one degree or another. There are a whole bunch of specific medical criteria used to diagnose a hoarder, which I've deleted from this book. If you're a medical professional, you know it. If you're not, it is boring. My rough-and-tumble definition of how to know if you're a hoarder instead of a clutterer is (oddly enough) under the heading "Hoarding" (page 142).

A Clinical Psychologist's View

I get calls from people who I would classify as a rather heterogenic population. Some are depressed, some have some OCD (obsessive-compulsive disorder). When I did an interview recently for a local news station, the reporter kept wanting me to talk about OCD. But I found myself saying several times that it just isn't that easy to break people down into their primary disorders.

I don't see cluttering or hoarding as specific to one disorder. Even people who cannot be classified with a certifiable mental illness via the Diagnostic and Statistical Manual of Mental Disorders IV (DSMIV) may accumulate a great deal of stuff.

It seems to me that we fill our lives with stuff if we have some spiritual vacuum that alcohol, sex, drugs, etc., doesn't fill.

People are complicated. It's not easy to have quick and simple equations for cluttering that translate into easy solutions. I have wished for the magic wand of treatment so that I could wave it for many of my clients, including the clutterers. However, not making the money of an Oprah, and having the ethics of a profession that would not approve a "clean sweep" therapy approach, I work with them a week at a time, some as they sort and clean, coming in with a proud report. Then the next week, or the next month, when they come in tearfully reporting that it's "worse than ever," I work with them to gain some perspective, work on correcting black-and-white, all-or-nothing thinking that says, if they can't be perfect, don't try at all.

Some clutterers are recovering alcoholics, some not. Some are recovering sex addicts, some not. I am not the first therapist to believe that as people get closer to their core issues, the more anxiety it generates. Thus, a clutterer I see almost has an anxiety attack when her adult sister who lives out of state tells her she's coming there and they are going to clean and throw out all that stuff. The stuff is them, not just material possessions. They have not severed the attachment to the stuff. It's important, and their self-esteem feels as if it will be shattered, were someone to come in and begin throwing out carefully saved newspaper clippings, stuffed animals from childhood, or mom's silver spoon collection.

Therapy requires of us self-honesty. It requires looking at ourselves over and over again and correcting the incorrect perceptions that helped us survive growing up in our families. However, most of the time those models of childhood survival are not adaptive for us as adults.

—Linda Neal, clinical psychologist, PhD,
Oklahoma City, Oklahoma

Anxiety and Depression

Most people get depressed now and again, or have a little anxiety in their lives. But there seem to be more clutterers who consider themselves depressed than the general public. Different surveys will have different numbers, but it's pretty safe to accept that a little less than 10 percent of the U.S. adult population is depressed at any given time. Not all of these are actually seeking treatment, so it's a self-diagnosis. Of people who have actually been diagnosed as having a major depression, 85 percent were diagnosed as having generalized anxiety disorder (*www.healthyplace.com*). Great. Now, not only am I depressed, but I'm also anxious about it.

Anxiety

One medical definition of anxiety is "a feeling of apprehension with no obvious, immediate cause." A hoarder with such anxiety holds on to his possessions for no real reason. However, he may well have rationalizations for his behavior, such as, "It will come in handy someday," "These things cost good money; it would be a sin to waste them," and, "I was taught to 'waste not, want not.'"

Anxiety is not fear. Fear is a reaction to a definite threat. New York psychiatrist Dr. Anthony Cozzolino explained it to me as follows: A soldier in battle has fear—fear of loss of life, fear of not performing well. When you are attacked by a mugger, your fear is real and has a definite form. You fear losing your possessions or your life. When the mugger goes away, the fear is gone. Someone with an anxiety disorder will believe that every stranger from that point on is a potential mugger.

Anxiety is indefinite, vague. People with anxiety worry that the fabric that holds their world together will be rent. Sometimes, anxiety is normal. Anxiety precedes growth. We all have anxiety when we change or grow. A normal person experiences anxiety when she begins a new job or moves to a new house. Someone with neurotic anxiety believes the job will be terrible, and she will fail and be fired. She worries that the house will have hidden structural defects, the neighborhood will go to pot, or a gang will move in next door.

Depression

Depression affects more Americans than cancer, AIDS, or coronary heart disease—according to the National Institute of Mental Health (NIMH). An estimated 15 percent of chronic depression cases end in suicide. Women are twice as likely as men to be affected.

Major depression affects 15 percent of Americans at one point during their lives, according to the U.S. Department of Health and Human Services. Its effects can be so intense that things like eating, sleeping, or just getting out of bed become almost impossible.

My own survey of 879 clutterers came up with a clear picture of the link between cluttering and depression/anxiety, or of the link between depression/anxiety and cluttering. Nearly half of my respondents admitted to having experienced depression and most of them anxiety to boot. Of those who admitted it, 30 percent actually sought treatment. Both numbers are much higher than the population in general.

So does this mean there's no hope, and I should crawl back into the hole I was hiding in before you came, you ask? Nope, Kemo Sabe. In fact, there is great hope. I've seen it happen time and time again. Someone comes into a Clutterless meeting, about as sad as a puppy who has lost his mother, and, in a few months, actually laughs and seems more truly at peace with himself. I'd like to say that the same thing has happened after one of my seminars, but my momma told me, "You can go to Hell for lying, the same as stealing," so I won't.

But I can say this: I have had a couple of people whom I've met months after they attended my seminars who have told me they were happier (and less cluttered) than they'd been since they were children. One fellow actually shared (in public, no less) that after putting the principles of my seminar into practice, he'd cleared a *field* of junk cars (hah! You thought I was bad with just one). When the field was cleared, he ran through it giggling.

So what's the deal? Does the sound of my voice magically cure depression? Nah. Facing your clutter and actually doing something about it certainly helps one feel less depressed. Don't you think that staring at your cluttered house, day after day, has to take a toll on your mental health? It certainly did on mine.

From a practical standpoint, a cluttered room is a setup for depression. We're less likely to be depressed in a light, bright environment than in a darker one. Suicide rates are higher in winter, or in places with dreary climates (such as Seattle, one of my hometowns). If your clutter has covered the windows in your house, the light can't get in. Even if the windows aren't covered, your stuff is sucking up the light. Physical items absorb light. The more stuff there is, the more light gets absorbed. Have you ever been in an empty house? Didn't it appear much brighter?

There are many reasons for depression, and plenty of books on them all. I don't know your reasons for your depression, but I do know that not feeling in control or not feeling that you are able to accomplish any of your goals might be a couple. By making a commitment to yourself to do one little thing about your clutter, you're taking back control, and you're accomplishing a goal. Sure, a few lousy pieces of paper or a mere square foot of desk isn't much in the grand scheme of things, but in our cluttered lives, they're huge steps. They may be baby steps to some, but we are babies at decluttering.

Another rational aspect of why decluttering can help with your depression is exercise. Everybody agrees (usually a dangerous statement) that exercise helps with depression. Well, decluttering may not be as good as a walk in the park, but it is physical, and it is more than most of us have done in quite a while.

ADD?

Everything catches my attention... I could get one in red and blue and cordless and for my nephews... I've forgotten that I already have a turkey baster or an adequate supply of white T-shirts because I (a) didn't put them with the others I have or where it belongs, or (b) it's still dirty from when I used it in a painting project, back in the garage... This year's version of the black cardigan sweater is more attractive than last season's... At a flea market or auction, my impulsivity gets more play than my reasonable mind... I am distracted by the grocery stores' deliberate attempts to derail me from my shopping list when they stick a lip balm display in the cereal aisle.

—A clutterer with ADD

Clutterers often ask if cluttering is related to attention deficit disorder. You'll see this written as AD/HD, ADHD, and ADD. Someone could be diagnosed as having ADD or ADHD, depending on symptoms. There is some debate in the medical community about what acronym to use, and each is used for different reasons. For clarity, I've just used ADD, unless quoting someone who uses another acronym.

The only way to know if you have ADD is to be diagnosed by a physician, but the short answer is, it is statistically unlikely. According to the Attention Deficit Disorder Association (*www.add.org*), "Approximately 4 percent to 6 percent of the U.S. population has ADHD." (Dr. Kathleen G. Nadeau, PhD, author of *AD/HD in the Workplace*, says it could be as high as 10 percent.) We clutterers often have ADD-like tendencies, but so do many people, to some degree. It's a question of how we handle them. When we learn not to clutter, we aren't as distracted by these tendencies.

Labeling can be a first step to identifying something that can be treated. But it's not an excuse. Saying, "I have ADD, so you can't expect me to be organized," is not acceptable, as anyone who works with ADD patients will tell you.

There are many successful and productive people who have ADD. They've learned how to use their unique ways of looking at things to their advantage. You can too. Being a clutterer means you have a different way of viewing the world. We are going to teach you to turn those "liabilities" into assets. You are not "bad." You are not "hopelessly disorganized." You just don't learn the same way as other people, or respond to "traditional" organizing techniques.

Dr. Amie Ragan gives a perfect explanation of cluttering and ADD on her blog, *http://psychologyofclutter.wordpress.com* (used with permission): "In my clinical practice I see a fair number of adults who have attention deficit disorder (ADD). Most seem to have outgrown the hyperactivity part of attention deficit/hyperactivity disorder (AD/HD). Some still have it, and others never did." (To review the symptoms of ADD and ADHD, please read this article by the National Institute of Mental Health: *www.nimh.nih.gov/health/publications/adhd/complete-publication.shtml*.)

As adults, there are a couple of key features of attention deficit disorder that make it quite challenging when trying to manage clutter. One of the hallmarks of ADD is "difficulty organizing tasks and activities." When trying to tackle a clutter problem, you have to think through the steps. Cynthia Friedlob introduced me to the great term *backward cascade*. You first have to think about what you want, and then back through the process to figure out where to start.

For example, if you want to clean out your closet, first you have to clear off your bed. You also need to be prepared with bags or boxes to put discards and donations in, or you will simply cause more piles. Someone with ADD may have the noble goal of cleaning out her closet, only to be discouraged by the state of her bedroom when she is done: Unwanted clothes piled on the floor in one corner. Donated coats and purses in another. *Never mind the stuff that shouldn't have been in the closet to start with—where does that go?*

Another reason why ADD and disorganization go hand-in-hand is the symptom of being easily distracted by extraneous stimuli. Someone might have the best of intentions, and start to clean out her refrigerator. The phone rings, she answers. After 30 minutes on the phone, she walks back to find that she left the refrigerator door open and the dog has helped himself to dinner. Instead of cleaning the fridge, now she has to mop the floor simply to have some sense of general cleanliness. No time left to clean the fridge.

Finally, for those bigger projects such as closets, cleaning cars, or basements, one of the major symptoms, difficulty sustaining attention in tasks, is a deal-breaker. The person with ADD will ping from one thing to the next often getting very little accomplished, although a great deal of effort has been exerted.

This is the reason many people with ADD are accused of being lazy—they never seem to get anything accomplished. However, if you watch someone with ADD, she is like a nonstop motion machine. This is with or without the hyperactivity piece. Being hyperactive just makes everything worse.

So is the person with ADD doomed to a life of clutter? Absolutely not. He does have additional challenges, but certainly he can overcome them with help. Most psychologists and therapists are trained to help people manage their symptoms.

Some professional organizers are even certified via additional training to help people with ADD. You can go to the National Association of Professional Organizers (NAPO) and click the "Public" tab. Then go to the left-side bar and click "Find An Organizer." You can select "Attention Deficit" as a specialty, and the NAPO Website will match you with organizers in your area.

If you are not yet ready to hire an organizer, please consider purchasing the book *Organizing Solutions for People With Attention Deficit Disorder: Tips and Tools to Help You Take Charge of Your Life and Get Organized*, by Susan C. Pinsky, or *Survival Tips for Women with AD/HD: Beyond Piles, Palms, & Post-its*, by Terry Matlen. The authors of both books have wisely written their information in mentally digestible chunks to accommodate short attention spans.

In addition, if you are not being treated with medication, talk to your psychiatrist or primary medical doctor. There are plenty of stimulant and non-stimulant, adult-friendly ADD medications on the market these days. You will either need a history of a formal diagnosis or go through some testing to ensure that you do have ADD before getting a prescription, of course. The bottom line is that your home can become better organized, and you will be more effective in school, work, and life.

Hoarding

Whether cluttering is a less-developed degree of hoarding is subject to debate. I do know that I have been in contact with several hundred clutterers in the past eight years. Some have been borderline hoarders. I've seen two of them "graduate" to hoarders. I've known four full-blown hoarders. One seemed to make progress in decluttering. So, out of several hundred clutterers, fewer than a dozen, at the most, have been hoarders. That's maybe 1 percent of a population that should be ripe for a diagnosis.

Cluttering is not the same as hoarding, but hoarding is more dramatic, so the people you see on TV shows are more often hoarders than not. I have been interviewed on a few TV shows myself, but have been asked to the prom more often than I've danced. The booking person always asks me to find someone who is really, really bad, so their show will be more dramatic. I know very few clutterers or hoarders who are willing to have their mess shown on TV, but the shows always find someone. Frankly, the degree of disorder is immaterial in terms of changing the behavior. But good TV and good sense don't always go together.

If you're a hoarder, it's unlikely that even a book as good as this one, by itself, is going to help you much. I've worked with a few hoarders in the past several years and, frankly, am not sure I did them much good. So if you have a family member who's a hoarder, God bless you. This book will give you a layman's glimpse into some of the corners of their minds, but not all. A clutterer's mental attic at least has more lights on, so you can see your way around the boxes of mental eddies. A site that I like about hoarding, because it is human and addresses the emotional pain of the children of hoarders, is *www.childrenofhoarders.com/bindex.php*.

Hoarding is a medical diagnosis. *Cluttering* is a layman's term. John P. Zak, MD, associate professor and director of clinical services at the University of South Florida's Department of Psychiatry, gave me this distinction: "The definitions of *hoarding* and *cluttering* are not clear; especially comparatively speaking. Probably clutterers can purge or 'excavate' the clutter with little or no anxiety/irritability involved. A hoarder finds it very difficult to get rid of the stuff without the occurrence of severe distress unless it is done in a very systematic, well-planned-out, therapeutic approach."

Dr. Randy Frost, whom I have had the pleasure of being with on a radio interview show, is another of the authorities on hoarding. He's the author of several papers and books on the subject. He defined compulsive hoarding as "the acquisition of and failure to discard possessions that appear to be useless or of limited value."

If your house/apartment is unsanitary, chances are you are a hoarder. (This means regularly, not just that you are a bachelor and didn't get around to taking out the old pizza boxes for a couple of weeks.)

The Good News

Dr. Zak believes that:

It is possible that a hoarder can completely recover without ongoing therapy. It is probably dependent on the quality of the therapy initially, and the personality structure of the individual hoarder. We must keep in mind that there is no absolute point at which we can determine what is hoarding and what is not. If there are absolutely no saving or collecting behaviors, we can state there is complete success, but if there are any of those behaviors, the perception of getting better lies within the individual—for example, if the person feels comfortable and experiences no dysfunction due to the minimal behavior.

Obsessive-Compulsive Disorder

There are several criteria that must be met to qualify a behavior as a case of OCD: The action (in this case, hoarding) must cause marked distress, be time-consuming (occupying more than an hour a day), or significantly interfere with one's occupational functioning or usual social routines.

Dr. Gail Steketee is one of the nation's leading experts on hoarding. She is professor and chair and interim dean at the Boston University School of Social Work. She has more than 20 years of research experience and is the coauthor of *Buried in Treasures: Help for Compulsive Acquiring, Saving, and Hoarding*, with Dr. David Tolin and Dr. Randy Frost, and *Treatment of Compulsive Hoarding*, with Dr. Randy Frost. She and Teresa Pigott, MD, were co-editors of what I think is the best primer on OCD for the layperson: *Obsessive Compulsive Disorder, The Latest Assessment and Treatment Strategies*. According to Dr. Steketee, "OCD is an anxiety-based condition. Hoarding has elements of both anxiety and impulse-control problems. Saving excessively can be driven by fear, and is compulsive. Impulsive alcoholics and overeaters have a drive to do something, and they overdo it. They drink too much or overeat because it is pleasurable. In many cases, this applies to the acquisition aspect of hoarding. Many people buy things they want even though [they] don't have a place for them. They have an appetite that is not fear-related."

Jean Goodwin, a Galveston, Texas, psychiatrist, calls hoarding "a knotty problem." She notes that psychodynamic treatment approaches (those based on the theories of Freud and his followers) are still useful, but are often combined with behavioral or cognitive therapies. In psychodynamic therapy, the emphasis is on the patient's relationships with others, and on a wide-ranging exploration of the psyche. In cognitive-behavioral therapy, specific coping and motivational strategies are emphasized. Goodwin believes that hoarding may be intertwined with other issues, such as low self-esteem, passivity, hesitation, and self-doubt.

"Cleaning is a common OCD symptom. Paradoxically, messiness, or not cleaning, can be a way to cope with the same set of obsessions," Goodwin says. Drug therapy is sometimes indicated. Because the medications take about three months to reach their maximum effectiveness, there must be "a good deal of commitment," on the part of the patient, Goodwin says.

The obsession of a hoarder to hoard things (whatever the reason) causes anxiety. He feels compelled to relieve the pain of the anxiety, but doesn't have the tools to do so. His behavior is not conscious. A hoarder's feeling of lack of control over his life—anxiety—results in his exerting control over his possessions. The irony of this is that the possessions end up causing more anxiety in his home life, paralyzing him.

Community Health Issues

Dr. Stotland notes that cluttering can significantly affect the community at large, "particularly [in cases of] psychotic patients, who may be kicked out of their housing because of all the clutter. They are not necessarily hoarding particular things." Also, community health officials are often called when someone's hoarding causes a significant odor, or when abandoned appliances and junk cars pose a danger to children in the community.

Sometimes, when the police are called in on domestic disputes, they see a situation of hoarding that requires social services to come out. There have been cases of families losing their children because of the unsanitary conditions.

I personally counseled a hoarder whose cluttering had brought him to the attention of the police. It started with shopping carts. He had two dozen behind his apartment. This led to the manager's knocking on his door. When she saw the clutter inside, she threatened to evict him. They got into a brawl. The shopping cart dilemma was easy to fix; there are services in large cities that collect the carts for stores. (The stores are happy to get them back and rarely prosecute the hoarder. If you have a stash of shopping carts, call a store manager and he will tell you what to do.) The assault charges and the eviction were more difficult to resolve. The man entered counseling, and eventually got better.

I've also worked with hoarders in their homes, some of whom were getting therapy. It's only safe to say that one got significantly better clutter-wise.

If animal control has been called because you have dozens of cats or dogs in a small living space, you're probably an animal hoarder. I am an animal lover and am involved with animal rescue, so this is a hard one for me to mention. I know people who have 20 rescued cats. I know people who have no-kill shelters on their property. But they have the room to do this. They live in the country, or at least have a few acres of land. That's humane. I know people who temporarily foster three or four dogs until they can be adopted. That's humane. More than 20 cats (it's more often cats than dogs, though animal hoarders could hoard any kind of animal) in an apartment, or even a house, is probably animal hoarding. Even 10 is pushing it. This, to me, is the saddest type of hoarding. Not only is the person and his family affected, but innocent animals are too. The only possible good thing about this scenario is that it should make it easier for people to understand that cluttering and hoarding are so often about love—or the lack thereof. Unfortunately, it's also about control. But whoever thinks he's in control over 20 cats doesn't know cats.

I did a radio show with WLS in Chicago once that lasted for three hours. One subject that came up was animal hoarding. After that, there were a lot of callers who kept their dead pets in the freezer for the winter until the weather thawed enough to bury them. Interesting as that was, I don't think it qualifies as animal hoarding. But then, I guess it would depend on the number of pets in the freezer, wouldn't it?

10 | Unpack Your Stuff With TCI

You can use this very brief primer on TCI, the Temperament Character Inventory, on your cluttering situation and see how it works for you. I believe it is a valuable tool in our decluttering arsenal. If this works for you, then you'll want to get Dr. Cloninger's book, *Feeling Good: The Science of Well-Being*. It addresses living a whole, fulfilled life. We've just adapted part of the concept here and applied it to changing our cluttering habits. Dr. Kathleen M. Wong, who once served as an assistant professor on a medical school faculty, works with clutterers among her patients, and she has recommended the previous edition of *Stop Clutter From Stealing Your Life* to them.

The following text was contributed by Dr. Wong, currently a psychiatrist in private practice in Fayetteville, Arkansas. Please note this does not constitute medical advice; it is a discussion of another means to understand cluttering and its causes.

The Temperament Character Inventory was developed throughout 20 years by C. Robert Cloninger, a psychiatrist who is the director of the Center for the Psychobiology of Personality, Sansone Center for Well-Being at the Washington University in St. Louis School of Medicine (https://psychobiology.wustl.edu). It is a tool utilized by mental health workers and others to understand the makeup of a person's personality. You can research the survey yourself and see the extent of related investigations and applications.

We're going to look at the factors it measures and how they might contribute to clutter. Further, we'll examine some constructive approaches to help someone quantitatively shift from one relationship to another approach, and, it is hoped, LESS CLUTTER!

The "T" in "TCI" is for Temperament—roughly a set of behavioral inclinations that are thought in part to be hard-wired, genetic (as I say, "your grandparents shining through you"), and fairly consistent throughout one's lifetime. Certain parts of you are true to the person you were in high school, and will be true of you at your 99th birthday party.

Let's briefly introduce each of the four factors. Of note, I want you to realize that it isn't a matter of maximizing or minimizing any of the factors. One doesn't "score high on all the 'bad' factors and low on all the 'good' factors." In fact, I want you to appreciate that the difficulties rest in the extremes—either too high or too low. That's when something may be more prominent—and more problematic in your functioning. Modulation—a slight shift toward the counterbalancing tendency—may make your relationship with stuff (clutter) less troubling and more favorable.

Novelty-Seeking: A Measure of Anger-Proneness

If low, you are more rigid, regimented, structured...organized! If you have a clutter problem, it might arise from holding fast to old rules, from doing it the same time every time—perhaps you're holding on to items because You're Supposed To...and perhaps, with revisiting with a new eye, you'll realize that there really isn't a service in that holding-on to old rules, etc.

If high, you are attracted to the new and the novel, perhaps the flashy. (You are more enthusiastic, impulsive, and extravagant.) You are less rule-bound and more excitable; by nature less conventionally organized; "disorderly" by some standards. Your attentions are inclined outward—so turning inward to contemplate yourself or the chaotic contents of the Everything Drawer is more of a challenge. In fact, the thought of the pristine, well-appointed orderly home might be...boring! So you see how we would want to corral your belongings broadly so that you can utilize and enjoy them better, save money, and find them more easily. We also need to recognize that this is in your nature, neither good nor bad.

Harm Avoidance: A Measure of Anxiety-Proneness

If low, you are less fearful, less prone to worry or fatigue, less cautious. Your clutter might arise out of a casual approach to your material environment, perhaps merely a lack of attention or concern...leaving the plate on the couch because I'm finished eating off of it...or the socks by the bed or the towel on the floor, or the empty soda can on the counter...

If high, then you are prone to fearfulness, fear of strangers, fear of the future, and fear of being hurt. These fears can serve well...or can paralyze you. OCD is rooted in this, and probably the majority of clutter cases. These folks are great at the "What If?" which had my Great Depression era/WWII, rationing grandparents stocked with reams of toilet paper and skids of canned peas (bought on sale!). I exaggerate, but you get the picture. Individuals high in Harm Avoidance often learn in one lesson: ONCE I had a party and ran out of drink cups...NEVER again will I run out of drink cups (or extra shoelaces, or out-of-state phone books, or paper clips, or gray socks). The individual with high Harm Avoidance has difficulty making decisions—so I can't decide which boots to keep and which to pass on. Many suggestions could be offered here (in the interest of space, I invite you to test yourself; push the comfort zone a bit). What if I don't *save every rubber band, what if I give away half my stationery supplies? Realize you can live without it, that you can tolerate—and maybe even be perfectly fine—without it.*

Take baby steps to gradually increase your levels of "discomfort." Take something out, record your feelings in your Decluttering Diary and watch your overall emotional level. It will probably rise as your level of physical clutter declines. If you get to the point that it's becoming seriously uncomfortable—i.e., you're taking too many things out the back door—then slow down. Get back to a level that's comfortable for you.

Reward Dependence: A Measure of a Social Dynamic

If high, this individual is more inclined to the "sentimental value" of things. Clutter may be an issue for holding on to items no longer useful or working, because Aunt Maisie gave it to me, or it's a big designer name (that cost me too much), but see, see, look at me have it! These people may hold on to birthday cards and mementos. Be deliberate and discriminating in these selections. Challenge yourself to be more practical, perhaps coolly calculating the worth of things, or being more realistic about available storage space and future service of the items in question.

If low, you may be more clinical, detached, and aloof in your interactions. You are more independent in your opinion, perhaps preferring to avoid dealing with many other people. It may be that your clutter creates company for you. You are less tuned than the individual described above to the social costs of disorder. Motivation for decluttering will have to arise from practical considerations for safety or convenience.

Persistence: A Measure of Ambition

Persistence is how we deal with a situation of intermittent reinforcement, a measure of how we deal with obstacles. I see persistence as a personal decision of how to apply our resources (time, money, muscle, attention...). I envision a poker hand. Persistence is the prudence behind the "Hold 'Em or Fold 'Em" question: Do I stick with this, or give up? At either extreme, clutter could trip us up. If persistence is too low, we may not be motivated to stick with anything, more inclined to put our energies toward a different task (such as surfing the Web), rather than folding laundry or sorting boxes of accumulated mail and papers. This is where I invite small, regular tasks to build your Persistence muscle—such as sorting the mail, ASAP, every single day—to work to conquer the clutter. Stick with a task, even after you've lost heart. Go back to the pile of whatever you'd been trying to make sense of—keep on with your clutter-busting a little bit more. Carve out a shelf or half a desk as your target, not the entire back room!

If persistence is too high, you may not be able to let go. "Gee, I was holding on to to those torn satin pants because the kids might use the fabric in an art project..." Let it go! You do not *need to keep every T-shirt or cocktail napkin from every place you've ever gone on vacation. Your clutter problem might derive from perfectionism: If I can't organize this material perfectly, it's not worth trying. So let yourself be okay with earnest attempts and well-intentioned efforts—you may find yourself pleasantly surprised!*

There's the spiritual aspect, which is equally important, but this short introduction will give you an idea of whether this is something that will help you with your cluttering.

11 | Alternatives to TV-Style Forced Decluttering

As you have probably guessed by now, I'm not a fan of TV shows that force clutterers (or hoarders) to get rid of their stuff. Neither are most clutterers I've talked to—and I talk to a lot of them. Neither are most of the medical professionals I talked with.

In fairness, some people who are cluttered enjoy those shows too, perhaps because they've given up on ever doing anything about their own cluttering. People who aren't clutterers think these shows are great, not because the people are cruel, but because they see a problem (a really disorganized house) and a solution (a neat and clean house). What I see are the human beings behind the clutter. The families who "volunteer" their relatives for these shows do so out of love and desperation. They just don't know what else to do. God bless them for caring.

I enjoy it when Oprah does a show on hoarders or clutterers. She's done more for daytime television, elevating the level of programming and addressing important issues, than anyone else. Oprah does also get a psychiatrist to come in, which shows that her heart is in the right place.

Oprah seems to have compassion, and she cares enough about these people to have them on her show and get them help. The organizers, however, seem to me to grandstand, and make entertainment out of public humiliation. Watch the faces of the audience members the next time you view one of these shows. You'll see a lot of shock and awe, but not a lot of understanding or compassion.

I have to admit that the hoarders pictured on these shows have some pretty serious problems. Where I differ from the "gurus" is that I respect the individuals enough to help them make changes in their behaviors themselves. I've seen the "expert" become frustrated and order the clutterer or hoarder to do something. Yeah, that works for the show, but how well do you think it works for the human being? I may be a very small voice, but I believe I'm speaking for us—real clutterers—when I say there are alternative ways to help.

I've personally known clutterers and hoarders who were forced to declutter on somebody else's timeline, though none who've been on national TV. Within a year, often less time, they were just as cluttered, and *more* possessive about their possessions, vowing never to let someone take them away again. Yes, I know that the show "Clean House" did a follow-up, and most folks (the ones they aired anyway) did keep their houses neater than before, but there's something in psychology called the Hawthorne effect. Essentially, it states that if people know they are being watched or evaluated, they will do "better." My own experience is that many clutterers who have had someone declutter their house felt violated, and hated the people who did it.

All that being said, I did a TV show with Debra Duncan in Houston, and I worked with a woman the right way, so that *she* made the decisions about what to get rid of, and we made tremendous progress. We decluttered a chair, which stayed "sacred" at least for the weeks between taping and airing. No, it ain't dramatic, but it is realistic.

The show was popular and aired four or five times afterward. I will admit that they did have to cut out the visualization part; that's about as exciting to watch as paint drying, but they did show that visualization was part of the process. I've been asked to be on some national TV shows where the host was a professional, and those involved said they wanted to seriously explore the problem, but none came to fruition. All of the clutterers I talked to were afraid that they

> **Wikipedia Says This About *Clean Sweep: Makeover Reactions***
>
> Some family members become emotional or even angry.... One such case featured [name deleted out of respect] and her daughter. This woman was so mad during the "reveal" of the makeover, she began crying and shouted, "I hate it, I hate all of it, I just want to leave!" The show claims that usually everyone is happy.

would be humiliated on air, because that was all they'd seen. I don't blame them, so I didn't try to talk anyone into it. I'd rather not be on a show than take a chance of harming someone emotionally.

I was on a show with Linda Cobb, the "Queen of Clean," a syndicated show on the DIY Network, and she understood and wanted real information on how to help people. So, not all TV hosts or shows are insensitive, just the most popular ones.

There Is an Alternative

The alternative way to stop your relative from cluttering is not as dramatic, and it's not good TV, but it is more humane. Because I am involved with animal rescue, I see an analogy there: There are two ways to combat the overpopulation of pets. The slower, but more humane way is to educate the public on spaying and neutering, and making these services available at low cost. The more dramatic, better-TV-ratings way, is to kill the offspring of un-spayed or non-neutered animals. Both achieve the goal—if the goal is reducing the population of animals in shelters. But the first stops the problem at its source, so there won't be more residents the next day. The second treats the symptoms. With that in mind, it was refreshing to encounter Dr. Amie Ragan's blog at *http://psychologyofclutter.wordpress.com*. Dr. Ragan works with clutterers and hoarders, and understands the psychology behind our behaviors. Here is a story, used with permission, that explains the right way to help someone with a serious cluttering problem.

The key points are that the clutterer decided what to eliminate, that her need to pass the things on where they would do some good for someone else were met, the clutterer's desire to shop again was met, and a compromise was reached. It's a rare clutterer who can stop shopping cold turkey, but we can slow it down and eventually stop bringing clutter in.

Ho-Ho-Holy Cow Look At All This Christmas Stuff!

I love Christmas decorations as much as the next person, but oh my goodness! Last year, while visiting a friend, I staged a one-person, impromptu intervention.

Let me set the scene: I stepped through the front door and was startled out of my skin by "Frosty the Snowman" blasting from the motion-detector snowman sitting next to the door. Putting my hand on the wall to balance myself—WAS A HAPPY JOLLY SOUL—I knocked off a Rudolph tapestry. Trying to recover my balance and stop the reindeer needlepoint from hitting the crystal nativity scene on the end table—AND TWO EYES MADE OUT OF COAL—I backed into the Christmas tree. Of course Frosty started blaring again, ornaments went flying, and I knocked the train circling under the tree off its tracks—THUMPTY THUMP THUMP, LOOK AT FROSTY GO.

*"What the heck (I didn't say heck) is going on in here?" I looked around, and not a single inch of my friend's living room was void of some form of Christmas paraphernalia. In addition to the snowman, tapestry, nativity, tree, and train, there were tons of lights, garlands, window stickers, old Christmas cards on a string, and a full Christmas town displayed on the once-functional coffee table. "It's Christmastime," my friend replied. "No shoot (**I didn't say** shoot). We need to talk."*

My friend loves Christmas. I do too, so I get the excitement. The problem comes in when she adds to her treasure chest of Christmas decorations every year. This happens when new stuff hits the store. Gotta have that! After-Christmas sales trigger more spending. What a bargain! In addition to what she buys, she gets Christmas stuff as gifts. Makes sense; she loves it, and it's in the stores at the right time. No deep thought and months of planning required for buying her a present.

*The problem is that my friend's living room, kitchen, guest bath, and dining room all become marginally functional due to the overwhelming amount of Christmas crap. She admits that she doesn't necessarily enjoy all the stuff, but doesn't know how to decide when she's put out enough. She simply pulls out the **17 (no joke) Rubbermaid bins** from the garage and the attic, and starts decorating.*

*After a long talk about how she wanted to get rid of things, but throwing Christmas stuff away felt really wrong, we came up with a plan. We went through and put everything that had sentimental value away, back in the bins. There were honestly **11 bins** of things that my friend could not bear to part with. Everything else was left out.*

From our discussion, which she called "free therapy," she decided to call a local battered women's shelter and invited the director over for lunch with the understanding that she would be donating decorations. Rather than deciding for her, the director was allowed to come over and choose those things that she felt would be able to spruce up the shelter without being overwhelming. **She left with two bins.**

Next to be invited was the executive director of a nursing home that is less than a mile from my friend's house. Same process, **three more bins gone.** The **last bin** worth of stuff was odds and ends that were gladly and graciously accepted by a low-income day care center downtown.

We came up with themes when we put away, in the 11 bins, for what she decided to keep. There was the blasted Frosty bin, a Rudolph bin, three Santa bins, a bin for Christmas linens (including towels, bed sheets, and tablecloths), and a bin for Christmas dishes. Three bins of Christmas ornaments. And one miscellaneous bin full of mostly handmade Christmas gifts and cards her children had made when they were young. She readily agreed that not everything from every bin need be displayed, but a few things from each would be sufficient. I think I was able to convince her that by doing this she would only be using items every few years thereby making them "new" again when their turn came due.

"So really, you don't need to buy any more Christmas stuff. Just admire it in the store and leave it there." She countered with "How about one thing a year?" I knew I was asking too much so I said, "Sure, one thing. Shop carefully and relish the purchase."

As I left, my friend's husband grabbed me in a big old bear hug and said, "You're a blessing; truly a blessing." I don't know about that, but this year I hope to be able to visit my friend at Christmastime without first checking to make sure my health insurance is paid.

12 | Living With Cluttering Kids and Spouses

With all thy faults, I love thee still.

—Samuel Butler

As clutter relates to families, I cannot tell you how many people I have met whose marriages are threatened by clutter.

—Jan Jasper, professional organizer

> *We credit these meetings* [Clutterless] *with saving our marriage. When Grace saw it in the paper, I figured, what the hell, nothing else has worked, why not try this? I didn't intend to come in, but Grace wanted me for company. We've both been coming back for three years now, and look forward to the meetings.*
>
> *Besides the companionship of other people with the same problem, just knowing you're not alone makes a big difference. Grace clutters; I don't, but I feel I get as much out of the meetings and your book as she does.*
>
> *Being able to understand why she's having such a struggle with decluttering has made a big difference in our relationship. I tell you, I was about to walk out the door when we found this. We make good money, and live in a beautiful home, and yet I was ashamed*

to have anyone over. It was like we had two different lives—our public life and our private one. We lived like we were junk collectors.

We've learned that Grace clutters because of other things going on in her life, and I have learned to be supportive without being a nag.

I'd like to say that everything is perfect, that we've completely decluttered our home, but that's not the case. I can see where she's made some progress and appreciate the effort she puts in, even when the results seem small. At least there is more going out than coming in now. Our home is decluttered enough to have friends over, though it is still cluttered.

More importantly, our marriage is on a more solid footing. We understand each other more now because she understands my frustration and I understand hers. Together we do something to ease each other's burden.

—Bill and Grace, clutterers

Let's face it: Clutter can be just as destructive to a relationship as anything else. The whole family is affected. The adults are ashamed of the way they live, and can't have friends or even other family over. The kids are ashamed of the way their family lives, and they won't have other kids over. It's a no-win situation for everyone. Cluttering is about control. In a household with a clutterer and non-clutterers, the clutterer always wins.

Married to a Clutterer

Married clutterers often grew into the cluttered relationship they have now. When you and your spouse first met, neither of you may have been old enough to have had a lot of clutter. Being a successful clutterer takes time. And aren't single people (especially males) expected to be messy? So basically, who knew?

Later, as you got more and more stuff, clutter just kind of crept in. It took time to become a problem, and by then you just didn't know what to do about it. As the husband of a clutterer said to me, "You don't throw someone away like a broken toy when they become sick. You still love them. You do the best you can, even when you don't know what to do. Finally, you just give up and hope for a miracle." (One man diagnosed with OCD told me that he didn't see how someone could live with a hoarder and not become one. His example was that his wife, who was the hoarder, started to collect hubcaps. Gradually, he began stopping on the freeway to pick up hubcaps to bring to her.)

Nagging never works, so why do we do it? We nag because we don't know what else to do. When our only tool is a hammer, we treat everything as a nail. Nagging often becomes the tool of choice for the nonclutterer. "If you would just listen to me, things would be better. Why can't you just take my advice?" Anyone who has ever lived with a nagging spouse knows how much sexual attraction there is in such a relationship. The clutterer hears the "gentle suggestions" as disapproval, and feels misunderstood. The clutterer also often feels that he or she can punish the nagging spouse by continuing the behavior.

The suggestions that follow can help resolve some of these issues, but this is a long-term situation to resolve, and it will not happen overnight.

Clutterers Married to Each Other

For clutterers married to each other, each one sees the other's clutter as "a real mess," and will be sure to point that out. The complaining, self-righteous one will soon blame his or her clutter on the weaker one:

"If only you weren't such a slob, I could clean up this mess."

"Your clutter is as bad as mine."

"No it isn't."

"Yes it is."

Nyah, nyah, nyah. And so it goes. Separate bedrooms are a requirement in such households, because there is only space for one person in any bed. If the couple lives in a one-bedroom apartment, one spouse ends up on the couch permanently. The couch becomes a nest, adding impossibility to the common area. If one spouse starts to clean up, the other will mess it up out of spite, like crabs in a bucket that pull any crab trying to make a break for it back into the bucket.

Dating

Remember when I mentioned that our beds are usually littered with books, magazines, dirty dishes, clothes, and so on? It doesn't take a PhD in psychology to figure out that this is a great way to avoid intimacy. Can you imagine meeting the man or woman of your dreams at a party, dazzling him or her with your wit and charm, and then inviting him or her to a boudoir that is more like a garbage dump? To even get there he or she would have to traverse the minefield of your living room, being careful to stay on the poorly marked paths to the bedroom. Forget it! Mood is everything in seduction, and you can't light candles because you might burn the place down!

One clutterer, whose problem had not become completely overwhelming, told me, "If it wasn't for dates, my house would never get picked up." Many clutterers simply use their clutter as a shield to keep people out of their lives, and ensure that no real intimacy ever develops.

Most single clutterers I know have such low self-esteem that they don't really date. They are so ashamed of the way they live that they do not invite even friends over, much less dates. Yet most clutterers are nice people, caring and supportive. They would make wonderful mates. They are sensitive, and, though they have isolated themselves, would secretly love to have a relationship with something other than their clutter. Our problem is that we have replaced people with things. We have denied ourselves love by surrounding ourselves with our self-loathing. We have traded intimacy for monuments to our insecurity.

Kid Clutter

Kids who grow up in cluttering families can go either way—they can become clutterers themselves, or excessively neat adults. While they are in the family, they can contribute to the problem or be part of the solution.

Much of what follows applies to both children and spouses (although you should probably not tell your spouse that).

Adults

Cluttering is often about control. Adults can control the other spouse (though probably without realizing it) through the cluttered common areas and cluttered bedroom. There's often a passive-aggressive aspect to cluttering that affects the dynamics of relationships. A spouse who is unhappy with life in general, or the home environment, but doesn't feel empowered to verbalize it, can express that discontent through cluttering up the house.

Once you and your spouse start working on the clutter, long-hidden emotions might come to the forefront. It might be tempting to keep the status quo, such that the disagreements were about the stuff rather than what's really bothering you, but most therapists would tell you that communication is important to a successful relationship.

The other side of this is that the cluttering spouse may feel that she has no control over the outside world (the same as kids), so she feels that she can control her home environment by cluttering, yet not be conscious of the effect it's having on the home or the relationship.

Kids

There are two sides to the battle for control with kids. Parents may try to control their kids by dictating what's acceptable and what's not, in terms of neatness. Children who chafe at that control may use their cluttering as a way of fighting back. In this scenario, both sides are fighting over control, not neatness.

Children feel they have very little control over their lives. Toddlers have the least, teenagers the most. But even with teens, most of their lives are directed and controlled by others. It's common for parents to use an analogy that a child's job is to go to school, just as an adult's job is to go to the workplace. Although this may work with smaller children, teens and precocious preteens will question this.

Adults have some control over their choice of work; children have none whatsoever. They go to the schools their parents choose, are taught what the administration decrees, and are rewarded according to a set of values they had no say in creating. The only control they have is whether to do the work or not. Doing it returns a positive reward, though the value of the reward may not be sufficient to motivate them. Not doing it returns a negative reward, which may seem more rewarding to them.

So it can be with their possessions. Regardless of what techniques you use to motivate your children, they need to feel that they have control over the "things" in their lives. Whether they choose to exercise that control in a negative or positive way is dependent, to a large extent, on how you, as a parent, motivate them.

Defining Control

It's a conundrum. If an adult or child chooses to clutter as an expression of controlling his environment, he *apparently* achieves control, but, in fact, loses it. When we let our stuff define us, we give power (control) to the stuff. If your children choose to keep their rooms messy, the mess determines a large part of their interaction with the family and robs them of true freedom. People's physical environment affects them, whether they're aware of it or not.

Clutter creates confusion and chaos on an emotional level. It fogs the mind, making it harder to do schoolwork or make decisions. Clutter's promise of control is an empty one. The clutter controls the reactions of their parents. If parents spend more time grousing about their children's messy rooms than complimenting them for a neat one, they're encouraging messiness. Negative attention is better than no attention.

When they leave their messes in the family areas, the children, in effect, control the whole family. They see the reaction of family members and gain a sense of power from having determined the condition of the house.

The same is true for adults. When the cluttered spouse maintains the clutter, she maintains control. Families walk around the clutter. They've learned that picking up after an adult leads to confrontations or emotional outbursts. For the sake of peace, they've forgone harmony.

Communication Is the Key to Changing Perceptions of Control

Do you feel that you spend way too much time complaining and nagging (wait, you never nag, you only make suggestions...sorry) your children or spouse to "do something about this mess"? How well has that worked so far?

The biggest problem with any behavior disorder is a parent's fear of addressing the underlying causes. There's a fear of inadequacy, fear that emotions are wrong. They have to get over the designations of right and wrong when it comes to emotions. Emotions aren't wrong. They just are.

—Kim Arrington Cooper, M.Ed.,
family counselor and neurobehavioral psychometrist, UTMB

Accentuate the Positive

My mother always saw the positive side of events. My father always saw the negative. She was happier and has lived longer. Psychologist Dr. Richard Wiseman, author of *The Luck Factor*, said that people who look on the bright side tend to be luckier, happier, and have more friends. By focusing on the positive, we have more positive experiences. Who knows? Maybe looking for the good in your clutterer's efforts will help you the next time you go to Las Vegas (although, to be honest, Dr. Wiseman says that is a different form of luck, but I believe that a positive attitude helps there too).

When your children or spouse actually pick up, recycle, or throw away something, congratulate them. If they've slipped into the negative mindset of cluttering, any improvement is a big hurdle for them to leap. We don't just wake up one morning and decide to change a lifetime of habits. We change slowly, replacing old beliefs with new ones.

The Compliment Two-Step

The Texas two-step is a fun country-western dance. The *compliment* two-step goes nowhere. "Boy, that's great, Johnnie. You picked your schoolwork up off the dining-room table!" (a forward step). "*But*" (whenever we place *but* as the first word in a sentence, we negate the entire previous sentiment), "why didn't you get those books off the end table?" (a backwards step). Instead, learn to stop with the first step. Clutterers will eventually learn to declutter for the inner (intrinsic) rewards that being neater gives them. At first, though, extrinsic rewards from family members will have much greater value. If they get negative praise, they'll feed into the negativity, thinking, "Even when I make an effort, it's not appreciated. I might as well not have tried. Nobody appreciates how hard that was."

If your spouse is the clutterer in question, I know it's hard to get excited about a tiny bit of progress. Your whole house probably looks as though you just moved in, or are moving out. (If you've got a hoarder in the family, your house will look like you should be evicted.) One stack of papers moved, a few newspapers recycled, or a book put away doesn't make a visible difference. When you're in the mindset of seeing only the mess, you can understand what a clutterer's life is like. We see the big picture—the whole house or room. We feel that we can't declutter the whole house; it's just too overwhelming. What we eventually learn is to see the individual piles of clutter and to narrow our focus.

Communicate Using *I*—With Both Spouses and Kids

Orders work just fine in the military; families are more akin to the United Nations. I understand that sometimes gentle persuasion doesn't get the job done.

Psychologists often have different ideas about how to approach things. Yet this is one area where most agree. When you make a statement using *you* or *your [action]*, you seldom get the results you want. *You* did this or that implies blame. Nobody wants to be blamed. Most people, including children, want to help. When your child is in a rebellious stage, you can throw that sentence out the window, but we'll have ways to cope with that later. Meanwhile, we'll assume that your children aren't perfecting their "whatever rebellious idol is popular at the moment" impressions yet.

The key points are to use *I* statements instead of *you* or *you should* statements, and to get your children to talk about how they feel about their clutter.

Not only were all our conversations turning into arguments, I was also telling my children over and over again not to trust their own perceptions, but to rely on mine instead.

—Adele Faber and Elaine Mazlish, from
How to Talk So Kids Will Listen & Listen So Kids Will Talk

Instead of: "You're a slob. Why can't you clean this room up?" Try (for kids): "I understand that your room is an expression of who you are. It's part of your individuality. But don't you think this room has created a new standard for messiness?" If you get a "nah" or some other form of negative grunt, try another approach: "This messy room bothers me. What can we do to make it neater?" Try (for adults): "I know how hard it is to declutter and that you don't want me to rearrange your stuff. Can we take just this small area of the room and work on it together? We won't make any changes unless you agree."

Although nothing may get discarded the first few times you do this, after a while, you will have built up a trust level so that your suggestions will be taken more seriously and less threateningly than before.

Kids and Rebellion

Dr. Michael Bradley, Ed.D, noted psychologist and nationally recognized expert on parenting, and author of *Yes, Your Teen Is Crazy!* and *The Heart & Soul of the Next Generation*, in an interview, put it this way: "Have the kids separate the rebellion aspect. You might have the Starbucks conversation [at a neutral place away from the home]. 'I know your blood runs cold when I talk about your room. But does this hurt you by making you feel anxious in the morning or at night?' Give the kid observations and direction. 'Do you feel happy like that?'"

A client with OCD with whom I worked once gave me a great insight: "When my father complains about the way I act, I ask him, 'Do you think I like living like this?'"

In the beginning, before you've reached the point of making an action plan, vagueness is acceptable. Pretend you're a jungle hunter sneaking up on a wild beast at a watering hole. You proceed slowly, because the prey is wary and will bolt if it gets the scent of a perceived enemy.

For both kids and adults, instead of: "You never pick things up around the house," try: "I get so frustrated and discouraged when I come home from work and the place is a mess. Can you help me? What can we do to fix that?" You've taken the onus away from your children and placed it on you. *You're* the one who's frustrated. You've taken the personalities out of what frustrates *you*. The mess or the stuff frustrates you, not your children.

You never know, your kids might come up with the obvious suggestion that they pick up after themselves. At least give them a chance. But that's a vague concept. To make it work, you've got to get specific. You've laid some groundwork here to gain their cooperation. You've taken the boring job of decluttering to the level of doing something nice for Mom and Dad. They don't understand a lot of the things they have to do to keep Mom and Dad happy, so this just gets lumped into the category of other inexplicable adult preferences. To them we are the ones from a different planet.

Keep Your Suggestions Short and Explicit

In the last example, we talked about a big room, or several rooms in the family area. Kids see the whole area and don't know what to do. The same is true for adults. Walk around the room that's bothering you with them and point out specific items that are their clutter. If your house is cluttered with other family members' stuff, your kids might point that out. Respond with something such as, "You're right, there is a lot of clutter here. Right now, we're working together on yours. Later, we can work with everyone else's."

"Is that your shoe?" "Are those your books?" "Are those your toys?" Getting your children to "own" their possessions is the first step. They can hardly deny it, unless they're really creative. Follow up with a lesson you've probably already taught. "Where do the shoes/toys/books live?" (Surprisingly, the concept of items "living" somewhere works just as well with adults.) This is still the information-gathering aspect of decluttering, and although your children and spouse have most likely figured out what's coming next, they aren't threatened with having to do something yet. Any salesman will tell you it's important to get a potential client to get into the habit of agreeing before popping the purchase question. That's why they ask you so many personal questions, and feed you questions that can be answered with a yes before telling you what their product costs. Consider this technique "parenting as a salesman." Sell the sizzle, not the steak.

Now, move in for the close: "You know, it wouldn't take you much time to put the shoes/toys/books back in their home when you're finished with them, would it?" Follow up with another yes statement/question: "It would make me so happy if you'd just do that. Will you do that for me?" "I guess so" may be the closest thing you'll get to a commitment, but it'll do.

Some parents follow up with a written contract (this is not recommended for spouses), something such as, "I agree to pick up my toys and other things from the family rooms when I'm finished with them—every time." Their theory is that this formalizes the commitment. When people put something into writing, it reinforces the commitment. But don't get too carried away with contracts or believe that a perfectly crafted contract will solve your problems. Dr. Bradley has a story in his book about a parent who thought he could solve all his rebellious teen's problems if he could just write a good enough contract for behavior that the kid couldn't find a loophole in. On the bright side, he may have raised a crackerjack lawyer.

Apply this same concept to their rooms. You already know that children have shorter attention spans than most adults—except perhaps your boss. Vague directions such as "clean up your room" are too broad. Look at your children's rooms as if there was a laser beam security system similar to the ones at museums. The entire room is intersected with beams of lasers projecting a grid. Within each square of the grid is a foot or so of clear space. Within each foot of your children's rooms is a square foot of clutter. Work on one foot at a time. "Juanita, this whole room is just too much to do at once. Let's pick one very small area and see how well you can do with that."

Don't worry, your children won't graduate from college before they get one room done. As they get positive strokes for little things, they'll want to do more to get more strokes, thus making it easier on you and perhaps preventing you from having a stroke from opening their doors one day and being crushed by a mountain of clutter.

Anxiety and Depression

When I feel full of energy, I like to be in a clean room. When I'm down, or feeling lazy, I like a messy room better.

—Megan, a preteen

It's normal for kids (as well as adults) to feel anxious at times. It's normal to feel "down" when things don't go right. Serious, persistent depression or anxiety needs to be treated by a psychological professional. According to Maurice Blackman, MB, Fellow of the Royal College of Physicians of Canada (FRCPC), "Recent studies have shown that greater than 20 percent of adolescents in the general population have emotional problems, and one-third of adolescents attending psychiatric clinics suffer from depression" (from *www.mentalhealth.com*, which is an excellent site for professionally written and researched mental health information of all kinds).

When a kid (or adult) is depressed, he's more likely to clutter. In fact, if your normally neat child starts to retreat to his room, and the room starts to get more and more cluttered, it could be a warning sign of a depressive episode. If the child has always had a challenge with cluttering, decluttering will help his mood. When people clutter, their environment contributes to depressed feelings. It's hard to be upbeat when you're surrounded by a mess. Clutter saps children's energy, just as it does adult's energy.

Does cluttering cause depression? Nah. The causes of depression are much more complicated than that. Does depression cause cluttering? It certainly doesn't help. Depressed individuals lose interest in their surroundings and are easily overwhelmed. Those feelings are common to the clutterers I've worked with. Decluttering requires a lot of decision-making, which can cause anxiety. By teaching your children why to stay uncluttered and to declutter their environment, you're helping them to create more positive environments for themselves and not add to their stress. Living uncluttered can help their mental health.

AD/HD

Rebellion and Purple Rooms—For Kids Only

Kids, especially teens, need to rebel in order to individuate, or define themselves. If they don't rebel now, they will later. By making compromises with your kids regarding their own private space, you enable them to express their rebellion in a safe, yet satisfying way. Don't compromise on the family areas in terms of your kids picking up after themselves, but you can compromise on when chores get done. Does it matter if the garbage gets taken out at 5 in the afternoon or 10 at night? As long as she's doing what needs to be done, let her do it when she wants.

When I asked Dr. Bradley about the rebellion aspect, he suggested a way to allow a little controlled rebellion: "Make a deal. 'If you want to paint your room purple and green, I will buy the paint and help.' Kids don't believe in drawers. How about crates? Let him make it art deco. It becomes the kid's room, like a studio apartment."

If your kid wants wild and crazy carpet in the room, let him put it in. Wait, that's probably too broad a statement. Let him *choose* it. (Speaking as someone who tried laying carpet, get someone who knows what he's doing to put it in.) You can rip it out when he leaves for college. Meanwhile, he feels that he has made his statement and successfully rebelled against your old, fuddy-duddy standards. You both win.

I ran this by several kids, from junior high to high school age, and they unanimously agreed this was a good idea. One father who followed through with this idea said this:

> *I thought the decorating ideas my son had were dumb, and we fought about it at first. Then it dawned on me that we were fighting about his wanting to be an adult and have control over his living space. He's a good kid, so why waste our energy and shut off communication over this? He is the one who has to live there.*
>
> *We made a deal. He agreed to keep up his chores and to pick up his shoes, clothes, and whatever else he brought into the family area. He agreed that he would still maintain a neat room. Guess what? He did keep it neat, and showed real pride in his room for the first time. He asked my advice on what kind of paints and brushes he needed. He didn't have a clue about how to put up shelves. We worked together to make his room the way he wanted it. It turned out the old man did know a thing or two. We talked while we worked together and I learned a lot about what was going on in his world. Our family stress level went down. He has his friends over more often. I'd rather they were here than meeting somewhere else. It wasn't such a dumb idea after all.*

Some Practical Tips for Kids

Rewards Work Better Than Punishment

> *Another thing I have found helpful is the A-B-C mnemonic for making a workable household rule. A stands for agreement, the initial buy-in to the rule with the child. It would work something like, "I make rules for myself to help me remember to do things like pay bills. I don't allow myself to go shopping until I have paid my bills. I thought of a way of making a rule to help us keep the household more livable." After the agreement, then there is a behavior (B), such as picking up the room at a specified time, or the opposite (failing to pick it up). This leads to C, the consequence. Positive behavior leads to getting ice cream; negative behavior leads to no TV, or something like that. The positive consequence is a way of getting buy-in to the rule. The child gets something they otherwise would not get, if*

they abide by the rule, in exchange for losing something if they break the rule.

—Dr. Terrence Early, MD

It'll be hard to teach your kids not to clutter, or to declutter the common areas, until the other cluttering members get involved. It's unmotivating to pick up your own clutter when there's so much of someone else's that you can't see a difference. Get in the habit of never leaving a room empty-handed. Something needs to go; pick it up and take it to the room it belongs in.

Hold a family meeting, because this is a family problem. Explain that the family rooms are for everyone, and if any one person clutters, it hurts the whole family. Ask for your kids' help. Explain that you have a tough enough time taking care of the house, and that their involvement would make your life easier.

There has to be a reward to get people to change. You could use a poker chip system with different values for different decluttering tasks, and the chips can be redeemed for predetermined prizes.

Dr. Michael Bradley has specific details of a reward system in his book *Yes, Your Teen Is Crazy!* His suggestions include: "Establish a bank account of points or poker chips or whatever you can think of that will work for your kid. Something tangible would seem to work best, as the reward is immediate and visible. For each decluttering activity carried out successfully, award chips or points."

He goes on to explain that it wouldn't hurt to provide visual clues at the same time, such as writing something down in a notebook as your child goes through the task. Let her redeem the rewards for something she really wants to do, establishing a higher point value for, say, a week at Disney World, than for getting to stay up half an hour later. Somewhere in between will lie the bulk of the rewards.

Clutter-Prone Areas

- **Kids' rooms.** The most important decluttering tip is that your children should help decide where things go as soon as they're old enough to have ideas of what they want. Because cluttering is about controlling our space, give them the opportunity to determine how their space is going to be utilized. Think about it: If your boss autocratically implements a system at work, are you as likely to follow it than if you had some input?

- **Closets.** Little ones can hardly be expected to hang up their clothes. Neither can older children, if the closet hanging rod is higher than they are tall. Why make it hard for them? Put in wire shelves that serve double-duty. They can hang clothes from them and stack stuff on top. Also, consider eliminating the closet door entirely. Most kids just think a closet is dumb. Depending on how your children feel about it, you can put up a drape, or leave it open to give a sense of more space. For teens, a closet without a door or drape makes their room feel like an efficiency apartment. That gives them a sense of being an adult.
- **Chest of drawers.** Some kids rank these on the scale of dumb adult ideas just below closets. Try crates. Heck, anything that makes it easier to put stuff away works.
- **Clothing.** If your kid "has to have" a new outfit, dress, or shoes, then she needs to make room for it. Sure, it seems as though she can cram an unlimited number of dresses into her closet (sound familiar?), but it violates some law of physics. A closet crammed full of clothes means that some are seldom, if ever, seen again. I've heard parents swear that, in the dark of the night, their children's clothes breed and make more clothes. I believe it.

This concept should be applied before you go to the store. When he first says he needs new clothes, games, shoes, and so on, even before you get into the discussion about whether he needs it, if you can afford it, or if it's appropriate, let him know that the rule is that he has to decide what to get rid of first. Ideally, "getting rid of" should mean passing it on to someone who can use it, not throwing it in the trash.

Make an Inventory

Offer guidance, but don't make the decision of what to eliminate. Give them a chance to change the biggest obstacle to not-cluttering. A major reason clutterers hang on to stuff is that they don't want to make decisions on the relative value of what they already own.

"But Mom, I need all my clothes. I might wear them someday."

"I'll tell you what," you might say. "Why don't you make an inventory of your clothes? Write down each item, the last time you wore it, and what special occasion you're saving it for."

If you're lucky, that'll keep them busy until they've grown another three inches. Then, the decision's already made. If it doesn't fit, it doesn't belong. Oh, if it was only that simple! Some of the clothing items, for boys and girls both, are kept because of the memories they trigger. That's also true for adults. A certain amount of "memory clothing" is perfectly normal. But when we have stuffed our closets with memories of the past, we leave no room for the present or the future.

Toys and Games

Designate shelves or floor space for these items. Remember the label idea to make it easy. Eliminating decision-making in decluttering is half the battle. You can win this one easily. Your kids may even get into the spirit of organizing by grouping the same types of games and toys with each other. This is an integral part of cognitive learning, so encourage it.

If your kids have so many toys that they don't have room for them, gently encourage them to pick out the ones they use the least (if at all), and give them to kids who don't have much. I favor giving things to women's shelters, because gifts to them go directly to kids who don't have much and have a hard enough life to begin with. Direct-donations to families you know who are struggling are perfect. Your church or civic groups may be able to give directly. Give where it counts. One thing that holds adult clutterers back is that they feel they have to donate things to "just the right person or organization." Giving directly makes donating easy.

Letting your kids choose the storage solution that makes sense to them is a common not-cluttering theme. If you insist that they use something that makes it harder for them to relate to, they won't use it. Take them to the office supply or computer store and help them decide which ones they like. Don't go overboard buying containers for CDs or anything else; the goal is for them to set reasonable limits on how much stuff comes in, and then get rid of items that are over the limit.

Make It Easy

Make it easy to put things up.

Brightly colored boxes are better than dull cardboard ones.

Put shelves and drawers at kid height instead of adult height. To figure out how high that is, watch your children as they try to put things away. Let their actions speak louder than anyone's words.

If they seem to balk at putting certain items up, either the item is too big or too heavy, and should go on the floor against the wall, or the designated space is too high.

Because this is a lifelong learning experience, adjust the height of the homes for stuff as your kids grow older, if it seems they're having a harder time putting their stuff away.

Darlene and I had another big fight about her leaving her stuff in the living room. It ended with her shouting at me, "Mom, how can you expect me to pick up after myself when it won't make any difference? There's so much of your mess around that I don't think it would make any difference if I were a neat freak. I'm ashamed to have my friends come over to this pigsty." Her words hurt, more so because they were true. After she left, I looked around and had to admit that she was right. I cried. I've always been a little messy, but it got out of control after her dad left. I just feel so overwhelmed that I don't know where to start. I've tried to get organized and it never lasted. I just don't know what to do.

—Mary Jane, a single mom

13 | The Organizers' View

An organizer knows you better than your spouse or mother. We know everything there is about you. We know your finances, your hiding places. You really need to know your organizer.

—Diane Snow, professional organizer

Many of us are able to get our clutter under control through the help of other clutterers and increased self-awareness, but a professional organizer has some distinct advantages. A good organizer is detached, has seen it all, and does not judge. (Though not all are willing to work with chronic clutterers.)

There are two main organizations of organizers: NAPO (National Association of Professional Organizers), at *www.napo.net*, and the NSGCD (National Study Group on Chronic Disorganization), at *www.nsgcd.org*.

Since the first edition of this book in 2001, the number of members of NAPO has grown from 1,400 to about 4,000. With this growth comes challenges. Although there is now an accreditation program, not all organizers are accredited, and not all organizers who claim to be accredited are. If you decide to hire an organizer, not only interview her, but also check with NAPO or NSGCD to verify her credentials. Not all organizers are members of NAPO.

Unfortunately, as in any business, some people will have a logo on their Website, but not be up-to-date with their accreditation. One very important thing is to ask the organizer how long she's been in business, and how many clients she's worked with. If someone says, "I've been organizing all my life," that doesn't mean anything. And just because an organizer has worked with 2,343 other people doesn't mean she will work for you, but there is something to be said for experience. The individual's personality, work methods, and skills should mesh with yours for this to be an effective arrangement. Keep these points in mind as well:

- Consultations with professional organizers are confidential.
- Organizers will be able to suggest new habits and systems to keep clutter from coming back.
- Fees range nationwide from $40 to $150 (and up) an hour, and depend on your location, the experience of the organizer, and the type of job she will tackle. (I use the pronoun *she* because most organizers are women, though there are more men in it today than previously.)
- People should turn to an organizer when their own attempts to declutter and stay decluttered have not borne fruit.
- Organizers may be especially helpful in the workplace, and some specialize in this area. Organizers specializing in time management and clutter control for companies are on the higher end of the pay scale.

Hiring a Professional Organizer

I asked Janine Godwin, a professional organizer, to give the organizers' view about what they can and cannot do. I've known Janine for years, and she knows how to work with clutterers.

She is the owner of Nooks and *Crannies* Professional Organizing in Katy, Texas. She provides the services of small business and residential organizing for those who want to make a positive change in their workplace or lifestyle. She will work with you to dispel the myth that you will never be organized. As an **accredited** member of both NAPO and the NSGCD, her focus is to guide you through the steps necessary to understand your disorganization, not just deal with the "stuff" cluttering your surroundings. Her Website is *www.nooks-and-crannies.com*.

A Professional Organizer's View of the Organizer

When Mike contacted me to write a few words for this book from the perspective of a professional organizer, I was more than willing to contribute. Mike and I have very similar views about organizing—it comes from within. I believe that disorganization and clutter is a physical manifestation of the turmoil that lies within a person's psyche, or is a direct result of what is happening in a person's surroundings. Each individual is like a snowflake; no two are exactly alike, and the solutions that a professional organizer presents will differ greatly from client to client. There is no general cookie-cutter solution for those who are clutterers to overcome their affliction. It's a continual work in progress.

Success vs. Roadblock

I don't like the word failure. *Nothing is more negative to a clutterer than that word. Actually, I refer to it as one of the "F-words" in organizing. To clutterers, their surroundings scream* failure, *so I don't use the word often. Instead, I prefer the term* roadblock, *which doesn't conjure up the same dismal feelings that the "F" word does. For those seeking assistance in getting a handle on their clutter, most will encounter roadblocks, but it's how they work through those roadblocks that is the key. A professional organizer can be a huge ally in breaking through things that are standing in the way of success for the clutterer. But the clutterer has to truly want the assistance, and be open-minded to the process, for it to be a success. When I speak to groups about clutter and organizing, one statement that resonates with people is, "Clutter is 90 percent emotional, and 10 percent 'stuff.'" Think about it: The clutter is an inanimate object, and it didn't get there on its own. It is a direct result of what the clutterer is feeling emotionally.*

Marie the Clutter Demon Slayer

Marie is a lifelong clutterer. She knew she could possibly benefit from the external help of a professional organizer, but didn't take the plunge in contacting one for many months. Why? She wasn't psychologically ready. Marie dabbled on the Web, and wrote down names of some organizers who could possibly assist her, but she wasn't convinced she needed an organizer just yet.

So she waited, until one day she decided to make the commitment to finally get her clutter under control. Enough was enough; she had procrastinated long enough, and she needed to make a drastic change and take charge of her cluttering ways. Marie was ready to take on the "clutter demon" once and for all. Nothing was going to stand in her way, and she made some calls. I was blessed to receive one of those calls, and now can add "Clutter Demon Slayer" to my list of clients. Marie is amazing. Why? She knew in her heart and soul she was ready to commit to the process, and because of this, she is making incredible progress in changing her lifestyle, habits, and surroundings. Yes, she has had many roadblocks along the way, but she has worked through them instead of being defeated by them. She is one of the most inspiring clients I have had.

Had I met Marie during her days of straddling the fence on getting assistance, I would have safely bet she would not have done as well as she has. Why? Quite simply, she wasn't ready to commit to making a change. She was still in the "I'm not sure what I need or want to do" stage. Once clients make up their minds that they want to improve their cluttering habits, it's amazing how well they respond to working with a professional organizer or clutter support group. Once clients understand and accept that it will take time and support to work through their situations, the success rate increases dramatically. They need to embrace the concept.

Preparing Yourself for the Organizing Process

You've made up your mind—you want to get organized and get a hold on the clutter in your life. Excellent! In order to make an educated decision about which professional organizer to hire, you need to do some research. But where do you begin? How do you go about finding an organizer for your project? Being prepared with information is your first step toward finding the right help. Knowing exactly what to expect, and how to go about choosing the right organizer for your needs, is what this section is all about—to educate you, and provide suggestions you should consider prior to contacting a professional organizer.

I often receive inquiries from individuals seeking assistance to put an end to their disorganization, and this is the key reason I wrote the following points. There are some key factors to consider prior to contacting a professional organizer, and the better prepared you are before you start your search, the more successful you will be in locating the right professional who will work with you to become more organized. Here are some steps to help guide you in the right direction:

- *Think about your objective. What is it you are trying to accomplish? Are you seeking help to get a handle on the clutter and learn how to take charge of the situation, or are you thinking more along the lines of just wanting someone to organize your surroundings? There is a difference. If you are looking for an Organizer to come in and "just make it work," then you need to convey this. If on the other hand you are seeking guidance to making a change in your lifestyle, let us know. Professional Organizers are extremely effective if we are aware of what your goals are. Since Professional Organizers vary in their knowledge, technique, qualifications, and experience, it is wise to communicate to those you do contact what your objective is so they understand if they can assist you in reaching your objective(s).*

- *Make a list of all the areas or things that you want organized, and be specific. For example, if you want your office to be organized, and have specific problems to be addressed, then write them down. Likewise for any other area or project you want to get organized. The more information you provide, the better understanding the organizer will have of what it is you want to accomplish. This will also allow the organizer to determine if he or she is the right fit for your particular project.*

- **Be realistic about the time you can commit to your organizing project.** *Do you have the time to complete your goal? The complexity of the project will determine the amount of time it will take to reach your goal. Anything can be organized with the right guidance, but is your timeframe for completion realistic? Will you be doing some of the work alongside the organizer, doing it alone, or wanting the organizer to do it for you? Any and all of these options are available, so ask the organizer how she works and sets up her sessions.*

- *Clarify your expectations. All professional organizers want to help you succeed, and you will, if **and only if** you are willing to work with them and **commit to the process**.* Don't expect an organizer to do all the work; you need to be actively involved in the overall process. Have you ever heard someone say, "I joined a gym, and that was a waste of money. I didn't see any results"? What they may not be telling you is, they joined the gym, and didn't give it enough time to see the results, as they didn't go long enough—or at all. In working with a professional organizer, you will see results, but as with anything you attempt, **you get out of it what you put into it**. You need to know up-front what your expectations are to truly benefit. Some organizers may not be a good fit for you, but once you find the right one for your needs, the relationship you form will be successful. You need to be accountable for communicating what your expectations are so you can get the most out of your experience.

- **Consider your budget.** Determine how much you can or are willing to spend to have the project completed. This would include labor and materials/additional services needed for completion to your satisfaction. Professional organizing doesn't have to be expensive, but your set budget will determine what type of service you can realistically afford. If you want a "magazine" look, you have to consider the materials, the labor, and so on, which can add up. Now, if you choose to do some or all of the work yourself, with a custom outline prepared by a professional organizer, that can be a very reasonable alternative versus working one-on-one at an hourly rate with an organizer until your project is finished. Again, this is based on the size of your organizing project. Always prepare a budget beforehand so you know what you can expect for your investment. Organizers will charge according to their level of expertise and knowledge in the industry.

- **Understand that organizing is a process.** Are you ready for the whole process? The areas in question didn't get to their present state overnight, and correcting the problem won't happen overnight either. There are various levels to organizing, and it will possibly take some time to obtain the results you are happy with. A professional organizer isn't simply clearing the area in question, but looking for ideas to set up systems designed specifically for you, and to assist you in coming up with a game plan that will help you maintain the area once it is complete. Some of the roadblocks you have encountered may be in the rethinking of habits, so it is a learning experience as well as an organizing experience. Are you willing to learn new ways to do things? Remember, organizing isn't about perfection, but rather what systems work best for you.

- **Think about how many people are involved.** Are there more people involved in your situation besides you? You may be tired of the clutter in your surroundings, and have decided the answer is to hire a professional organizer—that could be true; however, if there are others in your workplace or household who are completely comfortable with the surroundings that bother you, and they are not aware that you are thinking about contacting a professional, it could possibly backfire. Before you contemplate hiring a professional organizer, ask other members of the household/workplace (spouse, partner, colleague, family member) how they feel about it. Are they on-board for this as well? If they are, then your project will have a higher success rate. If there is resistance, you may not achieve the results you desired, and it would be a waste of your time and hard-earned money to try and change their point of view.

- **Evaluate whether outside intervention is best.** For those who are thinking of contacting a professional organizer on behalf of someone else **without his or her knowledge**, please think twice. Although I think your concerns are valid and intentions noble, it can send the wrong message. It could come across as, "Gee, I want to hire a professional organizer to get you help, because, honestly, I think you are a slob, and you need to get your act together." Whoa! Is this the message you want to convey to someone you care about? I doubt it. Understandably, the recipients may be put on the defensive, and I can't say I blame them.

    Instead, talk to the clutterers and ask if they are interested in seeking assistance of an organizer. If they are closed to the idea, don't push the issue. They may not think they have a problem, or may be too embarrassed about their situation, and not comfortable in speaking to anyone about it. In their eyes, they have "failed" to keep their surroundings in order. If someone *pushes them into dealing with their clutter and they are not entirely ready for it, they most likely will fail. Sadly, this will compound the problem even further, making them feel even worse. We want to build their self-esteem, not tear it down. Possibly the clutter is something that is bothering* **you**, *not the intended recipient. The only time I would suggest intervention is if the surroundings are bad enough to be a danger or health hazard of some type to your friend or relative.*

If the clutterers do seem interested, you can always assist them in finding an organizer that may be a good match for them, but **please** *don't choose their organizer for them; only they will know who and what feels right for them. The organizer who sounds ideal to you may not be the ideal candidate for the clutterers. Let the clutterers speak directly to the organizers, so the clutterers can choose who they feel they can trust. After all, it's their life, and they need to seek the assistance in order to become accountable.*

- **Consider the emotional, medical, or physical needs.** *For example, have you been diagnosed with ADD, AD/HD, or depression, and does this have a direct effect on your current situation? Are you chronically disorganized? Then you need to possibly think about working with a professional organizer who specializes in these areas. Make certain the organizer you are considering is affiliated with a professional organization in which she is educated in working with these disorders, and is a current member in good standing of the organization.* **Some organizers may state they work with ADD, AD/HD, chronically disorganized, or hoarding clients, but have no formal experience or education in this specialty.**

  If there are medical or physical challenges, you need to take this into consideration as well, and let your organizer know, so she is cognizant of your needs. You can always check with the National Association of Professional Organizers or the National Study Group on Chronic Disorganization to find individuals who specialize in your specific need. Not all professional organizers are alike. Remember, you are inviting someone into your life, and you need to be certain that the organizer you choose can show valid proof of her credentials.

If you have any uncertainty about the points presented here, you may not be 100 percent ready to tackle your project just yet. That's okay. It's better to think it through ahead of time by doing your homework than to not be informed. This may help you realize what is involved, and also gives the organizer a better feel for what your expectations are, as well when you are ready.

14 | The Spiritual View

> *In surrendering to one's own original sense of order and harmony, one's compulsion is abated.*
>
> —Mel Ash, *The Zen of Recovery*

Among those who've come (and come back) to Clutterless meetings, nearly every variety of belief has been represented: members of evangelical bible churches, mainstream Protestants, Catholics, Jews, Muslims, New Thought believers, atheists, and those of no particular faith. Cluttering cuts across all beliefs. Whatever your religious affiliation, you'll find something that will help you get closer to your God through decluttering. The visualizations taught are not meditation, and have no religious overtones. Meditations can be as spiritual or God-centric as suits you. The whole point is that, as we declutter, we open our physical and spiritual lives on a deeper level.

Spirituality is apart from any set of religious beliefs. I realize that it is dangerous to write about spirituality—I'm bound to offend someone. My goal is not to proselytize for any religion or worldview. It's entirely possible for someone with no religious beliefs to practice spiritual principles, and it's possible for someone who eschews both religiosity and spirituality to overcome his cluttering, using the other techniques and insights in this book. So, if talking about spirituality in a broad sense offends thee, to paraphrase a biblical quote, "cast this chapter out," and move on to the next.

A sloth is a three-toed mammal in South America, not the clutterer's original sin. The goal of decluttering is more than freeing ourselves from excess stuff in our lives; it is freeing ourselves from old ways of thinking that blocked the sunlight of the spirit from our souls. Our possessions were a physical manifestation of our limited, blocked lives. Our belief in lack (that we will never have enough in our lives), our fear-based mentality, and our lack of self-worth are all expressions of our distance from God. God wants us to be happy, prosperous, and free.

Purpose of Spirituality

The purpose of religion and spirituality (in my opinion) is to achieve peace and harmony in this life. "How can one be at peace with a cluttered mind?" asks the Reverend Roger Aldi of the First Church of Religious Science, in Houston, Texas. His spirituality is an amalgam of the practical, intellectual, and mystical. The first Clutterless meetings in Houston were at his church.

Fear of Letting Go

You must let go of a thing for a new one to come to you.
—Ralph Waldo Emerson

We clutterers are afraid to let go of our stuff because it involves risk (or "risk avoidance," as the psychiatrists call it), or a lack of trust in life or God (as religious people call it). A person who believes that God will provide doesn't look to physical items to do the providing. He believes that his God or a Higher Power will take care of the details as long as he does the footwork. Nearly everyone's heard the bible quote about the sparrows, which "neither sow nor reap," yet get fed. We have hundreds of sparrows flocking to our backyard, because we feed them. They (and other birds) expend an awful lot of energy just to eat. They may not be working the nine-to-five grind, but they are doing the work they're supposed to be doing.

There is an old story about a man whose house was being flooded by a river. An Army humvee drove to him when the river was lapping at his porch and offered to get him out. He refused, saying, "The Lord will provide." The levee broke, and he moved to the second floor. A Coast Guard rescue boat came by and offered to take him to higher ground. He refused, saying, "The Lord will provide." The water rose and rose, and finally he was on the roof. A National Guard helicopter came by, dangling a ladder. He refused to climb up, saying, "The Lord will provide." Finally, he drowned. When he got to heaven, he asked God why He had forsaken him. God replied, "Come on, man, I sent the Army, the Coast Guard, and the Air Force! You gotta do your part."

Even more than that, knowing isn't enough. We have to step into the humvee, grab on to the life preserver, and catch the ladder, or none of it matters. We clutterers are likely to *know* what we should do to change our lives; it's in the doing, or not doing, that we fall down.

We clutterers hold on to our possessions, despite offers of help from many sources. We keep moving farther and farther away from help, until only an act of God can save us—and we sometimes refuse that too.

Fear of letting go also happens because we become comfortable with the status quo, and because letting go involves risk-taking. This is scary, and paralyzing. The great unknown is too much to face alone, and that's when finding strength and peace from prayer, meditation, and reading the bible or other spiritual texts can help you find the answers you need. Some people who have come to support meetings have mentioned that seeing the ad in the paper for the group was God leading them. (This could also be true about seeing this book and choosing it instead of the dozen or so others on the same topic.) True spirituality also helps you see yourself as free from guilt and the yoke of oppression that comes from some religions that tell you you are a bad person or are guilty of the sin of sloth.

Not Just on the Physical Plane

The universe can't bring anything new into our life if we don't make some space.

—Rev. Roger Aldi

Cluttering is not just a matter of holding on to stuff on the physical plane; it is a reflection of our consciousness. We hold on to old grudges, old resentments, old loves, old disappointments, and old triumphs. That's a lot of "old." We make ourselves old and worn out before our time. If we carried all our junk on our backs day after day, we would soon have a bowed back, physical pain, and a sour disposition. What we manifest in the physical plane we first make real on the psychic plane. If we carry a spiritual suitcase of hurt and sadness, we will bow our soul's back, pinch our psychic nerves, and have a sour soul.

Few of us know, before we become enlightened, how much old psychic stuff we are carrying around. We think we can fix ourselves with more—more of everything physical—without realizing that having less inside will make us whole. We put our faith in a better job, more money, a better spouse, a bigger car, and so on. All the while, we are cluttering our souls with negativity. Some of us are filled with resentments because the job isn't good enough, our neighbor has more money, our spouse doesn't fulfill all our needs, the car breaks down, and so on. Others of us are cluttering up our spirits with envy. Some of us don't feel complete unless we have a lot of possessions. Every one of us is edging our God out because, for whatever reason, we're filling the hole in our soul with material possessions. We can manifest what we want and believe, but if our belief system is faulty, our manifestations will be too.

GOD—Good Orderly Direction

As I began to live more in the solution and less in the problem, I had to confront my own lack of faith. If I truly believed that God loved me and would take care of me, why did my actions belie my beliefs? For what it's worth, this didn't make me unique. Many people who are certainly more spiritual than I (Mother Teresa, for instance) have questioned their commitment to faith.

I had to let go of my lack of orderliness in order to make room for the good, orderly life I desired. I found out that I could not have a cluttered soul and a clean house. Sure, I could throw away lots of junk (and, in fact, that is where most of us start), but I soon found that I still felt heavy. I tried to meditate, and did so in the best way I could at the time—which is to say, not very well.

I learned that one concentrates on breathing or a candle during meditation not because either of those has magical properties, but because they teach us how little we are able to concentrate on the here and now. I became aware of the mind clutter I was figuratively tripping over while trying to attain a higher consciousness.

Resentments

In order to become cleansed and freed for many of life's problems, it is necessary to practice renunciation or release, especially in the human relations department.

—Catherine Ponder, *The Dynamic Laws of Prayer*

Support and 12-step programs, and most religions, believe that we heal by eliminating our resentments. When we begin to meditate and embark on a spiritual path, we find out how well we have done that. I discovered that I hadn't done as good a job as I thought. But before you start berating yourself, if you find you aren't as spiritually advanced as you thought (if indeed that is what you discover), remember that you did the best job you could at the time. The times have changed, and so have you. As you proceed in your spiritual quest, you may have to backtrack in order to go forward.

Just as I try not to bring new clutter into my home, I try not to bring new clutter into my soul. I acknowledge resentments when they happen, and let them lie around for a little while. Before they get too comfortable, I have to excise them. A psychologist pointed out that I may be 100 percent right 100 percent of the time, but life still doesn't always work out the way I want. Accept that, and you have taken a huge step toward eliminating new resentments.

So what about the old resentments that have made nests in your cerebrum? They are comfortable. They have been with you for a long time. Therefore, you have to work on your resentments one at a time.

As a kid in South Texas, I worked with my father, chopping Johnson grass from under the trees in our citrus grove. It was hot, sweaty work, and I hated it. I hated my father for making me do it. I chopped the tall grass (often taller than I) at the base, and went on. The old man said nothing. At the end of a week, he took me back to the trees I had first cleared. The weeds were already growing back. I'd thought they were gone forever. "Son," he said, "it don't do no good to hack away at just what you can see. You go to get to the roots, or you're just pissin' in the wind." Wise man, my father.

My resentment toward my father was one of my most deeply rooted. Even after years of recovery from my alcoholism, and attending meetings of Adult Children of Alcoholics, it was only when I began to recover from cluttering that I really, truly faced him, and unearthed the resentments I held for him. This came about while I was decluttering a box of my mother's memory items. When I saw him as a man and not a demon, his memory was no longer able to torment me. I let him go, and I am sure that he, looking down from heaven, was glad to be set free. After that, my meditations were clearer.

Anne Sermons Gillis, author of *Offbeat Prayers for the Modern Mystic*, wrote a wonderful prayer. I've abbreviated it a little here, but it can be found in its entirety on page 84 of her book:

> *Lord, I think that I am in prison because my mind keeps walking around the same little square.... My longing to know more of the mental state is as deep as my commitment to self-realization. I wander closer and closer each day to my goal.... Oh Lord of expectant beauty, lead me to freedom that I might break the beliefs that hold my mind in this tight restraint I call reality. Expand your infinite processes into my mind and guide me into the brilliance of everlasting light. Amen.*

Forgiveness

> *Inner peace can be reached only when we practice forgiveness. Forgiveness is letting go of the past, and is therefore the means for correcting our misperceptions.... Through true forgiveness we can stop the endless recycling of guilt and look upon ourselves and others with love. Forgiveness releases all thoughts that seem to separate ourselves from others. Without this belief in separation, we can accept our own healing and extend healing Love to all those around us.*
>
> —Gerald G. Jampolsky, *Love is Letting Go of Fear*

Forgiveness is an important step. We learn to forgive ourselves for our imperfections, and to forgive others for the hurts we feel they have caused us. We let go of the past to live in the present.

Surrender

Support programs suggest that we need to surrender to a Higher Power to get well. Whether you believe that your Higher Power is within you or outside of you, you must stop trying to fight the battle all alone. You have tried your way for years, and have not conquered the problem. Maybe it is time to get back to God.

Christ taught that the kingdom of God was within us. Buddha taught that we can all recapture our original natures. The Tao states we can free our minds and return to the root. Zen philosophy teaches us that we are already complete. Our original natures are free from disorder. Only as we grow in our earthly confusion do we bring disorder and disharmony into our lives. By realigning ourselves with God, we realign ourselves with our true natures.

Letting Go to Win

In giving up our cluttering problem to a power greater than ourselves, we release ourselves from having to fight our compulsions alone. If we can leave our problems in God's hands, we can go about the business of working the solution. We must take practical steps to get rid of the outside mess, and we must take spiritual steps to get rid of the spiritual mess.

By letting go, we win greater freedom and happiness. By allying ourselves with a partner with infinite power, we magnify the effects of our own efforts. Through prayer and meditation, we gain strength to face each day, and learn to concentrate on our successes and progress, rather than suffer in guilt and denial.

As Franklin Roosevelt said, "We have nothing to fear but fear itself." Our fear kept us prisoners of our stuff and our stuffed mentality. Our new way of thinking and living will free us to return to our true natures, our God-like natures that have been hidden underneath our clutter.

15 | Prosperity Is an Inside Job

I am come that they might have life and have it more abundantly.
—John 10:10

Abundance-thinking is hardly new. But it has seen a popularity in the past few years that's brought it from what some considered fuzzy New Thought to mainstream consciousness. This is due in large part to Rev. Joel Olsteen and other popular ministers telling their congregations that God wants them to be financially blessed as well as spiritually blessed.

Such ministers will be the first to tell you that a life built on the pursuit of material goods is an empty life. Clutterers have a real challenge here. We've made "things" the focus of our lives—either their accumulation, or, if we are living in the solution, their elimination.

Clutterers often believe in scarcity rather than abundance. We believe that we will never have enough, that what we have will not be replaced if taken away, and that we do not deserve better—more, perhaps, but not better. But we can change this thinking as we recover.

A universal truth is that we get what we believe we deserve. If we believe that we don't deserve the best, that we don't deserve a full and rich personal life with adequate material possessions, we will hoard those pitiful ones that we do have.

Be Grateful for What You Have Right Now!

Get grateful. We begin by realizing how prosperous we already are. Prosperity is not just stuff; it is people, health, pets, and how we feel. When we have decluttered our house and find all that loose change, we celebrate that. If you are similar to me and find $700, accept that this is a gift from God. Do you have a roof over your head? Enough food? Someone who loves you? A pet that loves you? (If you have a dog or a bird, definitely. If you have a cat...well, maybe.)

Spiritual teachers such as Jesus, the Tao, Buddha, Ernest Holmes, Catherine Ponder, Emmett Fox, Eric Butterworth, Ralph Waldo Emerson, Joel Osteen, and others have told us that God will provide, and provide abundantly. Practical teachers such as Norman Vincent Peale, Og Mandino, Dale Carnegie, Tony Robbins, Suze Orman, and countless others have told us, and demonstrated in their own lives, that if we change our minds, we can change our lives.

The Difference Between a Rut and a Grave

Okay, you're sitting in a messy house, surrounded by things that are treasures to you and trash to others. You're probably depressed. Your finances are a mess. You are alone. So how do you get out of your rut?

Sometimes it's hard to get grateful when surrounded by chaos. Getting out of our cluttered surroundings is always good. I like to go to a museum, where beauty and order can lift my spirits. Parks bring me closer to nature and the things that matter. Another tool is to read books that will point you in the right direction. Any of Catherine Ponder's books are a good start. I especially like *The Dynamic Laws of Prosperity* as a beginning. She is easy to read, and very practical. You don't have to believe; just have an open mind. Tony Robbins is dynamic and powerful, and his books and tapes have helped millions. Suze Orman is practical, and can help you get your financial affairs in order. Her books are uplifting and filled with no-nonsense prosperity tips.

Associate With Positive People

Check out social organizations such as the Optimists, Lions, Kiwanis, and so on, or just a group of people with the same interests. When people are interested in things besides themselves, they are more positive. Prosperity consciousness is a large part of their core belief and approach.

It is best to be selective in telling your current friends that you are changing your life. Chances are, you are associating with negative people. Such people love to bring others down to their level. So whenever people start talking about how hard times are, or how little they have, change the subject, or walk away. It does no good, at this stage of your development, to try to enlighten others. Their negativity will overwhelm you.

The Spiritual or Religious Approach

You may not believe in God, or you may have soured on the religion of your youth. I was the same way. But when at the end of my tether, I decided to give God another chance; it paid off in many ways.

If you are led to try a spiritual or religious approach, Hallelujah! (Sorry, I got carried away by the Spirit.) I mean, good for you. If your search leads you to a group or church that believes in positive thinking, so much the better. Positive-thinking church philosophies aren't limited to New Thought churches. Mainstream and some evangelical churches are addressing the issues of prosperity-thinking today. Joel Osteen (Lakewood megachurch, Houston, Texas, and on a TV near you) is evangelical, and he talks about God and money. He's in favor of both.

I can't think of a body of religious belief (other than some sects based on self-denial or vows of poverty) that doesn't want its members to have better lives, both in this world and the next. The important thing is to find a religious philosophy that speaks to you. Start believing that it is good to have material goods—just not as many as you have right now.

Change may not occur overnight, but it can. There is no time limit on how long or short it will take to start experiencing more prosperity. Most likely, you will have to start manifesting your new life a little at a time. Read the affirmations. Read them as often as you want. If you truly want to change, they will sink in. In *Unlimited Power*, Tony Robbins writes, "The world we live in is the world we choose to live in. If we choose bliss, that's what we get. If we choose misery, we get that too."

Money Flows

Money flows like a big river into an ocean of abundance. It cannot flow into a cluttered home or mind. You have got to take the physical action first to get the flow going. Imagine, as you declutter, that the pathways you open up in your home are riverbeds of prosperity. From a practical standpoint, you can prove that to yourself if you have a garage sale with the things you eliminate from your life. If a garage sale is too difficult for you, just get rid of things. When you donate them to the Salvation Army or Goodwill, get a receipt for their true value. Treasure this like a check. It is a check—from the IRS. See, already, prosperity has flowed into your life!

Part of prosperity is giving. Norman Vincent Peale said that giving is the secret of the law of abundance: "To receive the good things of life, you must first give." It is part of the natural flow of money—it flows into your life, and you let it flow out. More flows back—10 times more than you give. Jesus proved this with the loaves and the fishes and countless other teachings. If your funds are low, give of your time.

When I first started going to a church as an adult, I could barely squeeze out a dollar for the collection plate. It hurt. As I grew in prosperity consciousness, I realized that giving has to be done with a glad heart. A minister in Burbank, California, made it clear to me. She said not to tithe a certain amount until you were comfortable with it. If you give a large amount (to a church, organization, or individual) because you feel you have to, you will not reap any reward from it. She said she would rather someone gave a dollar with a glad heart than $100 grudgingly. Wow! A preacher who didn't make me feel guilty unless I helped buy a new rectory! But she said you get back what you give. You get back 10 times what you give, so if you want only $10 back, then give a dollar. Heck, I could do the math. I gladly dropped $2 into the plate. And guess what? I got an unexpected $20 in the mail shortly thereafter!

It doesn't always work that way, but it has worked that way often enough for me to keep it up. I know that whatever I get, I must give back to keep the flow going.

There isn't some spiritual calculator in the heavens making sure we all get our 10-times reward. The concept is just to give our poor little brains something to hang on to.

Money is not the only thing you can give to get the flow going. Give of your time. But be careful to only give what you can give with an easy heart. Clutterers often over-commit and don't make enough time for themselves. So make your first gift of time to yourself—for enjoyment. Go to the beach. Go to the park. Go to Tahiti. Just go. Then you can give to someone who needs the services you can offer.

Pray

Pray for prosperity. Make God your business partner. Every morning, I meditate and pray to God, first for peace and serenity, and then for money to flow in. Sometimes, the flow is restricted, but I try my best not to get nervous about it. I believe that it will flow, and it always has. Sure, there are people who insist that you are not to pray for yourself, or for material things. Let them think as they want. Even Jesus prayed for specific results. Bless your wallet or purse or checkbook. Hold it in your hand and say, "God, I bless this abundance represented here, and am grateful for the continuing abundance that flows into it, 10 times over." It will take awhile, but you will believe it once it starts happening.

A Prosperity Wheel

Got a dream? Make a prosperity wheel by drawing a circle on a large sheet of poster paper. Divide the circle into quarters. Label them *personal*, *financial*, *spiritual*, and *physical*. Then cut out pictures (from the magazines you have been hoarding) of something that represents each area of your life. Tape them to the wheel. Look at it every day, as often as you want. Say, "Thank you God, for [item], or something better, that is here, right now, in my life, and serves my higher good."

This will feel funny at first. How can you say something *is* when it clearly *is not*? The Universe can only say yes. It only knows the now. When you say something *is*, you tell the Universe to create it. Never vacillate with the Universe. Things are. If a loving relationship is what you desire, put up a picture of the way a loving relationship looks to you. Picture the way it should be in your mind. Picture the person. Feel the emotions of love that radiate between you and that person.

If it is money that you desire, be specific, just as you should be specific in decluttering commitments. Don't say, "a lot of money." The Universe doesn't know what that means. To some people, $100 is a lot of money. To others, it is $100,000. You can start with any amount that feels comfortable for you. Just make sure that it is an amount that you truly believe you deserve, and can handle. A million dollars tomorrow might be too much for your consciousness. You might only be able to be responsible for $1,000 or $100. You can always up the ante.

Rx: Have Fun

Most clutterers are afraid to have fun. Having fun means letting go, and that goes against our grain. Money is not what makes us happy. Things are not what make us happy. If they were, we'd be chuckling our cluttered fool heads off.

Money is a byproduct of being happy. Remember that. Money is not God. God is God. When we know that, and accept that, God can co-create whatever is for our highest and best good.

This may be the most important thing to carry away from this book: You deserve to have fun. Decluttering is not all life is about. A balanced life is also about enjoying yourself, whatever that means to you.

What Is Success?

Norman Vincent Peale, in *The Amazing Results of Positive Thinking*, defined *success* as "not mere achievement, but rather the more difficult feat of handling your life efficiently. It means to be a success as a person; controlled, organized, not part of the world's problems, but part of its cure...of being creative individuals."

Affirm for yourself that you *are* a success. Affirm that you are successful in getting rid of your clutter. If you are having a hard time getting started, be grateful that you are such a successful clutterer. Who else could have amassed such a collection of stuff?!

16 | Offices—Home and Otherwise

The birth of excellence begins with our awareness that our beliefs are a choice.
—Tony Robbins

Learn this, if nothing else: You don't need to print e-mails, Websites, or anything else that's on your computer. Got it? If we clutterers, who are such recyclers, would just stop doing that, we'd not only save the planet and maybe get an award from Al Gore, but we'd also keep our offices from becoming landfills.

We can save e-mails into file folders on our computers if we feel we'll need them. Usually we don't. We can copy the address of the sender to a database or contact-management program if we need to. Mail programs even save the names and addresses to a contact file if we want. So there's no reason to print e-mails.

Web pages are great. They change. The address stays the same. If you want to know how a Web page looked months or even years ago, use the Wayback Machine to find out: *www.archive.org/index.php*. Don't waste your ink printing them. You can save them on your computer if you need to.

Okay, enough preaching. On to the rest of the chapter.

Record Retention

I will discuss this first because this seems to bother more people than anything else. I also add this disclaimer: If you've got an accountant or bookkeeper, ask him exactly what applies to you and your business. I'm not either of those things, but have run a number of businesses (though not all successfully).

If you don't itemize expenses on your tax returns, you don't need to keep all your receipts, bills, and so on. I get so many questions about this from people who work at a regular job, yet want to save every utility bill there ever was. They say they want to compare their rates to what they used to pay. And why is that? And what good does it do? Why do we torture ourselves?

First of all, most things don't need to be filed. At least 90 percent of papers filed are never referred to again. Record retention mostly applies to people with businesses, where you need to keep most records for seven years (some businesses have longer requirements). If you're an average person, and if you've got seven years of files, that's probably way too much.

All you really need to keep is official stuff. Chances are, you're keeping every bit of correspondence, envelopes, and so on, when receipts, bills, tax stuff, and bank statements are about all that's necessary. (I met a woman at a seminar who was a landlady and won a case against the city because she had a water bill from nine years ago. Okay, good for her. But how much time did she have to spend going through nine years of water bills?)

Can a Clutterer Run a Business?

Have the following thoughts ever crossed your mind, or even been said to you by "friends"? "How can a clutterer run a business? You need the structure of an office run by a tyrant! You are so disorganized that you will fail." If so, take the advice of my mother, who said, "People will tell you 10 reasons why you can't do something. Ignore them."

We can do anything we want to do. We just have to change some beliefs and patterns of behavior. If you already have your own business and are overwhelmed by your cluttering, you can change that. If you are afraid to get out of a job you hate because of your cluttering, you can change that. Yes, it is tough to run a business, even for organized people. But we clutterers have an advantage that logical thinkers don't: We are inventive. We are able to devise all sorts of strategies to circumvent our disorder. We have the creativity to see things differently. If we are recovering, we can turn our greatest liability into our greatest asset. As Einstein said, "Imagination is more important than knowledge."

Admitting the Need for Change Is Not Admitting Defeat

Clutterers can be successful in any business they choose. I've known cluttered CPAs who didn't exactly inspire confidence when you visited their offices, but who were actually very good. After I worked with them, they were more successful and less stressed out.

Clutter is the biggest stressor there is. I've run two businesses at one time, even while I was in the midst of my depression and clutter. One of them was successful, and the other, I finally realized, was a money-loser. As I came out of my clutter fog, I tossed one of the businesses. Having a losing business didn't make me a loser; I was as much of a success as I could be, at the time. Dumping it was a statement of belief in myself—that I deserved more reward for my time.

Since I first wrote this book, I've consulted with a number of businesses, both large and small. It doesn't matter whether you're self-employed or work for a worldwide conglomerate, learning to get a handle on your cluttering will help you. So, here is what I have done, now that I have gotten better, to make a business work.

How to Make It Work

Walk into your home office and look at it with fresh eyes. Oh boy oh boy. You *need* all the stuff here, right? Wrong. I was ruthless with my home office when I moved, and I went through all my "necessary" stuff again when I moved up to a real office—rather than cart a lot of useless files, I went through them. Year-old information requests seemed valuable, because I thought I could use them for a mailing list. Then I thought about it: If I hadn't made a mailing list yet, what were the chances that I would do so in the near future? I chose to eliminate the clutter to let new business flow in. And guess what? It did.

Our home office is our expression of our confident, prosperous selves. It should inspire confidence in ourselves, even if we never receive clients. For years, I lived in fear that one of my suppliers would want to visit my office. In fact, I lost a big contract because one wanted to see my operation. There is no stigma attached to working out of a home office anymore, but a disorganized office will send people running. For one thing, it is easy to make mistakes in a disorganized office. It is also easy to waste inordinate amounts of time in a disorganized office. Declutter, and you will have all sorts of time to grow your business. You will also feel more like an executive, which is what you are. You are the president, CEO, and SFO, so act like it!

When Is Your Day Done?

Your day does not end until you have decluttered your desk. That is a rule. Clean it up, or you can't leave. Trust me, this one rule will make your life so much better.

Goals

Prosperity thinkers will have goals written down and taped to the walls, along with positive sayings. I have "Seven Steps to a Prosperity Consciousness," an anonymous piece given to me years ago in a church I no longer remember, taped beside my computer. Periodically, I write, "Today, I will create 10 new deals." There is nothing mystical or impractical about this. When I was a direct salesman, even the most unspiritual, greedy, economic successes I knew used these techniques. Og Mandino, who is revered by sales managers as a motivational god, stated, "The Second Commandment of Success: Thou must learn with patience ye can control thy destiny."

There are dozens of books about running an efficient office. Go ahead and get one or two. Once you get past the clutter mentality and apply these principles, you will benefit from them. Although most of the information is just plain common sense, these few suggestions will help clutterers deal with their special situations.

Keeping It Together

Information keeps flowing in. There are faxes to read and send; brochures to create, file, and mail; mail to be opened; bills to pay and send out. Once we learn to put everything in its place and deal with things as they come up, we can be efficient. Once we have decluttered and made space for success, we will want to keep it that way.

Filing Cabinets and Record Retention

How many filing cabinets do you have? If the answer is more than four, you are either very successful, or a clutterer—though a successful author friend of mine, Ralph Keyes (*Timelock* and 13 other books; see *www.ralphkeyes.com*), has dozens of filing cabinets in a 1,400-foot basement. Everything is neat and organized, and he can find anything. So there is no one answer. If you can actually get into the files, and they're not smashed up against each other, you are probably in pretty good shape. I currently have one two-drawer, lateral filing cabinet.

The key is to organize things so that you can find them. Simple, huh? Clutterers do best when they put things into "big pictures," because our tendency is to get bogged down in minutiae. You don't need to bother with color-coding systems, subsystems, and other complicated methods. Clutterers need to keep it simple. Like with like.

I've found that using different cabinets for different aspects of my work makes it easier. When I was writing a lot about Mexico, I had a whole cabinet devoted to this subject. Now it is one drawer. When I was promoting my "Mexico Mike" persona, I had two drawers of clips and ideas. Sure, it was great to have the clipping of me on the front page of the *Wall Street Journal* or the full-page spread in the *New York Times*, but I no longer send them out, so I don't need a hundred of each. Reviews of my previous 10 books are nice to keep for memories, but *Mexico From the Driver's Seat*, *Mexico's Colonial Heart*, and so on, are out of print, so why keep several copies? If I ever need one, I can photocopy it. [At least, before the fire, I could. See the sidebar on page 210 about the importance of papers.]

Hanging Files

If you can't get to your files, they are useless. A lot of space can be wasted with too many dividing hanging files and manila folders. You need a hanging file for each letter of the alphabet to hold miscellaneous information, but you don't need a manila folder for each bit of info if it is not something you refer to a lot. Don't crowd the hanging files. Make two or more hangers for a subject if it has a lot of manilas in it. And if you are saving a newspaper clipping, clip it! Don't save the whole page.

> ### How Important Was All That Stuff?
>
> As an example of how little we actually need all the stuff we keep: after the fire, obviously, I had none of the items I just listed. The *Wall Street Journal* story about me is online; I saved one copy of it in case I ever need it. The *New York Times* piece is available for a fee; I didn't want it that badly. My two books I got at library book sales. My birth certificate I got from the state records division. I got all my identification records, and am a bona fide official person again. The IRS even had copies of my tax records.

Software Registration Numbers and Backups

Most computer programs (software) have online registration today. That's good because it eliminates one area of procrastination—never getting around to sending in those paper registrations in the old days. Nevertheless, we may need to refer to those numbers again, so before you send off the registration to cyberlandia, copy the serial number to a plain text file, a database or spreadsheet, or an organizer where you will keep registration numbers. Because your home, too, could burn up or get flooded, it's also a good idea to send those numbers to yourself to an online mail account (such as Yahoo or MSN).

Computer manuals almost never exist anymore, being all online. That at least saves us some clutter.

If you're like me, you probably have more than one program DVD. Leaving them loose makes finding them impossible. I finally settled on a wallet-style CD/DVD case to organize them. Get the largest one you can. I tried using several small ones, "organized" by type of program, and it was a disaster. Divide the big one into sections such as "Business,"

"Web," "Photo," and so on. Allow several blank pages between the divisions. Put those gummed, clear, hanging-file-folder sleeves between them, and label them.

Online backup services have come and gone, but I'd trust one recommended by Kim Komando: *www.komando.com*. They're good to have in case of disaster. Having a portable hard drive to back up to is also a good idea.

Pens, Tape, Scissors, Paperclips, etc.

All these live in one place. Extra pens live in a coffee cup on the right side of my desk. Scissors and paperclips live in a drawer. If you don't use something every day, a drawer is fine.

Deal With It, File It, Toss It

When a fax comes in, try to deal with it immediately; make a decision, and file it. Not all faxes need to be kept. Throw away the ones that are not really necessary. A wastebasket should be your most-used filing system.

Phone messages need to be dealt with. If it's a one-time call, toss the number right away. Otherwise, enter it into your database and toss the note.

The mail needs to be read daily. Most of it should be tossed. Open it over a trash or recycling can. Unless you are truly interested in an advertisement, dump it. This will save you tons of time in deciding what to do with it. Bills should be put in a "bills to be paid" file, which should be looked at once a week, and dealt with.

Time Clutter

Clutterers have trouble with clock time. It is just too easy to imagine that we have all the time in the world to complete projects. A simple project-manager program enables you to define a goal, break it down into major tasks, and further subdivide it into individual subtasks to accomplish those goals. For example, my goal was "write a book," the major tasks I had to do were "research" and "writing," and the subtasks included "write introduction," "interview experts," "write Chapter 1," "write Chapter 2," and so on.

Get Visual

I know a clutterer who is a very successful businessman. He knows that his tendency is to "file and forget," so, being visually oriented, he had cubbyholes built behind his desk so he could see the messages and projects he needed to attend to. A big calendar on the wall (one with plenty of space to write on) is a good visual reminder. A corkboard is a great visual reminder, as long as you are ruthless about weeding it. Clear it out once a week.

E-mail

See my rant at the beginning of the chapter. Then read this too. We want to keep it all! Don't. Reply (leaving the original message attached), add the person to your address book, and delete the original. The copy is still there in your "sent" file. If you don't purge your e-mail program now and again, it will suddenly stop working.

Scanning Documents

Everybody asks me about this as a way to cut down on clutter. It *could* work, in theory. I've used scanners since 1990. I've just never been able to find a way to make them work right. It does make sense to scan articles and letters into OCR (optical character recognition) files in your word processor. However, scanning is not a cure-all for paper clutter, because it becomes too easy to scan everything—even useless items. The only difference between storing junk on your computer and in your paper files is that it doesn't take up as much room in your house. When you intelligently decide what needs to be saved and what needs to be pitched, then a scanner can work for you. The OCR programs have improved and can read most documents pretty well. If you have an intelligently organized filing system on your computer, these could be a good way to cut down on paper clutter. But remember, hard drives crash. If you don't back it up, those important documents could be lost forever.

Time Management Can Help

If you have employees who are clutterers, you are going to have to call out the big guns instead of the one-day seminars. There are three main options: You can hire a professional organizer who specializes in corporate work, you can hire a performance specialist, or you can send your employees to an intensive seminar for time management. Actually, a combination of all three might be called for, and may benefit all employees—not just the clutterers.

Catherine Jewell took the Franklin Quest course in 1993, and is still using it. She likes to implement the Franklin Day Planner time-management system. Some companies are mandating a specific organizing system through e-mail. They use only one system, which includes personal commitments with professional commitments, based on the theory that you've got to see how your whole life plays out for the week in order for your planner to be effective. Catherine has written a book, *31 Days to a Better Boss: Ways to Stop Whining, Start Planning, and Take Charge of Your Career Today*, which can be helpful in learning new techniques.

Disorganization May Signal Other Problems

"When I teach Covey's *7 Habits of Highly Effective People*, taught one day a week for three weeks, people reveal a lot about themselves," says Jewell. "The number-one issue is a struggle to maintain a home life and a work life. They feel guilty about not being the parents they want to be. Sometimes their marriages are falling apart because of all the above."

Jewell says that with proper time-management and goal-setting tools, people can overcome these drains on their business and personal lives, as well as their health. "I have met some extremely organized, capable people who seem much less stressed because their lives are organized," she notes. "They have boundaries, and they are assertive. I know a young man who is working in an environment where 50- to 60-hour weeks are the norm. He works 40. And he's been promoted three times in three years. Maybe it's matter of focus."

Jewell gives seminars and works with major corporations such as Dell Computers, Southwest Airlines, and Chase Bank on the issues of time management and goal-setting. "I work with mangers to get the best from their people," she says. "I work with individuals to find their life's inner passion.... Sometimes it is a change of workplace. Sometimes people don't need to be trained, [but] just to be given better tools or better motivation."

Changing corporate environments have also contributed to clutter by causing disorganization. Jewell finds that "everyone is a little bit" cluttered and disorganized. "What I've seen in a lot of corporate environments is a lot less storage space," she notes. "Where before people had six drawers, now they have two." Because of this, files tend to get crammed together without an organized filing system. Managers need to hang on to important documents, but they don't have the room for lots of file folders, so papers get filed in a general file, where it is impossible to find them quickly. When the important documents are needed, time is lost shuffling through others that *might* be important someday.

"There is a lot of movement within the corporate environment in general," Jewell says. "People move six times in four years. Because of that, many people do not have a reasonable filing system. So they remain disorganized until the move. Then they can give themselves permission to discard files." That is when all the CYA files get disposed of. People are aware of this, and thus don't have to own up to their disorganization.

Not Dysfunctional, Just Busy

Lynn Meyer O'Dowd, owner of All About Time in Chicago (*http://all-about-time.com*), is a professional organizer who works with corporations. She gets hired for professionals who are bringing work home and for whom the office has spilled over into their entire lives. "Then they travel like banshees," she says. "They don't have a system and it totally gets away from them. They are not dysfunctional, just busy." Often the employees feel that they are drowning, and that the boss has thrown them a lifeline. "There are times when I go in and the employees are so happy that the boss will pay for this," Meyer says.

Sometimes, however, Meyer O'Dowd meets with resistance. Her most important advice to employers who want to help cluttering employees is what *not* to do. Typically, she is hired by a "boss who calls me in and wants me to fix that person. I go in and meet with the employee. 'I don't have a problem,' is a common response. Resistance is monumental. They are balking and will do the opposite to spite you. What I have found is it is almost like an alcoholic. They have to admit they have a problem, [and say] 'This system isn't working for me.'" Meyer approaches the employee in denial with an is-there-anything-I-can-help-you-with attitude. She's found that most people come around when they don't feel that they are being singled out or threatened.

Some employers have suggested that their employees attend support groups such as Clutterless, or a 12-step program such as Clutterer's Anonymous. Whether this will help or not depends on how it is presented, and, of course, on the employee's motivation. I have known people who were recommended to treatment centers or Alcoholics Anonymous by their bosses, for whom the results have been truly amazing. Other times, it was wasted effort.

In my case, when I was impersonating an executive at a major international bank, my boss very kindly suggested that our insurance would pay for a treatment center to help me with my drinking problem. Outwardly, I said I would consider it, but inwardly, I thought, "I knew it! This is a way of getting rid of me. He wants to get me out of the office for a month and then hire someone else. Then there will be this big black mark on my personnel record. I'll show him! I'll find another job." And I did. A year later, the courts forced me to go to AA. I was still resentful, but had no choice. I went. It took. I stayed. So you never know.

At Clutterless meetings, there have been some members who were referred by their bosses. The bosses explained that this was similar to an ongoing seminar, and a tool to help the employee improve his performance and personal life. Because Clutterless is not a 12-step program, the employees were less resistant to it. In most cases, they have stayed, and their job performance (and lives) have improved. But, in cases in which the boss said "Go to these meetings or get out," the results were less than satisfactory.

It is important for bosses to understand that Clutterless meetings are not time-management courses or places where people go to get tips on cleaning out their drawers. Although specific decluttering issues are addressed during a meeting, the focus of the group is to deal with the emotional limitations that cluttering causes. Clutterless meetings are not a Band-Aid; they are gentle surgery. They augment the work of professional organizers, therapists, and time-management professionals, but they do not replace them.

Different Approaches for Different Types

If you have a variety of personnel types working for you, a cookie-cutter approach will not work. People who are artists, such as graphic designers in advertising agencies, aren't going to have pretty little stacks of papers. They won't respond to the same organizational tools as those in the accounting department. Moreover, just because something *looks* disorganized doesn't mean it is.

If you can find something at a moment's notice, you are not disorganized. Time management is a tool. If you are spending time looking for things, you need a tool to help you stop wasting time. Some people have messy desks and can still find things. Some people are very neat and can't find anything.

I disagree with the one-system-fits-all approach. Some systems will make sense to some people, and they will use it if they are motivated. Forcing a company-wide system that doesn't fit the individual will just cause some of us stress and resentment. But I am probably outnumbered here. If your company can tolerate employees picking systems that work for them, at least try it. I prefer to use a computer program called Maximizer as my organizer and personal information manager. It just makes sense to me, and has a feature that others didn't have when I was choosing which one to go with: It can search by first name, and I am more likely to remember someone's first name than last. Most companies use ACT! or Goldmine, or another popular brand. I have tried them all, and found that Maximizer works better and makes more sense to me. My productivity would decline from the resentment caused by having to use a program that I thought second-rate. My dedication to performing is enhanced when I feel I have some choice in making decisions. As long as your employees are not using this as an excuse to avoid changing their cluttering behavior, why not let them use what works for them?

Disorganization Affects CEOs Too

Jewell says, "I see disorganized people at all levels. I've seen administrative assistants who are picking up the pieces for their CEOs." Wilson agrees that most executives would be lost without their secretaries.

Meyer O'Dowd works a lot with CEOs. Her background was that of an executive secretary with a major hotel organization, and later a consulting firm. "When the [bosses are] disorganized, they are leading the team," she says. "Teach them how to work with their secretary. There is a lot of creativity and leadership in CEOs. They are not necessarily detail people. I tell them, 'You're supposed to be leading a corporation, and you are working out of a sticky pad? You run your corporation with a business plan, but how about your personal life?'"

Outsource Your Personal Life

According to Meyer O'Dowd, some companies, especially consulting firms, do recognize the stresses that extensive traveling places on the personal lives of their employees. One company she worked with, Anderson Consulting, has a concierge service for employees who travel. The concierge service outsources their personal life. When one executive had a car break down, for example, the concierge picked it up. "If you are organized," she says, "traveling is still difficult. If you are disorganized, you are sunk."

Jewell advises traveling businesspeople to streamline their personal lives. "Pay your bills electronically. Hire a lawn service that comes regularly, so you don't have to call them. I used to have seven phone bills, and now I have two or three. One thing I do is hire a money coach to pay all my bills."

Meyer says, "I liken myself to a personal trainer. We all can exercise. When you are not doing it, you hire a trainer." She considers it her role "to keep them going. Going through paper is the last thing they want to do after they go on the road. They tell me 'If you weren't here, I would never do it.' I give homework. People respond to the word *homework*. 'Your homework is to finish this drawer.' I give them three things they've got to do. 'Buy three containers. Finish this drawer on the left.' Very specific."

In Brief

KISS—Keep it simple: success!

17 | Hearses Don't Have Trailer Hitches

My biggest fear is that I'll die before I get rid of all this clutter. Then my children will have to take care of it. I can just imagine how well that will sit with them. If I die in the summer, when it's hot, they'll get all sweaty sorting through everything. If I die in the winter, they'll catch cold going in and out of the house, carrying boxes. Lord, let me die in spring. Or, they may not even try to sort through it. They may just throw it all away. That's awful. There are some valuable things in here. I just hope I make it long enough to sort through them.

—Ellen, a clutterer

Okay, let's stop talking about depressing stuff such as decluttering and talk about something fun, such as dying. Given the choice between decluttering and lying down and dying, some clutterers would have a hard time making up their minds. Clutter is not technically inevitable (though it may feel like it); leaving this earthly veil behind is.

Nobody likes to talk about death, and clutterers don't like to talk about their clutter. So right away, this doesn't bode well for this chapter to be one of the more popular ones. But you know what, if I'd just wanted to write a popular book, I'd only have compiled a list of tips. This was a hard chapter to write, because I had to find the right tone to motivate clutterers similar to myself to do something without making it sound like a guilt trip. There's no getting around it—somebody is going to have to deal with our clutter. Just because we die doesn't make it go away. If we leave this planet before we take care of our clutter, our relatives are going to have to deal with it.

If nothing else has motivated you to do something about your clutter, think of how you'll feel, rolling over in your grave, watching your family going through your stuff. Let's look on the positive side: By looking at this issue now, you can get some help in making decisions about what to get rid of.

Will You or Won't You?

Before you move on to the next step, start a will. In your will, list all of your accounts, both online and in the physical world. List the passwords for the online accounts and the location of any keys or combinations for real-world accounts. If you have pets, make sure that you have spelled out how they are to be taken care of. Ideally, they should go to someone who is a pet person, and who wants them. Make sure you discuss that with your designee, and don't just surprise them. If you don't have anyone to whom to give your pets, designate an animal rescue to take them, or a no-kill shelter. Also designate some money to the same institution. Your pets are your children. You wouldn't abandon or sentence your children to death, would you?

Make sure the will is somewhere people will be able to find it. That might sound silly to non-clutterers, but for us, it is essential. I'm not giving legal advice, so check with someone who can tell you, in your state, what to do. Lawyers have told me they don't want to keep wills anymore, so check with your own. In some states you can file the will with the county courthouse. If nothing else, file the will in a filing cabinet under "Will."

Putting your will into your safe deposit box may or may not be a good idea, depending on your state's laws regarding who can access a deceased person's safety deposit box. Even a co-renter may face delays in accessing your safe deposit box, so check with your bank and your lawyer about the best way to handle this.

Saving It for Your Family? I Doubt It

If you've been holding on to certain items because you want to pass them down to your family members, this exercise could be a Godsend. It won't work with every family, but surprisingly, does work for many. Dividing up the physical items in your life may sound ghoulish, but remember: stuff is just stuff. This is no more ghoulish than writing a will, except you are getting the input of those involved instead of springing a surprise on them after you're dead and gone.

The concept here is the same as in Chapter 6, on other people's clutter, but the focus is different. If you don't think this will work with your family without bloodshed, you can still have the ceremony, just without the extra players. You'll see what I mean in a moment.

Call a meeting of family members, announcing that you're going to divvy up your earthly possessions in advance. Obviously, this will work better if everyone lives in the same town, but that's not the norm in today's world. So you might have to schedule the dividing ceremony during one of the traditional holidays, such as Christmas (perfect—this goes with the sprit of the season) or Thanksgiving (appropriate—some of your precious items are probably turkeys in your family's eyes). Because, in many families, those holidays aren't the Hallmark moments they're supposed to be, there's nothing wrong with doing a little bit of family business.

Once everyone is together, and perhaps full of turkey and good cheer (but not too much of the liquid cheer), pass out magic markers and labels. Ideally, if you have different-colored labels for everyone, it will work best, but if not, just different-colored pens will do. (Okay, for those doing this without an audience, decide on a color label or pen for each family member, and write for them).

First of all, if you've been saving photos for the family, put them out on the table and ask everyone to take the ones they care about. Chances are (and I've talked to dozens of people who've done this exercise), there will be more pictures left over than were taken. Great. That means that there's one less decluttering decision for you to make. Immediately discard the photos that are left.

Using the same principle, bring out all the small items you've been meaning to sort and give to your children or grandchildren. Whatever's left is out the door.

Move on to the big or valuable items. If more than one person wants something, that's where this exercise ceases to be fun, so it probably wouldn't hurt to feel everyone out beforehand regarding the big stuff. Even here, you are probably in for surprises. This is when not having everyone gathered can be a blessing.

You can do this either of two ways, whatever works for you. You can tell certain family members that you'd like them to have X, but only if they want it; or you can ask who wants what. Here's where the labels and markers come in. Ask everyone to write their name on the items that are going to them, and affix it to the back of the item. If more than one person wants the same thing, put the names in a hat and have a lottery.

Now, for the hard part: With everyone there, pick an executor of your estate, who is going to have to declutter what's left behind.

This exercise may not completely get rid of your clutter, but it will make it a lot easier to make decisions—which is really the hard part of decluttering.

Once you and your family get in the mood, this would be a good time to ask someone to take out those stacks of magazines and newspapers you've been saving. Those things can be really heavy, so why not use help while you've got it?

If your family can actually take some of the things they're going to inherit away from the house (without making you feel empty, that is) right now, all the better. But if the stuff gives you joy to have around you, then they'll just have to wait.

18 | Maintenance Steps

This is not the end. It is not even the beginning of the end. But it is, perhaps, the end of the beginning.

—Winston Churchill

Hooray! We did it. We've made some progress in our physical decluttering, and our mental blocks that enabled our re-cluttering. We may not have a "perfect" house right now, but we've got the best house we can have at this moment. We're always improving. We're almost always moving forward.

Daily Maintenance

If we follow these daily habits, we will spend a lot less time on major cleanups, and we will keep our lives and souls clutter-less. We won't be able to do all these maintenance steps every day, and sometimes they won't even apply. Do what you can every day until it becomes a habit.

While practicing these habits, I found that I became bored, or felt myself slipping into a rut. I even wondered if I had become obsessive about neatness (okay, maybe that is a stretch). So I tried not to do any daily maintenance. The next day, I didn't feel as good about myself. I let everything go for two days, and felt that old, somewhat depressed clutter-thinking returning.

We all have times when we just don't want to do these things. So we won't! There, we showed that clutter who was boss! This temporary declaration of independence is like canceling a check to a creditor—we pay far more later. For myself, I find that I am good about keeping the kitchen and bedroom in perfect order, but slack off in the other areas. Oh well, I am getting better. So are you.

Newspapers

I love newspapers. I used to write for them, so I have a special passion for them. With all the news about newspapers dying due to a declining subscription base, I wonder if clutterers are the only ones still taking them. Remember that they are *daily* papers. Read them that day, and throw them away. There is nothing in them that is not available online or in libraries. If you must save an article (and my advice is not to), clip it immediately (keep a pair of scissors next to where you read), file it immediately, and recycle the rest of the paper immediately. I now clip half a dozen articles a year. It's just not worth it.

Most people get at least one weekly paper, which contains calendars and reviews of the weekend's events. Use the calendar and throw the rest away on Tuesday or Wednesday. Put the calendar on a bulletin board, throwing away last week's.

I get a real charge out of recycling newspapers, but if you know anyone with a bird as a pet, give the papers to them.

Mail

Open mail over a trash can or shredder. Immediately toss the junk. If it looks as though it is junk, it probably is. Generally, you will toss 30 percent of incoming mail. Take what is left and deal with it. If it is a bill, put it in the "to be paid" basket immediately. Set aside a time each evening to respond to personal mail and any business mail that you saved. File it or toss it when done. There is really no way to totally get off junk mail lists, as there are more than one. But it will at least help to write to: Mail Preference Service, Direct Marketing Assn., P.O. Box 9008, Farmingdale, NY 11735-9008.

E-mail

Read, respond, delete. Be ruthless. I get hundreds of e-mails a day. Even if I saved them, I could not find them if I needed them. Set up a filing system in your e-mail program for those items that are worth saving. Don't just dump everything into "my e-mail" or "my documents." Take some time to organize several directories.

Dishes

If you've got a dishwasher, there's really no reason or emotional excuse for putting the dirty dishes in the sink instead of the dishwasher. If you do them by hand, wash them at least once a day. It takes less time to wash them every evening than it will if you let them go for a few days. I tried it, and not only does procrastinating take more time later, but you face a mess every time you go into your kitchen. This can set up feelings of being a failure and lead to recurrence of old behavior. If you make coffee in the morning, get it ready in the evening. I have to wash my espresso stuff and regular pot before I can put fresh grounds in them, and as long as I am at it, I use the soap and time to wash the rest of the dishes. Time spent: seven minutes. Peace of mind: enormous.

Yes, you can soak dishes to make them easier to clean, but my experiments showed that soaking for an hour did just as much good as soaking for two days.

Clothes

It's easy to leave the clean clothes in the laundry basket after washing—forever. Folding clothes is boring. If you can't fold them when you get them out of the dryer, do it in front of the TV. Same for ironing. I bought my first iron two years ago, and I found that ironing's not that bad. Hang up the ironed clothes right away.

Old clothes, towels, and bedspreads are very much welcomed at animal shelters.

The Bed

If you read in bed, put your books on the floor, and not on the bed. If you eat in bed, get up and put the dishes in the sink. These little habits will pay off big time. In the morning, making a bed without books or ice cream bowls in it is a lot easier. You don't have to make your bed military-style—unless it makes you feel better. Just pull the sheets and bedspread up over the pillows, and it will look 100 times better. Your dog or cat will be happier too.

The Bathroom

If you keep a sponge by the tub, you can give the tub a quick wipe just before you get out, and that nasty ring won't show up for a longer time. Give the faucets on the sink and tub a quick wipe with a dry towel before you leave the bathroom. It will do wonders for your self-esteem when you come home from work.

The Living Room

Don't use that coffee table for a bookcase or filing cabinet. Put things where they belong. Newspapers love to mingle on coffee tables and sofas. Send them to a newspaper singles bar—the trash/recycle bin. They will be happier together. How much time does it take to pick up the evening's glasses and cups? About two minutes. Ashtrays are particularly gross. Dump 'em.

The Dining Room

That was a really nice dinner you prepared in your clean kitchen. Now pick up the dishes, as you are going to wash them anyway. Wipe the table. Time: perhaps five minutes. If you live with someone else, he or she will generally be very happy to help with this chore. He or she is so happy about the progress you are making.

A Small Investment

We have now spent about 15 or 20 minutes spread throughout our day to give ourselves a better life. That is a very small investment for a very big reward. If we let these things slide, we can look forward to losing a good couple of hours of our weekends doing the same things. Personally, I would rather be fishing. How about you?

18 | Backsliding

What will happen if we backslide?

We will have periods when we just don't care. It's not the end of the world. No one is perfect. After you have decluttered, you will feel great. Then, slowly, it starts... A newspaper is left out. Dishes go unwashed. One book for nighttime reading is left on the bed. Then his pals join him. Then they have a party and invite their friends. Before you know it, you are overwhelmed again. Don't panic. Sliding backwards is not the end of the world. Getting back on track is easier, because you don't have as much stuff as when you started.

This is a good time to reread your Decluttering Diary. Find out what area of your life or your clutter is causing the problem. See if you dealt with either one before. Do what worked the last time, and see if that helps.

Reasons for Backsliding

Let's see why you might have slid back down that slippery slope of being cluttered.

> **Visualize and Get Vision**
>
> Remember the visualizations you did when you first started to declutter? Did they help? Well, then, do them again. Visualize yourself living in a clutter-free house. Visualize yourself confident and proud and able to take care of the problem. Read the affirmations in this book. Make up your own.

You didn't just wake up cluttered; certain behaviors and thoughts led to your cluttered state. You chose to abandon the lifestyle that made you feel good for one that was comfortable. You left your new lover for the old one. Why? Only you can answer that, but here are some possible reasons. If you recognize the thoughts leading up to this negative action, you will be able to stop them in time the next time...or the time after that.

My Problems Aren't That Serious, My Stuff Is Just out of Control

That fits most of us when we backslide. We let one thing go and it doesn't seem that bad. It may start in your bedroom, your sanctuary. You can still invite others to your house—just not in your room. Then it is the coffee table. Then the whole living room. Then it is just all too much.

If you can, start picking up where you started putting down. If trying to remember where you started will slow you down, start anywhere. No matter where you start, or when you start, just start! The task isn't as daunting as you think it is. Only you make it so. You can do it.

A Major Trauma

A loved one died or left you. You left a loved one. Your beloved pet died. These are awful events, and you are entitled to grieve, or to be angry. But is your cluttering going to bring them back? If the trauma is that someone died, and you loved him, don't you think he would want you to have a clutter-less life instead of retreating into clutter as a way of mourning?

If it is an ex-lover who set you off, is your living in depression going to help you get even with her? If you start making your own life miserable, aren't you giving her power over you? Do you really want to give her the power to ruin your life again?

You will love and be loved again. If you are emotionally healthy and clutter-free, your chances are greatly improved. Give yourself a break, give yourself a chance, give yourself your life back. Get back on the program.

As you begin to clean up the wreckage of your present, toss some stuff. Start with those things that remind you of the one who is gone. If you hate the person now, view it as throwing him out of your life. If you lost loved ones, view it as helping them move on. If you love them, you still have the memories. If you hate them, get rid of any objects that could trigger memories.

What happens if you reconcile? They will either understand or they won't. If they don't, that is their problem, not yours.

You Went on a Trip and Left a Mess

This happens a lot. Before you go, you put your house into disarray when you are packing. You don't have time to clear it up. You live out of a suitcase while on the trip, and when you get back, it's hard to unpack. The suitcase lies on the floor. You rummage in it for stuff. You get used to walking around it. The other stuff in the house never gets put away. More stuff ends up on the floor.

This is typical. So many of us have to travel for business today that it's hard to keep up with any kind of routine. Often, after a trip, whether for business or pleasure, I would be disoriented for about a week. When I surfaced, clutter had reared its ugly head. I have vowed not to let that happen again. Now, I get the suitcase unpacked within a day or two.

Start with the suitcase: Toss the brochures that you don't really need. File the papers you do need. Wash the dirty clothes. Ditch the plastic hotel sacks they were in. Return the suitcase to where it lives. Then get busy on the rest of the room, and then the rest of the house. Remember, this is a minor setback compared to where you have been.

Financial Setbacks Have Paralyzed You

This happens to all of us. A business deal didn't work out. You lost your job. The stock market went down. You had unexpected expenses from an illness, a child's illness, home repairs, car trouble, and so on. This is life. It happens to everyone.

First of all, get your financial house in order. Figure out your true financial situation. Not knowing is scary. It leads to mental clutter. Clear off your desk and get out the checkbook and the bills. If you are seriously behind, do what normal people do—sell something, cut back, get a part-time job. Make a plan to get out of the financial mess. With that off your mind, you can start working on getting rid of the physical mess.

Money flows. It cannot flow to you if your life is cluttered. Give it a chance.

Nothing Matters Anymore

Depression happens. You are in a fog, nothing has meaning, and you don't seem to have purpose anymore. You feel worthless, so why care? You wonder if anyone cares what happens to you. Your life is such a mess on the inside that it's hard to care about the outside.

But you *do* have purpose, and someone *does* care, even if it is only I. What is going on in your physical realm *is* happening in your mental realm. If you take action in one, the other will follow.

Finding Your Way Back Out

Pets Can Help

If you have a pet, you have a perfect depression-reliever. If you have a cat, she will love it if you stay in bed all day; you can comfort each other. Your dog will try to talk you out of it. Snakes and fish aren't much help, though your boa might hug you... Birds seem to understand when you talk to them about it. They at least pretend to listen.

Talk

I have suffered from major depressions, even to the brink of suicide. So I know that when we are in that frame of mind, we cannot use the tools we have. If you have a therapist, make an appointment. Then hang on. Don't take the permanent solution to a temporary problem. If you feel you can't afford a therapist, there are community services that can help you. There are crisis hotlines you can call. Your clutter buddies will listen. You are not alone, though you may feel that way.

If you can't do it on your own, seek professional help. God gave psychiatrists and psychologists their gifts to help people such as us. Good ministers are there to help their flocks through trying times. Call yours.

Read

Read something. Some of us can't deal with anything more challenging than mystery novels when we are down. But if you can, try some uplifting books. Whether you pick up something by Tony Robbins, the Dalai Lama, or your favorite romance or mystery author, pick up something. Stop listening to depressing music. Stop looking at the news. Rent some funny movies. Stop worrying about the whales, global warming, or the devious Republicans or Democrats in Washington. You may be able to do something about those things when you are your old self, but right now, you need to get yourself together.

Take Action

If you do nothing else, pick up your clothes off the floor. It will help you as much as a therapy session. You are in control of your stuff, not the other way around. Don't give up. I want you around to buy my next book. Don't let me down, okay?

Write a letter. Express your feelings without reserve. Put all your anger, fear, self-pity, loathing, pain, and any other emotions you have into it. Hold nothing back. Then, on a new page, write any solutions you can think of. If you can think of nothing better, just write "better." Write down how you would like your life to be. Be as optimistic and positive as you feel you can be at this time.

Then take the letter outside into the sunlight, to the beach, to the mountains, or wherever you feel is a blessed place. Hold it in your hand and say something along the lines of, "Here, God (or Buddha, Tao, Jehovah, Great Spirit, Universal Intelligence, or whatever your Higher Power is called), please take these things. I can no longer deal with them. I give them, and the solutions, to You." Feel the release as you say these things. Then burn the letter. As it goes up in smoke, feel that your blackened spirit is being burned out of you too. I always feel a great sense of peace after doing this ritual. I hope you do too.

You may feel an immediate release, or it may take days. But it will come. Upon your return home, try to not pick up the problems you just burned. Get busy when you get home and throw one thing out. Pick up and put away one thing. If you have a spiritual program, start it again.

You didn't get into the woods in one huge step, and you won't get out of them in one giant leap. Just start walking and looking for that sunlight at the end of your dark trail.

20 | Support Groups

Not everyone is a groupie. Wait, that sounded wrong. Oh well, a little support group humor might lighten up this topic. The point is, it would be a good thing if you tried a support group.

The number of clutter support groups is tiny in comparison to support groups for other issues. That could be because clutterers are loners, because people don't know about them, because clutterers just don't do groups. All I know is that those who make the effort get a heck of a lot better. You've been trying to change your cluttering habits yourself, all alone, for how many years? So what's it going to take to get you to try something different? Trust me, as good as this book is, you're going to get over your cluttering a whole lot faster if you join or start a group. Another benefit is that you will help others. Clutterers are so introverted that we appear selfish; we are actually quite caring, once we come out of our shells.

Helped by Self-Help Groups

The group based on the 12-step principles of Alcoholics Anonymous is Clutterers Anonymous (*www.clutterersanonymous.net*). They are strictly and traditionally based on the 12 steps and 12 traditions of AA. They have between 30 and 50 groups nationwide, depending on the attrition rate that month. If you aren't willing to start your own meeting, then these folks might have a solution in your town. I recommend them.

The group I founded is Clutterless Recovery Groups, Inc., a 501(c)3 nonprofit support group, not a 12-step program (check out *www.clutterless.org*). Both groups are sincere, and each benefits from different personalities.

Clutterless Recovery Groups is based on the principle that psychological tools combined with practical decluttering methods works best. The concept is that we are equals who share our feelings about cluttering and how it affects us. We spend part of each meeting on practical solutions during an open discussion, and part on sharing your own feelings about how cluttering is affecting your life. Anything shared there is kept confidential, and is thus anonymous. Freedom to express oneself and to be heard without blame or shame are the cornerstones of this group.

Clutterless Recovery Groups is based on the principles of positive thinking—visualizations and affirmations—as tools to improve one's self-image. It can benefit those who haven't gone over the top with their cluttering, as well as those who are in therapy. It does not promote any one way of dealing with the clutter in our lives. Sharing by clutterers is the basis of it, but professionals, from psychologists and psychiatrists to professional organizers, are welcome to come and present their insights. We have found that we have had little success with diagnosed hoarders, though they are certainly welcome.

As of this writing, we have three groups in the whole country. Whoopee! We had more than a dozen at one time, but I guess everyone got better. Seriously, as I explained earlier, we're just a hard group to organize, more like cats than dogs.

When this book comes out, there will be a flurry of people starting meetings. Maybe the time was not ripe in 2000, and the world is ready for Clutterless groups now. There is a free meeting kit with complete instructions on starting a meeting on our Website, *www.clutterless.org*. Check there for a meeting in your area, and if there isn't one, start one. Otherwise, try Clutterers Anonymous.

Maybe clutterers are too disorganized to start meeting. Maybe the 12-step group has more meetings because people who gravitate to it are already in some sort of group and are used to starting meetings. We did have a surge of meetings start across the country after my world tour of seminars, but they died one by one. If you want to start a meeting, go to the site and download the free meeting kit. Then call me or e-mail me. But don't call me and ask if you can be notified if someone else starts a meeting in your area. You *are* the someone else.

Commitments Are One Advantage of a Group

If there's one tool that will lead you down the right road, it's commitments. No, I'm not intimating that you should be placed in an institution. Making a commitment to another human being, especially another clutterer, can motivate you to do something. I tried making a commitment to my dog, but it didn't work very well. And although a nonjudgmental friend (obviously) isn't going to judge you, there's something about having to tell a person your success, or lack thereof, that motivates you more. I knew that Fluffy would adore me whether I decluttered the bedroom or not. I suppose there is an upper limit to how nonjudgmental a friend should be.

When I first wrote about commitments in the first edition of this book I felt proud that I could share a surefire solution that would motivate millions into joining the ranks of the uncluttered! (I just had a vision of "joining the ranks of the uncluttered," to becoming "joining the ranks of the undead." I saw a town filled with grateful clutterers shambling down the street in rags, arms outstretched, crying plaintively, "Clutter, clutter, my soul for some clutter." When you die, you can't take it with you, darn it.) But instead of this being as effective as the invitation on the Statue of Liberty for clutterers to arise and join me in a new land of Clutter-lessness, it didn't cause the wholesale urge to commit. As far as I know, the masses of clutterers are still cluttered and fettered.

Why didn't my words about groups and commitments work? The theory is sound, but the practical application seems to be threatened by the laws of the cluttering nature. (Now if that's not the beginning of a science-fiction plot, or a politician's testimony to Congress, I don't know what is.) Clutterers are loners. We don't like to join groups. We don't like to talk about our clutter. We are in denial. Because of the first two reasons, we don't have anybody to commit to, and the third reason keeps us from committing even if we could. The last one keeps us from ever starting. We rationalize that, "If it gets really bad, I'll do something about this clutter. Meanwhile, I can still find my way around the paths in my home, so it's all okay. Tra-la-la."

This aversion to groups probably cuts more people off from overcoming emotional limitations than anything else. There are support groups for nearly anything that bothers just about anyone, now. Some say there are too many. Some say cluttering doesn't deserve a group. After all, it's not serious: All you have to do is get motivated and clean up! In fact, one national TV psychiatrist said just that: "People who clutter either don't know how to clean, or just aren't motivated." Unfortunately, we clutterers buy into that negative thinking. "Groups are for losers. We could spend the time we'd waste on going to a group decluttering." If I had a nickel for every time I heard that one, I'd be driving a nickel-plated Mercedes.

When I lived in Los Angeles, the *LA Times* did a feature on support groups, and I was the front-page poster boy for clutterers. Being on the front page of your local newspaper because you've got a problem is probably not how you want to be remembered, but what the heck, I figured it would help somebody, and I like being in the newspaper (as long as it's not the obituaries or the police blotter). In that story, they informed the public that there were hundreds of different types of self-help groups in Los Angeles County. As a person who didn't have all of the issues some groups focused on (there were both fear-of-success and fear-of-failure groups), I had to admit to being a bit judgmental. Similarly, since I started Clutterless Recovery Groups, I've seen people pooh-pooh the idea of a group for clutterers. But I've never had a problem with support groups. Once I finally crossed the threshold to my first group, a light dawned in my head. I was a loner as well. What I realized is that a group is just a place where others similar to you in one aspect of their lives get together to solve one of life's many problems. After nearly three decades in a support group, I've come to realize that groups help in so many unintended ways. I pity those who don't have any groups to go to. You see, when you've got a group to go to, you can spend an hour focusing on what's wrong and how to fix it. When you don't have a group, you can spend your whole life focusing on what's wrong and never find a solution.

People who come to groups often have far more emotional issues than that of cluttering. They're lonely, depressed, and anxious, they have low self-esteem, feel alienated, and experience nearly every other feeling you can think of that keeps them from living full lives. The cluttering is just a manifestation of these other things.

When people come in, they are so damn serious. After a while, they lighten up. You know, "facing an issue" sounds so intimidating. We don't "face issues." We face ourselves. In the light of self-examination and hearing how others deal with the same challenges, we learn that you'd have to be dead to not laugh at some of our coping behaviors. I've seen dozens of dour, self-absorbed, emotional basket-case clutterers come to meetings and turn into quick-witted and funny people. We lovingly laugh at ourselves. In laughter there is healing. We may not "get well" right away, but we surely as heck get a lot better.

One of the great aspects of a group is that we make a *commitment* to the group to do one thing about our cluttering, and then report on our success the next time we come. We have a saying: no matter what we do (or don't do), we are a success because we faced our cluttering behavior. Instead of whining about it, we face it head-on and try to do something about it. The power of knowing that you'll go back to the group, which is nonjudgmental, and report, makes us want to do something. When we didn't have a group, there was no extrinsic reward for decluttering. With a group, there is, even though it's only applause from others at our successes or an understanding nod when we fall short. But we never fail.

Online support groups seem to help some, though I personally have my doubts about their long-term efficacy. I started one on Yahoo and eventually turned it over to one of the moderators. I had one on the Clutterless Website for a couple of years, and let it go out of frustration: I saw too much concentration on the physical aspects of cluttering ("I cleaned my desk today, hooray!"), and too little on the emotional growth that is more important. These are stop-gap measures, because one of the issues that real clutterers have to face sooner or later is our isolation. The anonymity of the Internet is no substitute for face-to-face contact with real people. In fact, the Internet can contribute to our time-clutter. Those who are involved in Internet support groups are the same people who say they don't have an hour a week to go to a real support meeting. Beware: There are other "groups" on the Internet that purport to be support groups, but in fact are just vehicles to sell someone's organizing products.

I will probably try a live online group again. Maybe the time is right. Stay tuned to the Website or join the mailing list.

Appendix I: Decluttering Diary

The purpose of this diary is to help you see patterns in your cluttering behavior, and solutions to those patterns in your decluttering behavior. It is a map of my journey from living a cluttered life to learning to live clutter-less.

There is a temptation to use it as a life journal. Don't. We clutterers are too easily distracted, and will do just about anything to get out of decluttering.

There are a few rules, but they are not egregious.
1. Do not journal on scraps of paper or loose sheets. You will lose them.
2. Do journal in a full-sized spiral binder or on a computer.
3. Don't worry about spelling, spacing, or anything other than getting the thought out.
4. Do be honest. If some deep-seated emotion rears its ugly head (and at least one will), accept it, and write what you feel. If something pops up that seems, well, stupid, write it down. So what? Living the way we have is hardly an expression of our intellectual prowess, is it? If we can accept the reason we're holding on to something as stupid, then we can deal with it and stop doing it.
5. Oh heck, that's enough rules. If you can, have fun with this.

Because clutterers are often frustrated creative types, you may find yourself doing wordplay when you write, or waxing poetic. Heck, go for it. Clutter's been blocking you on all levels, so it's natural that decluttering should unblock you on all levels.

Copy the format of the bold lines into the pages of your own notebook.

Day:__ Time: From __ to __. Total Minutes: __. Session # __.

The first day will be Day 1. The second will be Day 2, and so on. The idea is that this is not a one-time deal, that you are on a quest. The time element is important. If you start at 5:30 and go to 5:45, be honest. The idea is to track the number of minutes you use decluttering, both to keep you honest and to help you chart what works best for you. If doing three 15-minutes sessions works best, then do that. If one 45-minute session works better for you, then do that. Same with mornings or afternoons or nights. You've got your own rhythm; find it and use it. Some people may hate this exercise. They may write, "Before I started this decluttering session, I felt angry. I am angry because I have to write this stupid diary." Hey, it's not going to hurt my feelings. Say what you feel. But try to stick with it for 15 days. (I'd like to say 30, but that seems close to forever.) I bet somewhere in there a real thought comes sneaking out. Also, by making this part of your new habit of decluttering, you've set yourself up for success.

Before I started this decluttering session, I felt:

Use full sentences or pithy words. You may say, "I am enthusiastic/ overwhelmed/ anxious/angry/no real emotions." Then be a little more specific. "Overwhelmed because _____ . Angry at _____ . Anxious about_____." Oh, by the way, this part of the diary is similar warming up for exercising: It doesn't count against your decluttering time. Having writer's block won't get you out of your commitment. Sorry.

My Goal This Session:_____ .

Be as specific as you can. Don't just say, "Clear out this room." That fairy tale's not going to happen—at least not at first. "Clear off half the desk," might come true. The whole idea is to make a commitment that you can achieve, so that you will feel successful. You've come here with feelings of failure regarding decluttering, so give yourself a break for a change. Yeah, you can set the bar as low as you want. You can always raise it later.

Type of Clutter: _____ .

Paper, clothes, mail, tools, photos, what have you. The idea is to chart how well you do with different types of clutter.

Emotions: When I Start to Deal With This, I Feel: _____ .

This is the nuts and bolts of this diary. What the heck is going on when you deal with certain things? Why are they there in the first place? Why are they still there? Why are they so hard to get rid of? (Conversely, some things will be surprisingly easy to get rid of. You may want to start with those items and work your way up to the emotionally "heavy lifting" items.)

Emotions: When I First Bought (or Was Given) This Item, I Felt Good Because: _____ .

These are the tough ones, and these are the answers you will need to face to stop cluttering in the future. When you bought X, it made you feel good because: "I was down because I'd just had a fight with my boyfriend/spouse/friend/parent/bill collector, and this made me feel pretty/sexy/successful/rich." It's important to acknowledge the reasons we shop so that we can do something about it. If we know that our tendency is to buy things when we're angry with someone else, we can channel that energy into some other activity, and stop buying to fill the holes in our souls.

Sometimes there's no deep psychological reason we bought something, but there's often a clutterer's reason. You may have bought an extra claw hammer (unless you are a demented murderer, it's hard to get emotional about a claw hammer) because you couldn't find the other three you already owned. If that's the case, then the issue to work on is, plainly and simply, organization.

When This Session Was Over, I Felt: _____ .

Good? Bad? Ugly? Tired? Energized? Stupid? Angry with myself? And so on. You feel what you feel. Another area that we are generally blocked in is the ability to admit what we are feeling. We have been stuffing our emotions the way we've been stuffing our clutter. After about two weeks of keeping this diary, you'll probably find that your answers get more real. At first, our inner critic tends to make us say everything's "fine."

You'll find that some types of clutter affect you in different ways. You'll find your own rhythm for decluttering. Marathon or sprinter, the choice is yours. Most importantly, you'll find out how you feel about different types of clutter, and then be able to change that behavior from the start.

Picture Journal

Have one page of "before" pictures of your whole house or office. That's the Big Picture.

Each day attach a before and after picture of the area you worked on. That's the Little Picture.

You don't have to print them in color (which will save you ink and money). In fact, printing them in black and white is more dramatic. Keep the pictures on your computer, and, if you can, put them into a slide show. There are very inexpensive and even free programs that will do simple slide shows for you. When you get depressed about not making any progress, watch the show.

Appendix II: Affirmations and Promises

Affirmations

- I live in a clutter-free environment, mentally, spiritually, and emotionally.
- I see beyond my clutter. I see the orderliness that lies within.
- My life is filled with beauty and organization.
- I am perfect as I am today. I constantly improve my definition of perfection.
- I allow myself to be imperfect in the eyes of others, knowing I am a perfect me.
- Clutter is the past. Order is the present. Peace and prosperity are the future.
- I start my day over whenever I need to.
- No task is overwhelming to me. I have the strength to overcome every limitation.
- My finances are in perfect order.
- There is always enough money in the Universe for my every need. I now claim my fair share.
- Oops, I had a slip! It is not serious. If I can do it, I can undo it.
- I am a perfect expression of Universal love.

- Time is a precious gift. I do not waste it on people, places, or things that do not contribute to my growth.
- Thank you, Great Spirit, for the prosperity that right now flows to me like the rivers flow to the ocean, and the ocean flows back to the shore.
- The longest journey begins with the first step. I confidently take that step, knowing I am guided in the right direction.
- There is plenty in the world for me. I lovingly release those items that are no longer useful, knowing, in truth, that what I need has already been provided.
- Money flows into my life according to the space I allow it.
- G.O.D., Good Orderly Direction, is my guide on this journey to orderliness.
- Clean, clean, clean, that is my house.
- Nest, neat, neat, that is my life.
- As I clear my physical clutter, I clear my mental and emotional clutter.
- My life is clutter-free on all levels.

The Promises of Living Clutter-Less

1. You will know more happiness and freedom from worry.
2. You will know the joy of not having to hide your shame.
3. You will feel more self-confident and secure.
4. You will feel as though a whole new world has opened up for you.
5. You will stop beating yourself up for your disease.
6. You will stop blaming others for what is your responsibility.
7. You will stop being afraid of letting people know the real you.
8. You will develop a more spiritual manner of living, which will help you in all areas of your life.
9. You will want to share your experiences with others, to help them and yourself.
10. You will accept your imperfections as expressions of your humanity.

Bibliography and Resources

Ames, Patrick. *Beyond Paper: The Official Guide to Adobe Acrobat*. New York: Adobe Pr, 1993.

Ash, Mel. *The Zen of Recovery*. New York: Penguin Putnam, 1993.

Bradley, Michael. *The Heart & Soul of the Next Generation*. Gig Harbor, Wash.: Harbor Press, 2006.

———. *Yes, Your Teen Is Crazy!* Gig Harbor, Wash.: Harbor Press, 2003.

Brink, Susan. "Sleepless." *U.S. News and World Report*, October 16, 2000.

C., Roy. *Obsessive Compulsive Anonymous: Recovering from OCD*. New Hyde Park, N.Y.: The Obsessive Compulsive Foundation, 1997.

Cloninger, C. Robert. *Feeling Good: The Science of Well-Being*. New York: Oxford University Press, 2004.

Fox, Emmet. *The Sermon on the Mount: The Key to Success in Life*. San Francisco: Harper San Francisco, 1989.

Gillis, Anne Sermons. *Offbeat Prayers for the Modern Mystic*. Spring, Texas: Easy Times Press, 1998.

Hay, Louise. *Love Yourself, Heal Your Life Workbook*. Carlsbad, Calif.: Hay House, 1990.

———. *You Can Heal Your Life*. Carlsbad, Calif.: Hay House, 1999.

Holmes, Ernest. *Science of Mind*. Marina Del Rey, Calif.: DeVorss and Company, 1995.

———. *Living the Science of Mind*. Marina Del Rey, Calif.: DeVorss and Company, 1997.

Jampolsky, Gerald G. *Love is Letting Go of Fear*. New York: Bantam Books, 1998.

Jasper, Jan. *Take Back Your Time*. New York: St. Martin's Press, 1999.

Jewell, Catherine. *31 Days to a Better Boss: Ways to Stop Whining, Start Planning, and Take Charge of Your Career Today*. Austin, Texas: Copyright Success Address Press, 2000.

Kolberg, Judith. *Conquering Chronic Disorganization*, 2nd Edition. Decatur, Ga.: Squall Press, 2007.

Kolberg, Judith, and K. Nadeau. *ADD-Friendly Ways to Organize Your Life*. New York: Routledge, 2002.

Matlen, Terry. *Survival Tips for Women with AD/HD: Beyond Piles, Palms, & Post-Its*. Plantation, Fla.: A.D.D. Warehouse, 2005.

May, Rollo. *The Meaning of Anxiety*. New York: Washington Square Press, 1979.

McCorry, K.J. *Organize Your Work Day in No Time*. Indianapolis, Ind.: Que Publishing, 2005.

Obsessive Compulsive Disorder: A Survival Guide for Family and Friends. New Hyde Park, N.Y.: Obsessive Compulsive Foundation, 1993.

Orman, Suze. *Nine Steps to Financial Freedom*. New York: Crown, 1997.

———. *The Courage to Be Rich*. New York: Riverhead Books, 1999.

Osteen, Joel. *Become a Better You*. New York: Free Press, 2007.

Peale, Norman Vincent. *The Power of Positive Thinking*. Englewood Cliffs, N.J.: Prentice Hall, 1978.

———. *The Amazing Results of Positive Thinking*. Pawling, N.Y.: Peale Center for Christian Living, 1987.

Pinsky, Susan. *Organizing Solutions for People With Attention Deficit Disorder: Tips and Tools to Help You Take Charge of Your Life and Get Organized*. Beverly, Mass.: Fair Winds Press, 2006.

Ponder, Catherine. *The Dynamic Laws of Prosperity*. Englewood Cliffs, N.J.: Prentice Hall, 1962.

———. *The Dynamic Laws of Prayer*. Marina del Rey, Calif.: DeVorss and Company, 1987.

Robbins, Anthony. *Unlimited Power*. New York: Fawcett Columbine, 1987.

Schwartz, Jeffrey M. *Brain Lock: Free Yourself from Obsessive-Compulsive Behavior*. New York: ReganBooks, 1986.

Shenk, David. *Data Smog: Surviving the Information Glut*. New York: HarperOne, 1998.

Steketee, Gail, and R.O. Frost. *Treatment of Compulsive Hoarding*. New York: Oxford University Press, 2007.

Steketee, Gail, and Teresa Pigott. *Obsessive Compulsive Disorder: The Latest Assessment and Treatment Strategies*, 3rd Edition. Kansas City, Mo.: Compact Clinicals, 2006.

Tolin, David, Randy Frost, and Gail Steketee. *Buried in Treasures: Help for Compulsive Acquiring, Saving, and Hoarding*. New York: Oxford University Press, 2007.

Van Noppen, Barbara L., Michelle T. Pato, and Steven Rasmussen. *Learning to Live With OCD*, 4th Edition. New Haven, Conn.: Obsessive Compulsive Foundation, 1997.

More Resources

Websites

- *www.clutterless.org*: Homepage for Clutterless support groups. It has ideas for dealing with clutter in our lives, and information on starting a Clutterless group in your city. Very uplifting.
- *www.clutterersanonymous.net*: Homepage for Clutterers Anonymous, a strictly 12-step approach to recovery.
- *www.childrenofhoarders.com/bindex.php*: A site that I like about hoarding because it is human and addresses the emotional pain of the children of hoarders.
- *htttps://psychobiology.wustl.edu/coherence.html*. Dr. C. Robert Cloninger's TCI scale test.

Organizations

- **Clutterless Recovery Groups, Inc.** Clutterless meetings provide a safe place to be heard, discussions of ways to get out of the clutter trap, and practical suggestions. Clutterless is neither 12-step nor religious. All information about meetings and starting them is on the Web at *www.clutterless.org*.
- **Clutterers Anonymous**
  PO Box 91413
  Los Angeles, CA 90009-1413

CLA is a 12-step group specifically for clutterers, based on the principles of Alcoholics Anonymous. Send a large self-addressed, stamped envelope for information. Check them out on the Web at *www.clutterersanonymous.net*.

Professional Organizers

California
- Suzie Glennan, The Busy Woman, Thousand Oaks, Calif. *www.thebusywoman.com*. (805) 375-1144.
- Karen S. Oldroyd, The Organizer, Danville, Calif. *www.karentheorganizer.com*. (925) 383-2456.

Colorado
- K.J. McCorry, Officiency, Boulder, Colo. *www.officiency.com*. (303) 517-5300.

Georgia
- Judith Kolberg, Fileheads, Decatur, Ga. *www.fileheads.net*. (404) 231-6172.

Illinois
- Lynn Meyer O'Dowd, All About Time. *http://all-about-time.com*. (773) 202-9394.

New York
- Jan Jasper, Jasper Productivity Solutions. *www.janjasper.com*. (212) 465-7472.

Texas
- Janine Godwin, Nooks and *Crannies* Professional Organizing, Katy, Texas. *www.nooks-and-crannies.com*. (281) 450-5196.
- Linda Durham, Organizing Matters, Houston, Texas. *www.organizingmatters.com*. (281) 304-0695.

Organizing Associations
- National Association of Professional Organizers: *www.napo.net*.
- National Study Group on Chronic Disorganization: *www.nsgcd.org*.

Index

abundance-thinking, 197
action, take, 233-234
AD/HD and kids, 172-173
ADD (attention deficit disorder), 140-142
    disorganization, 141
    medications, 142
Aldi, Roger, 190
Alzheimer's, moving to an assisted living facility because of, 89-90
animal hoarding, 146-147
anxiety, 137-138
anxiety and depression, kids and, 171-172
Attention Deficit Disorder Association, 140
attention deficit disorder, *see* ADD
auctioning your relative's things, 97
backsliding, reasons for, 229-232
bathroom, daily maintenance for, 226
bed, daily maintenance for, 226
books, organizing, 43, 53
Bradley, Michael, 169, 172, 174
budget for organizer, 184
business, clutterer running a, 206-207
Capacchione, Lucia, 118
Carnegie, Dale, 121
Carrasco, story of Joe King, 131-133

categories of stuff, 98-99
CEOs, disorganization affects, 216-217
CHAOS junkie (Change Hurts And Organizing Stinks), 31-32
children,
    clutter and our, 84-85
    clutter and our grown, 25
Christmas stuff, story about decluttering, 157-159
Clean Sweep: Makeover Reactions, 156
Cloninger, C. Robert, 15-16, 149
clothes, daily maintenance for, 225
Cluterless Recovery Groups, Inc., 236
clutter,
    going through your parents', 90-93
    grown children's, 25
    physical, 58-59
clutterer,
    fear-driven, 29-30
    home or office, 24-25
    procrastinating, 30
    questions to determine if you are a, 17-18
    rebellious, 28-29
    situational, 26-28
    uncontrollable, 32

clutterers and hoarders,
    the difference between, 94-95
Clutterers Anonymous (CLA), 123,
    127, 235
clutterers clutter, why, 65-66
cluttering and our consciousness,
    191-192
cluttering, degrees of, 23-24
Clutterless, 80
Clutterless or Clutterer's Anonymous,
    employers suggest employees
    attend, 215
clutter-prone areas for kids, 174-175
Cobb, Linda, 157
collector, definition of a, 66
color-coding, 111-112
community health issues, 145-147
compliment two-step, the, 167
compulsive shopping, 75-77
control, communication as key to
    changing perceptions of, 166
control and cluttering, 164-165
control with kids, defining, 166
corporate environments, changing, 214
Cozzolino, Anthony, 138
daily maintenance, 223-226
dating and clutterers, 163-164
decision, making a, 62
decision-making in kid cluttering,
    eliminating, 176
decluttering,
    combination of the practical and
        emotional, 20
    TV-style forced, 61, 155-156
    xtreme, 18-21
Decluttering Diary, 59, 61, 80, 81-82
decluttering in a nutshell, 54-57
depression, 138-140
    and anxiety, 34
    as reason for backslide, 232
dining room,
    daily maintenance for the, 226
dishes, daily maintenance for, 225
disorganization, chronic, 34

disorganized, mildly, 24
Duncan, Debra, 156
Durham, Linda, 87-88
Early, Terrence, 173-174
economy size, buying the, 76-77
e-mail,
    daily maintenance for, 225
    decluttering, 212
    printing, 205
emotions and things, 96
emotions, decluttering and facing, 60-61
failure, feeling like a, 80-81
family, divvying up your stuff to give
    to, 220-222
family history, 43-44
family member, clutter of a, 27
fear
    and clutter issues, 67-69
    and decluttering, 19
    of letting go, 190-191
    of making a mistake, 69-70
    of someone in our past, 72-74
fear-driven clutterer, 29-30
feeling overwhelmed, 78
feeling unloved, 70-71
15 minutes to change your life, 57-58
file paper, ways to, 108-111
files, hanging, 209-210
filing cabinets and record retention,
    209-211
filing myths, 106-107, 112-114
financial setbacks as reason for a
    backslide, 231-232
Fluffy, the Declutter Dog, 41-42
forgiveness, 194
Frost, Randy, 33-34, 144
Gillis, Anne Sermons, 194
giving as part of prosperity, 200
goals and prosperity thinkers, 208
GOD (Good Orderly Direction), 192-193
Godwin, Janine, 180
Goodwin, Jean, 145
group, commitment to a, 237, 239

Index

groups,
   aversion to, 238
   online support, 239
guilt as stumbling block, 78-79
harm avoidance as a measure of anxiety-proneness, 151
hoarders, the difference between clutterers and, 94-95
hoarding, 33-34, 143-147
hoarding and cluttering, definitions of, 143
home office, 208
I statements, 168-169
information junkies, 31
insecurity and fear, 70
intervention, 95
Jewell, Catherine, 213-214, 216, 217
kids
   and anxiety and depression, 171-172
   and clutter, 165
   and rebellion, 169, 172-173
kids,
   clutter-prone areas for, 174-175
   practical tips for, 173-177
   suggestions for, 170-171
Lao Tse, 15
learning style,
   questions to find your, 101-103
learning styles, types of, 104-105
letting go, 195
living room,
   daily maintenance for the, 226
losing it all, lessons from, 40-41
mail, daily maintenance for, 224
Maltz, Maxwell, 121
Mandino, Og, 208
marriage and clutterers, 162-164
Maslow, Abraham, 62
Matlen, Terry, 142
meditations, 189
memory by association, 108
mental clutter, 81
methods of approach, different, 35-36, 43

Meyer O'Dowd, Lynn, 214, 216-217
mistake, fear of making a, 69-70
money, 200-201
moving, 48
NAPO (National Association of Professional Organizers), 142, 179
National Study Group on Chronic Disorganization, *see* NSGCD
Neal, Linda, 136-137
negative talk, 73
Neuro Linguistic Programming, *see* NLP
New Though churches, 199
newspapers, daily maintenance for, 224
NLP, 104
novelty-seeking as a measure of anger-proneness, 150
NSGCD, 179
obsessive-compulsive disorder (OCD), 144-145
online support groups, 239
OPC (Other People's Clutter), 87
Oprah, 155
organizer,
   contribution from a professional, 181-187
   hiring a professional, 180
organizers, points to keep in mind about, 180
organizing process,
   preparing yourself for the, 182-187
Orman, Suze, 50
Osteen, Joel, 50, 197, 199
over-committed clutterer, 83-84
overwhelmed, feeling, 78
paper clutter, 106
   computer-based solutions for, 106-107
parents' clutter, going through your, 90-93
Peale, Norman Vincent, 200, 202
people, associate with positive, 199
perma-clutter, 23
permission to discard things, getting, 96-97

persistence as a measure of ambition, 152-153
personality, using TCI to determine makeup of a person's, 149-153
personnel types, different approaches for, 216
pets as depression-reliever, 232
Pigott, Teresa, 144
Pinsky, Susan C., 142
Ponder, Catherine, 50, 198
prayer and prosperity, 201
problem, recognizing the, 36-37
procrastinating clutterer, 30
project-manager program, 83
prosperity, be grateful for, 198
prosperity wheel, make a, 201-202
psychological issues, 65
psychologist's view, a clinical, 136-137
Ragan, Amie, 141, 157
"rainy day," saving for a, 74-75
reading as depression-reliever, 233
rebellious clutterer, 28-29
record retention, 206
recycling, 59
relationships and clutter, 162
relatives clutter, why, 93-94
relatives' clutter, dealing with, 87
resentments, heal by eliminating, 193-194
reward dependence as measure of a social dynamic, 151-152
Robbins, Tony, 104, 200
Roosevelt, Eleanor, 118
Roosevelt, Franklin, 195
Roosevelt, Teddy, 78
sacred space, declaring, 59
scanning documents to declutter, 212
self-esteem, low, 80
situational clutterer, 26-28
software registration numbers and manuals, 210
spiritual or religious approach, the, 199-200
spirituality, purpose of, 190
spirituality and decluttering, 189
spouse,
    cluttering, 164-165
    punishing a nagging, 163
Steketee, Gail, 33, 144-145
success, definition of, 202-203
support groups, 67
surrender to a Higher Power, 194-195
talking as depression-reliever, 232
TCI (Temperament Character Inventory), 149, 150
    scale, 15
terms for cluttering, 34-35
time clutter, 82-83, 211 [Hyphen?]
time-clutterers, 30-31
time management, 212-213
to-do lists, problem with, 83
Tolin, David, 144
toys and games, kids and, 176
trauma as reason for backslide, 230-231
TV decluttering, 61
TV-style forced decluttering, 155-156
uncontrollable clutterer, 32
unloved, feeling, 70-71
value of items, determining, 27
visualization during filing, 109-110
visualizations, 189
visualizing and meditating, 82
Warren, Lynda, 81
will, create a, 220
Wiseman, Richard, 167
Wong, contribution by Kathleen M., 149-153
Zak, John P., 143, 144

About the Author

MIKE NELSON has worked with hundreds of clutterers and families since founding Clutterless Recovery Groups, Inc., in 2000. As a reformed clutterer himself (he's eliminated more than a ton of no-longer-needed items from his life), he understands that helping people understand *why* they clutter is more important than telling them that simple rules and systems will solve their cluttering challenges. Working from the inside out has more lasting effects than concentrating on the stuff itself.

He's been a guest of the Dr. Laura Schlessinger Show, the American Association of Retired Persons (AARP), and Associated Press news shows, as well as radio and TV stations across the country. He's been profiled for his work with clutterers by the *Los Angeles Times*, *CNN*, *Houston Chronicle*, and the *Galveston Daily News*, and has been quoted for his unique perspective by the *Motley Fool* and *Atlantic Monthly*.

Nelson has lectured on cluttering from a psychological perspective to civic, business, and church groups nationally, and presents workshops coast to coast. He can be contacted through *www.clutterless.org*.

He lives in McAllen, Texas, and has published 18 books.

Mike and Fluffy
Photo by Nicole Nicotra.

Also by Mike Nelson

Stop Clutter From Wrecking Your Family
Clutter-Proof Your Business
Spas & Hot Springs of Mexico

And many more. See *www.mexicomike.com* for his latest releases.